WILDFIRE POLICY

T0293274

During the five decades since its origin, law and economics have provided an influential framework for addressing a wide array of areas of law ranging from judicial behavior to contracts. This book reflects a first-ever forum for law and economics scholars to apply the analysis and methodologies of their field to the subject of wildfire. It brings together leading scholars to consider questions such as: How can public policy address the effects of climate change on wildfire, and wildfire on climate change? Are the environmental and fiscal costs of ex ante prevention measures justified? What are the appropriate levels of prevention and suppression responsibility borne by private, state, and federal actors? Can tort liability provide a solution for realigning the grossly distorted incentives that currently exist for private landowners and government firefighters? Do the existing incentives in wildfire institutions provide incentives for efficient private and collective action and how might they be improved?

Karen M. Bradshaw is a Judicial Clerk for the Honorable E. Grady Jolly of the Fifth Circuit Court of Appeals.

Dean Lueck is a Professor of Agricultural and Resource Economics at the University of Arizona. Prior to his academic career, he was a smokejumper with the USDA Forest Service in McCall, Idaho.

WILDFIRE POLICY

Law and Economics Perspectives

Edited by
Karen M. Bradshaw
and
Dean Lueck

RFF PRESS
RESOURCES FOR THE FUTURE

First published in paperback 2024

First published 2012
by RFF Press
605 Third Avenue, New York, NY 10158

and by RFF Press
4 Park Square, Milton Park, Abingdon, Oxon OX14 4RN

RFF Press is an imprint of the Taylor & Francis Group, an informa business

© 2012, 2024 selection and editorial matter, Karen M. Bradshaw and
Dean Lueck; individual chapters, the contributors

Library of Congress Cataloging in Publication Data
Wildfire policy: law and economics perspectives/edited by
Karen Bradshaw and Dean Lueck.
    p. cm.
    Includes bibliographical references and index.
    1. Wildfires—Law and legislation—United States.   2. Wildfires—
    Economic aspects—United States.   3. Wildfires—Prevention and
    control—United States.   4. Wildfires—Prevention and control—
    Government policy—United States.   5. Wildfires—Prevention and
    control—Australia.   I. Bradshaw, Karen.   II. Lueck, Dean.
    SD421.3.W537 2011
    363.37′9—dc23   2011023588

ISBN: 978-1-933115-95-5 (hbk)
ISBN: 978-1-03-292667-4 (pbk)
ISBN: 978-0-203-15304-8 (ebk)

DOI: 10.4324/9781315871844

Typeset in Bembo and Stone Sans
by Florence Production Ltd, Stoodleigh, Devon

ABOUT RESOURCES FOR THE FUTURE *AND* RFF PRESS

Resources for the Future (RFF) improves environmental and natural resource policymaking worldwide through independent social science research of the highest caliber. Founded in 1952, RFF pioneered the application of economics as a tool for developing more effective policy about the use and conservation of natural resources. Its scholars continue to employ social science methods to analyze critical issues concerning pollution control, energy policy, land and water use, hazardous waste, climate change, biodiversity, and the environmental challenges of developing countries.

RFF Press supports the mission of RFF by publishing book-length works that present a broad range of approaches to the study of natural resources and the environment. Its authors and editors include RFF staff, researchers from the larger academic and policy communities, and journalists. Audiences for publications by RFF Press include all of the participants in the policymaking process—scholars, the media, advocacy groups, NGOs, professionals in business and government, and the public.

CONTENTS

FIGURES AND TABLES

Figures

Tables

EDITORS AND CONTRIBUTORS

Contributing Editors

Karen M. Bradshaw is a judicial clerk for the Honorable E. Grady Jolly of the Fifth Circuit Court of Appeals. She has conducted dozens of ethnographic interviews about wildfire and has published law review articles on the subject, including "A Modern Overview of Wildfire Law" and "Backfired! Distorted Incentives in Wildfire Suppression."

Dean Lueck is a professor of Agricultural and Resource Economics at the University of Arizona, where he is also a founding codirector of the university's Program on Economics, Law and the Environment. His current research includes studies of the economic function and effects of property law, the demarcation of land, and the behavior of state wildlife agencies. Prior to his academic career, he was a smokejumper with the USDA Forest Service in McCall, Idaho.

Authors

Sarah E. Anderson is an assistant professor at the Bren School of Environmental Science and Management and Department of Political Science at University of California–Santa Barbara. She was the W. Glenn Campbell and Rita Ricardo-Campbell National Fellow in 2006–2007 at the Hoover Institution, Stanford University.

Terry L. Anderson is the executive director of the Property and Environment Research Center (PERC), a research institute in Bozeman, Montana, and a senior fellow with the Hoover Institution, Stanford University. He is an economist whose research helped launch the idea of free market environmentalism and has prompted public debate over the proper role of government in managing natural resources. His publications include coauthoring *Free Market Environmentalism*.

Jeff Bennett is a professor at the Crawford School of Economics and Government, Australian National University; a distinguished fellow and past president of the Australian Agricultural and Resource Economics Society; director of the Environmental Economics Research Hub; coeditor of the *Australian Journal of Agricultural and Resource Economics*; and principal of the consulting group Environmental and Resource Economics. He currently leads research projects investigating the use of nonmarket techniques to estimate the value of the environment, the use of auctions to encourage land use change in western China, and private sector conservation initiatives.

Kirsten Engel is a professor of law at the University of Arizona James E. Rogers College of Law, where she teaches and researches in the field of environmental law. Prior to that, she held numerous permanent and temporary appointments within academia and in the public and nonprofit sectors, including the U.S. EPA, the Massachusetts Attorney General's Office, and Harvard, Vanderbilt, and Tulane Law Schools. She is the coauthor of an environmental law textbook and the author of numerous articles and book chapters.

Richard A. Epstein is the Laurence A. Tisch Professor of Law at New York University School of Law, the Peter and Kirsten Bedford Senior Fellow at the Hoover Institution, and the James Parker Hall Distinguished Service Professor of Law Emeritus and a senior lecturer at the University of Chicago. In 2005, he was named by *Legal Affairs* magazine as one of the 20 leading legal thinkers in the United States. His book publications include *Design for Liberty: Private Property, Public Administration, and the Rule of Law* (2011) and *Simple Rules for a Complex World* (1995).

Jason Scott Johnston is the Henry L. and Grace Doherty Charitable Foundation Professor of Law and Nicholas E. Chimicles Research Professor of Business Law and Regulation at the University of Virginia School of Law. He was previously director of the Program on Law, Environment and Economy at the University of Pennsylvania, where he coordinated the Penn Workshops on Markets and the Environment. He has published in leading law reviews and peer-reviewed economics journals, on subjects ranging from natural resources law to torts and contracts, and is editor of *Institutions and Incentives in Regulatory Science* (forthcoming, 2011).

Jonathan Klick is a professor of law at the University of Pennsylvania. He is also a senior economist at the RAND Corporation, Institute for Civil Justice. His work focuses on identifying the causal effects of laws and regulations on individual behavior using cutting-edge econometric tools. He has published papers in law reviews and articles in numerous peer-reviewed economics journals.

Carolyn Kousky is a fellow at Resources for the Future in Washington, DC. Her research focuses on natural resource management, decision-making under uncertainty, and individual and societal responses to natural disaster risk. She has examined how individuals learn about extreme event risk, the demand for natural disaster insurance, and policy responses to potential changes in extreme events with climate change.

Thomas W. Merrill is the Charles Evans Hughes Professor of Law at Columbia Law School. From 1987 to 1990, he served as deputy solicitor general in the Department of Justice, where he represented the United States before the U.S. Supreme Court. His teaching and research interests include administrative law, property, and environmental law. He has published several articles that explore the roots of administrative law and coauthored *The Oxford Introductions to U.S. Law: Property*.

Sheila Olmstead is a fellow at Resources for the Future. Before coming to RFF in 2010, she was an associate professor of environmental economics at the Yale School of Forestry and Environmental Studies. Her research focuses on natural resource management and pollution control, with a particular emphasis on water resource economics. She is author or coauthor of numerous articles, book chapters, and other publications, including the 2007 book *Markets and the Environment*.

Andrew Reeves will serve as a judicial clerk for the Honorable Christine Quinn-Brintnall of the Washington State Court of Appeals beginning in August 2011. He was the 2009–2010 Sol Resnick Water Resources Fellow at the University of Arizona and a fellow with the Rocky Mountain Mineral Law Foundation. He is interested in energy and environmental law and has published on the subject, including a recent law review article he coauthored titled "Solar Energy's Cloudy Future."

Roger Sedjo is a senior fellow and the director of RFF's Center for Forest Economics and Policy. His research interests include forests and global environmental problems; climate change and biodiversity; public lands issues; long-term sustainability of forests; industrial forestry and demand; timber supply modeling; international forestry; global forest trade; forest biotechnology; and land use change. He has written or edited more than a dozen books related to forestry and natural resources.

Jonathan Yoder is an associate professor at the School of Economic Sciences at Washington State University. His areas of research include environmental and natural resource economics, econometrics, and contract theory and public policy. His journal articles include "Liability, Regulation, and Endogenous Risk: Incidence and Severity of Escaped Prescribed Fires in the United States," published in the *Journal of Law and Economics*.

ACKNOWLEDGEMENTS

We would like to thank the following organizations for their generous support of the Symposium on Wildfire: Economics, Law and Policy held at the University of Arizona on November 15-16, 2010: The John M. Olin Program in Law and Economics at the University of Chicago Law School, and at the University of Arizona, the Program on Economics Law and the Environment, the Institute for the Environment, and the James Rogers College of Law. These supporters enabled us to generate the original works published in this volume and created a stimulating environment to broaden the discussion and to improve the original manuscript.

ACRONYMS AND ABBREVIATIONS

BIFC	Boise Interagency Fire Center
CAA	Clean Air Act
CAL FIRE	California Department of Forestry and Fire Protection
CFA	Country Fire Authority (Victoria, Australia)
CFS	Country Fire Service (South Australia)
EPA	Environmental Protection Agency
FACTS	Forest Service ACtivity Tracking System
FAIR	Fair Access to Insurance Requirements (Plan)
FEMA	Federal Emergency Management Agency
FHSZ	Fire Hazard Severity Zoning
FMP	Fire Management Plan
GFAs	government land management and fire agencies
GIS	geographical information system(s)
ha	hectare(s)
HFI	Healthy Forests Initiative
HFRA	Healthy Forests Restoration Act
KCFAST	Kansas City Fire Access SofTware
LFO	large fire organization
LRA	Local Responsibility Area
NAAQS	National Ambient Air Quality Standards
NAFC	National Aerial Firefighting Centre
NIFC	National Interagency Fire Center
NOAA	National Oceanic and Atmospheric Administration
NPS	National Park Service
NSW	New South Wales, Australia
PDSI	Palmer Drought Severity Index
PM	particulate matter

PM_{10}	particulate matter of 10 micrometers or less
$PM_{2.5}$	particulate matter less than 2.5 micrometers in diameter
RFS	Rural Fire Service (New South Wales, Australia)
RPF	registered professional foresters
SIP	State Implementation Plan
SMP	Smoke Management Program
USFS	USDA Forest Service
VHFHSZ	Very High Fire Hazard Severity Zone
WUI	wildland-urban interface

INTRODUCTION

Karen M. Bradshaw and Dean Lueck

The increasing incidence and intensity of wildfires over the past two decades have resulted in enormous expenditures for suppression efforts by state and federal governments and imposed substantial environmental and fiscal costs on an assortment of stakeholders. More and more, wildfires have been capturing the attention of the media, the public, and politicians, and questions abound about how best to deal with them. This focus will become more acute as wildfires worsen and the attendant public attention on managing them continues to grow. *Wildfire Policy: Law and Economics Perspectives* represents the first coordinated effort by top legal scholars and economists to identify key questions and suggest possible answers to the quandary of modern wildfire policy.

Policy-makers face considerable public pressure to respond to the increasing risk and damage of wildfire. Yet few parties involved in on-the-ground wildfire suppression are familiar with modern theoretical approaches studied in policy-making, political processes, or legal systems. There is currently a void of insight into wildfire policy issues from legal scholars and economists on whom policy-makers rely in other arenas. Thus, a substantial need exists for careful scholarly considerations of the complex issues underlying current practices and policy proposals. This book meets this need by bringing together leading legal scholars and economists to provide detailed scholarly analysis of the important public issues surrounding wildfire. As such, it should serve as a powerful resource not only for scholars, but also for others engaged in wildfire policy decisions, such as political figures, governmental agency leaders, and natural resources experts.

To introduce much-needed empirical analysis and innovative policy recommendations in the field of wildfire, we used a simple strategy: we invited well-regarded leaders in various academic fields to learn, think, and write about an aspect of wildfire law that interested them. Then the academics joined with an experienced group of natural resources and wildfire experts to discuss and edit their works. The result is a collection of unique and thought-provoking works from people representing fields as eclectic as property law and climate change, science and natural resources. These diverse perspectives lend creative approaches to the previously overlooked issue of wildfire strategy and policy, an area in which academic legal discussion has largely been absent over the past fifty years. Collectively, the chapters lay a foundation for critical thinking about wildfire issues.

This book also contributes to a vibrant field of legal academia: the school of law and economics, a well-established field that focuses on incentives arising from legal (and related) institutions. This field is known for blending rigorous empirical analysis with traditional areas of law. Over the five decades since its inception, it has provided a valuable framework for addressing a wide array of areas of law ranging from judicial behavior to contracts. Yet environmental and resource economics have remained relatively untouched by the law and economics approach. Consequently, the ideas generated by the authors of this book provide a substantial contribution to the robustness of resources economics and law and economics.

Regardless of the reader's area of expertise, we believe this book should prove useful to anyone with an interest in wildfire, law, or economics. Although it answers some vital questions of wildfire policy, it, like all scholarship, raises many others. We invite you to join our team of authors in thinking through new approaches to fighting wildfires and how to achieve better outcomes.

1

COMMON LAW LIABILITY FOR FIRE

A Conceptual, Historical, and Economic Analysis

Richard A. Epstein

The tort law governing fire is a peculiar amalgam that adjusts the general principles of tort law to the particular context of fire. This chapter examines the different principles of tort law as they apply to both wildfires and fires set by human agents. In particular, it looks at how, in this context, the law treats such perennial issues as the act/omission distinction, the role of privilege for private and public actors, the application of principles of vicarious liability, the choice between negligence and strict liability, and the laws of causation and affirmative defenses. The possibility of huge consequences from small antecedents is one of the great challenges in this area. Yet at the same time, the universal recognition of the danger of fire has led to the development of a body of common law rules that, although rough around the edges, is reasonably adapted to the challenges of both earlier and modern times.

Fire in Context

One major function of the law of tort is to supply redress to individuals who have suffered physical damage to their person or property. It is a huge field that is amenable to study in at least two different ways. The first articulates those general theoretical conceptions that can be brought to bear in a wide number of situations that, on the surface at least, bear little relation to each other. The second starts from the other end of the barrel, by looking at discrete kinds of harms that merit special attention. The dominant mode of academic study today surely follows the first path, as lawmakers and scholars alike face the constant question of how to define the function of tort law in the abstract and then integrate it with various systems of administrative control. Oftentimes, however, the second approach may yield some insights on how the various components of law of torts mesh with each other, by looking at the evolution of tort law as it applies to the various instrumentalities capable of causing harm.

This tradition of looking at liability rules by the origin of harm is very much alive in the common law of torts, which can be divided, for instance, into the law of animals, cars, railroads, filth, water, and for these purposes, fire. That approach is evident in, for example, Lord Blackburn's opinion in *Fletcher v. Rylands* (*aff'd* 1 Ex. 265 [1866] *rev'g Fletcher v. Rylands*, 3 H. & C. 774, 159 Eng. Rep. 737 [Ex. 1865], *aff'd sub nom. Rylands v. Fletcher*, 3 H.L. 330 [1868], 3.4; 5.12; 13.3), when he writes:

> The person whose grass or corn is eaten down by the escaping cattle of his neighbour, or whose mine is flooded by the water from his neighbour's reservoir, or whose cellar is invaded by the filth of his neighbour's privy, or whose habitation is made unhealthy by the fumes and noisome vapours of his neighbour's alkali works, is damnified without any fault of his own.

Other opinions link together water and fire. In the *Tithe Case* (Y.B. Trin., 21 Hen. 7, f. 26, 27, 28, pl. 5 [1506]), Chief Judge Rede brackets the two together when he addresses the appropriate legal response "where things are in jeopardy of loss through water or fire and the like," a question to which we shall turn presently. Each of these modalities of harms raises questions that are not found in connection with the others. Animals, for instance, have wills of their own, whereas water and fire do not. Both water and fire can arise from natural sources or be unleashed by the hand of man. But each also has distinctive properties of its own. For example, it is far easier to store water than fire. It is also possible to fight fire with fire—an issue that gives rise to profound issues of liability. Yet it is difficult to understand what it would mean to fight water with water. Backfires, by which one fire is used to block the spread of a second, often make sense; back flooding does not. These differences work themselves out in a variety of ways in particular cases.

The first question with regard to wildfire is whether it poses any tort issue at all. Most wildfires are started by natural events, frequently called "acts of God" in the earlier cases. It is, after all, "a familiar principle in the law of torts that no one was liable to make compensation for injuries that were attributable to some entirely providential cause," such as harms brought about by tempests, earthquakes, or fires of spontaneous origin (Arnold 1979). In connection with the law of fire, the strict application of this principle could lead to the uneasy conclusion that natural accumulations of undergrowth impose no duties of care on the landowners, even if they create potential tinderboxes.[1] But appearances can deceive, and the extensive set of common law rules necessarily shows that the topic is more complicated. First, some accumulations may, in a fact-specific sense, be attributable to a landowner who, say, erects a barrier that could prevent the wind from carrying away debris. Second, many fires in the wild are of human origin, caused by such things as sparks from railroads. Third, some fires are jointly caused by natural and human events. And fourth, liability may attach to the failure to deal with even those fires that were created by natural events. It is therefore appropriate to see how the traditional issues of tort liability play out in the special context of fire.

The topic is one in which there has never been serious doubt about whether the harms in question are of a sort that should be actionable (i.e., subject to suit). In this regard, these physical losses are quite different from economic harms suffered by the loss of customers, which for sound reasons of policy should not be actionable in court no matter what their magnitude. It is painfully clear that no one regards the uncontrolled spread of fire as a good thing. Flames kill people and destroy houses and livestock. They often do so with a magnitude far out of proportion to the modest culpability of those individuals who are responsible for either setting the fire or, as is commonly the case, letting it spread. The danger of uncontrolled fires, moreover, gives rise to extensive debate over the degree to which human backfires should be used as a method of fire prevention, and if so, whether the parties who set those fires under government auspices should be responsible for any damage that they cause (see Chapter 3).

Yet no matter how great the risk of harm by fire, the zero-tolerance solution that bans all use of fire is a dead loser as well. Just as fire means death and destruction in some circumstances, it means heat and light in others. In both primitive and modern times, the need of fire for cooking, warmth, and clearing fields is too evident to require much comment. In more modern times, the risk of fire comes not only from fires themselves, but also from the use of various kinds of heating or electrical equipment, for example, whose faulty design, maintenance, and use carry with them severe risks of dangerous consequences to others.

It is this love-hate relationship with fire that has made the question of its proper regulation a salient one from the earliest times. From the Roman era to the present, fires have always been subject to regulation with respect to the construction of various structures, their spacing, and the kinds of activities—from weaving to blacksmithing—that are allowed in particular places; for example, dangerous activities may be allowed only at the periphery, downwind from the main establishments (for a summary of these laws, see Klitzke 1959). In some isolated communities in Norway, strict rules prevented individuals within a commune from making their own fires (see Epstein 2009). All cooking was done in a single guarded centralized facility to reduce the risk of fires that could quickly spread to annihilate the entire community, which did not have the luxury of living in brick houses. Quite simply, the need for fire led to the greater reliance on a regime of common property for powerful safety reasons.

In dealing with the common law of fire, this chapter necessarily omits the huge part of the story that deals with the direct regulation of activities that could give rise to fire. Tort law typically provides damage remedies for fire after the fact. Unlike direct regulation, it is not an effective source of injunctive relief for the simple reason that the arc of potential danger is so wide that no single person has a distinctive interest in bringing suit for private injunction, for which he or she would bear the full cost, only to receive a small fraction of the potential gain. A simple set of numbers tells the familiar tale. Let the cost of bringing an action for injunction be 100 and the expected social benefits of getting that injunction be 1,000. The individual who garners all the gain from that suit would be prepared to pursue it if there were more than a 10 percent chance of success. But if those benefits were equally distributed across a population of 1,000, that same person would not pursue that action for injunctive relief even if he or she had a 100 percent chance of success, given that no one invests 100 to recover 1. But if the state could impose a tax of $0.10 per person, it could (ignoring some transaction costs) bring that action, because now the numbers are reversed. The tax collects the needed $100, which allows the action to go forward. A new set of transaction costs clouds the equation, but these costs do not do so in a way that shipwrecks the entire venture. Thus, if the administrative scheme costs $50 to run, the needed tax would rise to $0.15 per person, which is still much less than the $1 per person gain available.

In practice, however, the situation is far from perfect if public officials seek to obtain injunctions on behalf of the public. Under standard law, all injunctions are issued only in the face of an imminent peril. Relying solely on that approach is unwise even for public authorities, because fire presents the mirror opposite situation. The huge expected losses derive from a low probability of very high losses, which does not mesh well with the standard requirement that injunctions be issued only in cases of imminent peril. With fire, when the peril is imminent, a private injunction is useless. One spark from a mundane activity could set a large and immediate conflagration. Whereas it is easy to stop the operation of a factory that spews pollution on a regular basis onto a neighbor's land or into the public space, it is far harder for private injunctions to stop a person from lighting a match in a windstorm or storing kindling on his or her own land.

Instead, direct regulation has a major advantage in this area, because it overcomes these free-rider problems by allowing the state or some smaller group to exert constant oversight for the benefit of the public as a whole. In addition, laissez-faire concerns about excessive regulation sound hollow when dealing with fire, as the general police power concerns with health and safety give the government the greatest power to act in these cases.[2] The extensive precautions against the spread of both wildfires and fires of human origin thus became a part of the very fabric of the community long before the rise of the modern era.

It would, however, be a mistake to regard direct regulation as the only alternative to tort liability, for once again the distinctive physical properties of fire open up the way for huge gains from voluntary cooperative action. In the absence of any liability for fires that start naturally on someone else's property, there are strong incentives for someone, indeed anyone, to take steps to mitigate the risks of future fire. It therefore makes sense for neighbors to informally agree to engage in various kinds of cleanup or suppression activities to reduce the occurrence of fires for which they would *not* be held liable. Fires can start just about anywhere and can spread with the wind in just about any direction. The mitigation efforts in question yield especially high returns to many parties. Landowners who take antecedent precautions benefit both themselves and their neighbors. A person who puts out a fire on a neighbor's property protects not only that neighbor, but also himself and everyone else in the vicinity. As noted in Chapter 5, "There exists a strong norm—one landowner called it 'absolute'—that any person spotting a fire must immediately engage in firefighting activities to try to stem the fire, regardless of whose property the fire is on." Therefore, so long as all landowners share the same objective of preserving the value of harvestable timber, for example, these cooperative efforts should mature, as indeed they have. It is only when the government as landowner deviates from the goal of harvesting timber, as it has in the last 50 years or so, that the cooperative efforts break down. The government is no longer willing to take the same kind of preventive efforts as its neighbors, which violates the implicit norm of reciprocity on which the long-term stability of these arrangements rests.

In effect, a three-tier system is involved, which includes government regulation, local norms, and tort liability. As a general matter, the first two seem, in different proportions, to be more central to the enterprise than the third. Nonetheless, owing to the evident risks of fire, even the tort law plays an important part, which is evident from the number of well-known tort cases that either involve liability for fire or discuss that issue in connection with other matters.

Private Remedies for Fire

The ubiquitous threat of fire is a problem that must be addressed by every legal system. Indeed, the incidence of fire was even higher in bygone times than it is today, so it is no surprise the early case law contains extensive discussions of the topic. The plan of attack in this chapter is to follow the standard inquiries in tort theory, which conjure up the usual topics: liability for acts or omissions; the choice between strict liability and negligence for accidental harms; vicarious liability for the actions of others; the theory of causation—factual, joint, and proximate—for the harms so caused; and the set of affirmative defenses available to a defendant. These issues range up and down the entire law of fire in all its aspects. Although some fires could be classified as urban and others as rural, these broad distinctions seem to do little to explain the structure of the law, which subjects all fires to the same general rubric. The refusal to subdivide fires thus allows the legal system to avoid the hapless task of deciding which set of fires belongs to which class.

By way of introduction, the key questions tend to line up as follows. The initial inquiry is whether the defendant has committed some action to which tort liability attaches or, in the alternative, is subject to some affirmative duty to act (normally an exception in the tort law). The question of liability for both acts and omissions runs across the full range of tort law, and it is closely matched with the doctrine of privilege in cases of necessity, both public and private, where the law often imposes a duty to act especially on public officials.

Closely allied with this question is the topic of vicarious liability, somewhat neglected in the modern tort law, for the principle today is usually applied only against employers (masters, in the earlier argot), who are responsible for the wrongs of their employees (servants) arising out of and in the course of their employment. The principle, however, can be stated in a more general fashion to ask when one person should be held responsible for the actions of another and can thus include liability not only for employers, but also for independent contractors and all persons who are on the land of another—something that is particularly important for determining liability for fires set either in the home or in the field. In performing this analysis, it is sometimes critical to note that all employers are not treated alike under the rules of vicarious liability, as certain government agents receive the benefit of sovereign immunity, which insulates them from liability for some but not all kinds of conduct. In addition, public utilities often operate under special charters that impose distinctive limitations on the types of liability that they have to bear. I shall add some brief comments about this exhaustive topic.

In connection with fire, it is also necessary to revisit the perennial choice between strict liability and negligence, a topic on which I have written extensively (for the bookends, see Epstein 1973, 1974, 2010). Once the defendant's conduct is within the frame of liability, the next question deals with the standard of liability, which normally involves an application of the perennial choice between strict liability and negligence. The former is understood to impose liability (subject to affirmative defenses based on plaintiff's conduct) for those actions that cause harm to the person or property of the plaintiff, wholly without regard to whether those actions were done with the intention to harm or whether those harms could have been avoided if the defendant had taken the requisite level of care under the circumstances. In contrast, the negligence theory requires, in the absence of some intention to harm, that the defendant failed to act with reasonable care under the circumstances.

Once the issues of liability have been resolved, the question then turns to three interrelated types of causation: causation-in-fact, joint causation, and proximate causation. The last is normally, if incorrectly, thought of as a limitation on the unbounded liability possible under causation-in-fact, believed to invite a "but for" view of causation that treats any necessary condition for the occurrence of some harm as one of its many causes, except in the case of joint causation. Once that issue is done, what remains are the affirmative defenses that can be raised in fire cases, all of which concentrate on two questions. The first is the extent to which a plaintiff may have contributed to his or her own harm that arises from a fire set by another, and the second is the extent to which the plaintiff is under a duty to take measures to make sure that his or her activities do not cause or contribute to his or her own harm. Let me take up these questions in order.

Acts and Omissions

The initial inquiry in the tort law is whether the defendant has committed some act or omission that is responsible for the harm in question. This section addresses that issue solely in connection with private parties, holding off for the moment on the discussion of the privilege afforded to public actors for dealing with fires, including wildfires caused by natural events or other fires attributable to the actions of ordinary individuals. In the case of private parties, the usual act requirement is sufficient to hold accountable in tort those persons that have set fires that burn down the property of other individuals. Yet at the same time, as noted earlier, that requirement prevents any defendant from being held liable for the natural conditions on his or her land, in the absence of any statutory duty to that effect (see Chapter 3). That judgment is as old as the law itself.

The question first arose under Roman law with the Lex Aquilia, whose first and third chapters dealt with various sources of liability. In the first chapter, the question was whether a slave or a herd animal had been killed (*occisus*) by the act of the defendant. This Latin word for "to kill" carried with it the connotation of a killing by cutting, but the term was easily extended by analogy to other forms of direct harm, which surely included setting fire directly to slaves or animals so that they perished. The same topic was covered more explicitly in the third chapter of the Lex Aquilia, which covered those forms of damage that were not covered by the first section of the statute, including bodily injury but not death to slaves and herd animals, as well as other fire damage to other forms of property (Watson 1998, 9.2.27.5).

In dealing with these matters, the most famous of the Roman cases on fire asks the question of how liability should be assigned when one person sets the fire, and then turns it over to the next person to watch. The second person does not tend to the fire adequately, in consequence of which the fire spreads and causes damages to the property of another. Who should be liable: the first party, the second party, neither, or both?

Given the ways in which fires can spread, this case poses an obvious challenge to the usual legal rules. The first party is the only one who performed some act in setting the fire. Yet he did not do anything "wrong," as the fire remained contained in its designated place until he passed control of it to a second party. The second party, by his or her neglect, let the fire spread without doing anything at all. As related in *Justinian's Digest*:

> [I]f one man lighted the furnace but another watched it carelessly, will the one who lighted it be liable? For he who watched it did nothing, while the one who lighted it properly was not at fault. What is the answer? I think that an *actio utilis* lies as much against the man who fell asleep at the furnace as against him who watched it negligently, nor can anyone say that he who fell asleep was only afflicted with a normal human failing; for it was his duty either to put out the fire or to take such care that it did not escape.
>
> (Watson 1998, 9.2.27.9)

As this passage indicates, it is difficult to hold responsible the culpable party for his simple omission without some fancy legal footwork. But in this instance, the Roman law made the effort to bridge the conceptual gap, which was signaled by its use of the *actio utilis*—an all-purpose procedural device that is invoked for those cases that deviate from the paradigmatic wrong of the killing of another person by the direct application of force. The Roman law standard of liability has close parallels to modern product liability cases, where the question is whether the maker of a product could be held liable when its user suffers injury from some open and obvious danger.

The traditional modern law response to this question was in the negative (see *Campo v. Scofield* (95 N.E. 2d 802, 804 [N.Y. 1950])). The second party had full information about the nature of the dangerous condition and thus was in a position to make a judgment whether to accept the risk or not, given the alternatives that were available. The obvious nature of the alleged defect thus ruled out any theory based on fraud or misrepresentation: no trap, no potential liability. The key extension from this point is what happens if the second person uses a machine in a manner that hurts a third person. The proper answer is the same result as before. The full transmission of the information in question protects the initial actor against tort liability. The only source of liability thus arises from statutes that, for example, forbid the sale of a gun to a minor, who then uses it to injure another (see, e.g., *Henningsen v. Markowitz* (230 N.Y.S. 313 [N.Y. Sup. Ct. 1928])). But in those cases where the handoff is executed without trouble, the liability stops with the last actor.

In dealing with the two sequential actors under the Roman law, the key point is that the second party has assumed custody of the fire and thus should be understood to have stepped into the shoes of the initial actor, who is now outside the chain of causation, unless and until there is a flaw in the handoff of control from one person to another. That flaw, which raises questions of "negligent entrustment," could take place if the first person knew that the second person was not competent to oversee the fire, or if the first person knew of some particular latent danger associated with the fire that was not passed on to the party who followed.[3] These are parallel to the entrustment decisions in modern tort cases and should be decided in the same fashion. The transition of custody is, in my judgment, sufficient to alter the direction and dynamic of the case. We are not dealing with a simple case such as the failure to rescue a drowning person in position of peril.

The question of acts versus omissions also arose in quite a different context in the near legendary case of *Moch v. Rensselaer Water Co.* (159 N.E. 896 [N.Y. 1928]), where the question was whether a water company could be held responsible for the destruction of property by fire when it failed to supply the local firefighters sufficient water pressure at the hydrant to put out the fire. The company had a contract of service with one of its customers, who did not sue (possibly because there was a contractual limitation against suing for consequential damages under these circumstances), but instead was sued by the party next door, who neither paid consideration for the protection nor would have been bound by any contractual limitation not to sue as was commonly found in contracts between water companies and their customers. As fate would have it, it turns out that one of the key objections to private fire departments was that they would not put out fires in houses that were not owned by their subscribers, with the obvious external hazard. (For further discussion, see the Chapter 2 endnotes, where Merrill criticizes

McChesney 1986 for overlooking this weakness, among others, in the volunteer system.) In dealing with this problem, Judge Cardozo did not touch on these grander issues, but he did write a mysterious decision that placed far too much weight on the misfeasance/nonfeasance distinction, holding that this particular wrong had not gone far enough to cross the supposed line to result in liability for the water company.

But in fact, *Moch* had little or nothing to do with the misfeasance/nonfeasance line, given that any party charged with public responsibilities has some duty to act. The best way to think about this decision is to ask whether, if there had been an immediate contractual arrangement between the water company and the plaintiff, the plaintiff would have been prepared to pay the defendant a premium sufficient to cover that risk. On the buyer's side, that price is likely to be stiff. On the seller's side, it is not credible to think that any defendant would have agreed to extensive liability to third parties, either for negligence or breach of promise, when it resists that liability to its own customers. The strong instinct that drives Cardozo's analysis has nothing to do with misfeasance or nonfeasance. It stems from the conviction that this defendant did not receive sufficient compensation for services rendered to fund tort liability to a stranger who did not contribute a penny to the operation of the fire company. As Charles Gregory (1951) wrote, "Cardozo thought the sum of $42.50 insufficient to warrant the conclusion that a negligent water company should be made to relieve a fire insurance company from bearing the ultimate risk of loss by fire." Yet that no-liability determination could easily flip over for any deliberate refusal to supply service, or even a reckless indifference as to whether that service could be supplied. Cardozo could have answered that question for the purposes of intellectual incompleteness but diplomatically refused to address it at all. Note, moreover, that the issue in *Moch* applies with equal force to wildfires. To be sure, no injured party could have a direct action for losses caused by a fire without a human origin. But the duty on any defendant to protect against fire should be the same regardless of the fire's origin. It therefore follows that the negligent failure to provide that protection should be excused from liability, leaving unsettled the question of what should be done when a reckless disregard for the welfare of the plaintiff is the force that animates the defendant's conduct.

The range of questions raised in *Moch* is not just of historical curiosity, for the same problem can arise today, and indeed it has occurred in recent times, most prominently in rural Tennessee in the fall of 2010, when firefighters from the nearby town of South Fulton refused to put out the fire of one Gene Cranick because he had not paid the annual $75 fee for fire protection (Dykes 2010). The company refused to respond even though it had been called to the site by a subscriber to the local service. The clear danger in this particular case is that of free riding. Surely it would not do for the distressed homeowner to pay the policy amount only after he knew that he was exposed to risk. But what was striking about this situation was that the fire force missed a profit opportunity, for, far from free riding, Cranick offered to cover their full expenses, which would have reduced the company's losses from answering the call in the first place. And there is an additional reason to respond in this instance: to guard against the risk that the fire could spread elsewhere to third parties, whether or not covered by this particular fire company. Whether the company could be held liable for that loss is an open question, but I would be inclined to impose that liability at least where the immediate victim was prepared credibly to cover costs. Indeed, the third-party risk might be so great that the optimal approach is to mandate that the company respond when in a position to do so, only to give it a lien on the property of the homeowner in the event that the property is saved, plus a kicker that gives the company an incentive to answer the call.

Privilege and Necessity

The common law rules that relate to acts and omissions need one important qualification to deal with the absolute privilege normally given to public figures charged with containing fires. In many fire cases, the blaze is of natural origin, to which no human agency can attach. But the absence of individual responsibility does not make the spread of that fire a matter of indifference. It is therefore of no surprise that government officials are often dispatched to manage the blaze, at which point the potential for human error arises, for the government decision to fight fire carries with it the risk that government action will destroy property either by choice or by mistake. Setting backfires to contain wildfires is a common illustration of this practice. In other cases, the fire containment efforts sometimes miscarry, causing a fire to spread farther than it should have.

The central question here asks whether the necessity to combat fire justifies some form of privilege against tort liability. That question in turn can be answered only by asking who is acting, and for whose benefit. The standard case of private necessity involves one individual who takes or uses the property of another in order to save his or her own. The rule that prevents the owners of property from blocking the efforts of strangers to engage in self-help, as in *Ploof v. Putnam* (71 A. 188 [Vt. 1908]), makes eminent good sense, considering the relative value of the stakes. The owner of a dock should not be allowed to cast a ship in distress out to sea if the owner of the distressed ship refuses to pay some extravagant toll the dock owner demands. Yet at the same time, that privilege is typically conditional on payment after the fact for the damage that the outsider inflicted on the owner's property, as decided in *Vincent v. Lake Erie Transportation Co.* (124 N.W. 221 [Minn. 1910]).

The dynamics of the situation change rapidly, however, when a defendant acts in order to provide a benefit to a distressed plaintiff. The early decision in the *Tithe Case* held that an interloper is responsible for any property losses sustained by the plaintiff, even if the interloper increased the chances that the plaintiff's property would be saved. This creates all sorts of perverse incentives that would be eliminated by making that privilege to handle the goods of others, which would otherwise be a trespass, absolute (for the argument, see Epstein 1993). The defendant's act has a positive expected value to the owner of the property, by reducing his or her risk of loss. It makes no sense to adopt a legal regime in which the putative rescuer faces a negative expected return from a socially desirable activity. To be sure, that loss could be offset in part by allowing some recovery by the rescuer under a theory of restitution, perhaps in the event that the rescue succeeds. But even if that element is factored in, the divergence between private and social costs remains, because the sums allowed for restitution will not equal the value of the property (which would leave the owner indifferent to its rescue) but would extend only to the expenditures incurred in making the successful rescue effort. Granting an action for losses in the event of a successful rescue helps, but probably not as much as a defense against tort liability when the rescue effort fails.

Yet another variation on the same issue asks whether various corporations that operate under government charters should be entitled to some protection against tort liability for their operations. This issue, which first arose in the second half of the nineteenth century, continues to divide courts and legislatures today. On the one hand, the argument is that any group that is forced to provide public services should receive protection against liability for harms that are beyond their control, at least if they comply with the statutory conditions under which they labor. This issue came to a head in connection with sparks from railroads that caused fire damage to plaintiffs' land. The judicial decision in *Vaughan v. Taff Vale Ry. Co.* (5 H. & N. 679; 29 L. J. [Ex.] 247 [1860]) took the position that because all the requisite precautions had been taken, the statutory authorization excused the defendant from liability. That position was sharply contested in yet another fire case, *Powell v. Fall* (5 Q.B. 597 [1880]), in which Judge Bramwell thought that the compliance with the statute afforded no defense. In one sense, the issue is closely balanced, for if the statute sets the right standard for all circumstances, the railroad has the incentive to take the same level of optimal precautions under either rule. But statutory standards cannot take into account the local variations that railroads can perceive in their own operations. And railroads might well have sufficient clout to persuade the legislature to adopt standards that are subpar for the purpose, at which point the common law rule of strict liability will give better incentives. The railroad now has the incentive to take whatever precautions it deems best no matter what the statutory mandate. At this point, the low statutory standard does not expose any party to undue risk. And if the statute demands excessive precaution, the issue could be resolved by political means with the liability still intact.

The same debate can apply to other forms of public utilities, where the same resolution seems correct. In addition, it is useful to note that the question of stranger liability for fire (and other harms) has also arisen with respect to charitable immunities. On this score, the courts have often drawn a sensible distinction: the willingness to serve a needy clientele for little or no money may be a good reason not to impose liability for services that were wrongly tendered.[4] But at the same time, the care of the patient or other needy person does not come at the expense of harms to strangers who are protected from their activities, in the same manner as applies to railroads and other kinds of franchised public organizations.

Perhaps the most important variation on the necessity theme asks whether public officials should receive some sort of immunity for their various acts and omissions in fighting fires. Here again the basic logic in favor of immunity starts from the ex ante perspective, when the expected value of the intervention is positive. Any regime that holds the public body responsible for the losses therefore places these gains at risk, by encouraging public parties to steer clear of danger. The problem of privilege, moreover, looms especially large when these public officials labor under certain affirmative statutory duties to take steps to prevent and control these fires. The dangers of public inaction for want of immunity were stated quite eloquently in one of the early American fire cases, *Respublica v. Sparhawk* (1 U.S. 357, 362 [Pa. 1788]), where the court wrote:

> We find, indeed, a memorable instance of folly recorded in the 3 Vol. of Clarendon's History, where it is mentioned, that the Lord Mayor of London, in 1666, when that city was on fire, would not give directions for, or consent to, the pulling down forty wooden houses, or to the removing the furniture, &c. belonging to the Lawyers of the Temple, then on the Circuit, for fear he should be answerable for a trespass; and in consequence of this conduct half that great city was burnt.

One can understand why anyone should fear mixing it up with the lawyers housed at the English Inns of Court, who were in no position to give consent to the destruction of their property. But the strong institutional response to this dilemma has been to pair the statutory duty to act with a well-nigh absolute privilege for dealing with these public necessities, whether of natural or human origins. That position was adopted in no uncertain terms in *Mayor of New York v. Lord* (18 Wend. 126 [N.Y. 1837]), where the court held that it was "well settled" that the privilege afforded to public officials was *absolute*:

> [I]n cases of actual necessity, to prevent the spreading of a fire, the ravages of a pestilence, the advance of a hostile army, or any other great public calamity, the private property of an individual may be lawfully taken and used or destroyed, for the relief, protection or safety of the many, without subjecting those, whose duty it is to protect the public interests, by or under whose direction such private property was taken or destroyed, to personal liability for the damage which the owner has thereby sustained.

In his treatment of this issue, Professor Francis Bohlen (1926) put the point as follows: "Since the benefit is solely social, there is no reason why one who acts as a champion of the public should be required to pay for the privilege of so doing." It is important to note that the privilege in this context is limited to public necessity cases and need not be extended to the routine forms of government land management, which expose other individuals to risks of loss. In those cases, the current law protects the government with the far broader "discretionary function" privilege, which applies to a broad class of government actions, including land management decisions of government actors.[5] I have relatively little sympathy for this privilege when the government acts as an ordinary landowner of, say, parkland, whose management techniques increase the hazard of fires to neighbors. But these concerns do not apply when the government intervenes in times of crisis, when it is critical for the law to align the private incentives with the public welfare. When the underlying actions have a positive expected value, the private return to the persons who act should not be negative, which is just what happens when they can collect nothing from the persons whose lives and property are saved, but must bear the full risk to those whose property or persons were endangered or lost.

This creation of absolute government privilege for routine actions has two negative consequences. The first is that it denies property owners an obvious source of compensation for their wrongs. In most cases in which these losses are incurred— when public bodies are acting in times of necessity—the problems of working the compensation system are acute. In principle, the ideal response is to have the ultimate burden of the loss fall, whenever possible, on those persons whose property was spared by the losses in question. The system looks a bit like the principle of general average contribution in maritime situations, where the cargo and hull are charged back in proportion to value for the property that is cast off in order to lighten the ship.[6] In this context, the rule in question has the great advantage of giving all parties the incentive to honestly value their property at the time that it is loaded.

In principle, a variation on the rule of general average contribution could be applied to charge property saved to cover the loss of property sacrificed in a fire. Unfortunately, when the old rule is transferred to fires that spread to wide and indeterminate areas, its administrative disadvantages become manifest. As a factual matter, it is impossible to give an accurate determination of which structures were saved by the intervention and which were left unaffected. The vagaries of wind and weather necessitate an inquiry that receives no acceptable answer. In addition, the first-party insurance market for losses set by governments in times of necessity obviates the need to go through this exercise (see Chapter 2). In the first-party market, all individuals purchase coverage from reputable insurance companies for the types of losses that might otherwise be compensated by government action. This coverage is relatively easy to administer because it turns only on the fact of property damage, not on any complex issue of whether government agents should be liable for the loss in question. So long as no one from behind the veil of ignorance knows whose property is destroyed, everyone is better off by resorting in the ex ante position to the general insurance scheme.

The use of first-party insurance in turn still has the serious negative consequence of removing all tort incentives from these actors, who could well act with massive incompetence or even actual malice. But the law, which grants an absolute immunity from tort liability, need not remove all legal incentives for proper conduct. After the fact, it is always possible to examine the behavior of the parties to see if some more modest sanctions are appropriate, such as in the form of job loss or administrative fines for deliberate failure to follow certain procedures. But even here, the punishment should be narrow both in scope and in severity, lest it undo the benefit of the absolute privilege. Imposing punishment should take more than negligence, such as actual malice as determined by reckless disregard or actual hatred, which is found at most in a tiny fraction of these cases. Otherwise, the privilege holds firm in these public necessity cases, as it does for all private parties who seek to help public officials contain private fires.

Vicarious Liability

Returning to the question of private parties, one of the major issues in tort law deals with problems of joint control, where it becomes necessary to sort out the relative contributions of the parties. One version of this problem relates to the issue of vicarious liability, where one individual organization is held responsible for the wrongs of another. It is just this doctrine that is brought into play when a railroad is responsible for a fire set by its engineer, or the government is held liable for work done by public officials. Yet another branch of the vicarious liability rule holds individuals responsible for the conduct of other persons who are on their property with their permission. The cast of characters that could fill this second role could be relatively long, and it includes everyone from the household guest that makes a fire in his bedroom to the independent contractor that uses a blowtorch to unclog frozen pipes (see, e.g., *Balfour v. Barty-King* (1 Q.B. 496 [1957][Goddard, C. J.])). The question in all cases is whether the owner of the property should be liable to outsiders for the actions of those persons who enter onto his or her land with the owner's approval.

The historical answer to that dates back to the 1401 decision in *Beaulieu v. Finglam* ((1401), Y.B. 2 Hen 4, fo 18, pl 6, 36 *Digest* (Repl) 78, 416; the text can be found in Fifoot 1949). That case made it chillingly clear that a landowner's liability could attach to all guests and servants, but that the liability in question did not extend to strangers:

> I shall answer to my neighbour for each person who enters my house by my leave or my knowledge, or is my guest through me or through my servant, if he does any act, as with a candle or aught else, whereby my neighbour's house is burnt. But if a man from outside my house and against my will starts a fire in the thatch of my house or elsewhere, whereby my house is burned and my neighbour's houses are burned as well, for this I shall not be held bound to them; for this cannot be said to be done by wrong on my part, but is against my will.

This decision provoked an anguished response from the defendant's lawyer, who—as his case did not fall within the stranger exception—said that the defendant would be "undone and impoverished all his days," for, if this action were allowed, then 20 more like it would follow. To which the answer came: "What is that to us? It is better that he should be utterly undone than that the law be changed for him."

This notable toughness of mind is indeed correct on economic grounds for reasons that are not made explicit in the opinion. The vast number of these fires are likely to be set by someone lawfully on the premises. These fires will almost always be set accidentally, because neither owner nor servant nor guest wishes to burn down the premises on which the action takes place. Yet it is virtually impossible for any outsider who has been damaged by the fire to determine which of the many people lawfully on the premises were, either jointly or singly, responsible for the fire in question. The strong vicarious liability rule removes that burden from the individual stranger and allows him or her direct access at the party who is easiest to identify—namely, the owner of the property.

The use of this strategy simplifies litigation, because it prevents the introduction of evidence, either real or manufactured, that the responsibility for the fire lies in the hands of someone—invited guest or servant—who is long gone from the locale. In addition, it eliminates the need to process complex negligence cases, because the theory assumes that the owner entrusted the fire to someone who was not competent to handle it or provided facilities that are dangerous when lit. In this case, as in so many others, the adoption of the vicarious liability rule eliminates the need to chase down the tenuous causal connections that routinely characterize a negligence system (see Epstein 1986). The owner is armed with greater information and remains free to pursue these actions against the person who was in direct charge of the fire. These latter cases normally raise difficult questions of proof, given the divided responsibility in the control of the premises, and could easily depend on how some casual remark could allocate risk between these parties. But indemnity suits are the rare exception, not the routine case, so it is far better to reduce the number of cases where the issue remains live by allowing the injured party to skirt free of these causal complications.

On the other hand, cases involving fires set by strangers range from those of arson to poor souls seeking warmth in a property owner's barn. In these few cases, it should be permissible for an owner to deny responsibility for the overall loss, so long as he or she could prove the point with some degree of clarity, which may well be done if the stranger is apprehended by public officials at the time of the fire or thereafter. It is hardly wise to say that a person whose property has been wasted away by a stranger—a consideration caught by the phrase "whereby my house is burned"—should be required to bear not only his or her own costs, but also those of all other persons adversely affected. The rulings in the early cases seem therefore to have set just the right balance on these matters, and indeed, they work better than the modern rule, which, aside from the fire cases, tends to limit the principle of vicarious liability to employees acting within the course of their employment, to the exclusion of other guests, which complicates the proof issues for little or no reason.

Strict Liability versus Negligence

Even more so than questions of initial responsibility, the choice between rules of strict liability and negligence is one of the fundamental moves of the tort system. In dealing with fires, as with animals, there is a pronounced tendency to favor what is best termed a modified strict liability system. That position is also consistent with the Roman law materials, which speak in the language of strict liability by noting that "if you throw a lighted torch at my slave and singe him, you will be liable to me. Again, if you set fire to my orchard or my country house, you will be liable to me" (Watson 1998, 9.2.27.6–7). No evidence in these texts would suggest that the defendant had some intention to bring about that result or failed to take reasonable care to see that it did not happen. The verbal connections are straight and simple.

The situation is usually a bit more complex in a modern system, where a strict liability rule is often treated as an exception from the general negligence norm, which has to be justified on some special consideration of public policy. That view is expressed by the position that strict liability rules are usually applicable only for abnormally dangerous or ultrahazardous activities.[7]

In my view, this convenient rationale is flawed, because it makes the choice of a liability system depend on questions of degree, namely of antecedent culpability, which are better excluded from determining liability. The level of anticipated loss is always relevant to the question of whether some precautions against the spread of fire should be taken in the ex ante position—which is why fire has always been subject to extensive schemes of public regulation. But it hardly follows that the ex ante probability of loss in any given case should have any influence on determining liability for those fires that have already occurred. The defendant who takes a higher level of precautions may lose in the few cases when the fire has spread. Yet that additional level of precaution generates a high level of benefit to the defendant by reducing the number of occasions on which those losses will occur. The shifts in probabilities necessarily determine the frequency of any compensable event. But there is no coherent theory in which small changes in these probabilities should determine who bears the risk of loss once the fire has occurred. Just as the clean rules work best in dealing with matters of vicarious liability, so too they work best in dealing with the standard of care of any person whose conduct is associated with the harm in question.

The actual situation on the ground, however, is somewhat more complex because of the complication noted earlier of multiple possible actors. The party who set the fire may not be in charge of it at the time that it escapes and causes damage. At this point, the transition of control over the fire becomes the critical issue, so that the guest who sets a fire in a farmhouse is not liable if it spreads after he or she has left the premises, if the guest has properly placed the fire in the care of someone else. In these contexts, the natural focus of liability should be on the party who retains custody over the fire, which thus challenges the notion that strict liability can be imposed for wrongful acts. In some situations, it is said that the defendant should be held liable if he "negligently and improvidently kept his fire," which looks as though there is a disjunction between the rules of liability for setting and watching fires. But in most cases, that difference is more apparent than real, because in many fire cases, negligence is conceded and the issue of basic liability does not arise. *Tuberville v. Stamp* (3 Ld. Raym. 250, 92 Eng. Rep. 671 [K.B. 1697]) saw a rerun of the negligence/strict liability debate with respect to fires set by an owner on his own land or those there with his permission. Judge Turton thus ventured: "That effort to introduce a negligence system of a contextual basis was, however, firmly rejected by the judicial major which treated this as a special case of more general propositions." But Judges Holt, Rokeby, and Eyre wrote:

> Every man must so use his own as not to injure another. The law is general. The fire which a man makes in the fields is as much his fire as the fire in his house; it made on his ground with his materials and by his order, and he must at his peril take care that it does not, through his neglect, injure his neighbour. If he kindle it at a proper time and place, and the violence of the wind carry it into his neighbour's ground and prejudice him, this is fit to be given in evidence.

Note that on this account, the operative rule is a cross between strict liability and negligence. In both of these settings, it is clear that the "violence of the wind" counts as an act of God, which should excuse from liability. From that observation, it follows first that if there is no act of God, then the strict liability rule applies, so that the level of antecedent precaution is irrelevant. Yet the converse proposition does not hold, for a defendant is not necessarily *exonerated* if the fire spread through an act of God. Rather, in these cases, the question of antecedent precautions is always an issue, such that a defendant that has warning of the violent wind is then under a duty to put out the fire before it has a chance to spread. In this regard, the rules follow those generated under the earlier law of "inevitable accident," which received a cryptic explanation in the celebrated case of *Weaver v. Ward* (80 Eng. Rep. 284 [K.B. 1616]), where the proposition was put as follows:

> As if a man by force take my hand and strike you, or if here the defendant had said that the plaintiff ran against his piece when it was discharging, or had set forth the case with the circumstances so that it had appeared to the Court that it had been inevitable, and that the defendant had committed no negligence to give occasion to the hurt.

Note the sequence that a general strict liability rule is followed by an inevitable accident defense, which in turn can be overridden by noting an antecedent negligence that set up ("occasioned") the harm. That is exactly the pattern here. If an act of God occurs, the antecedent levels of care matter. If not, they don't. It is a mixed position that pays due attention to the complexities of custodia—the rules that impose liability for safekeeping—without throwing out the strict liability position in the many cases where the act of God issue is never raised.

Causation

The next stage in any tort litigation involves the proof of causation in all its manifold guises. These are, respectively, the cause-in-fact question and the proximate cause question, which covers cases of causal intervention, joint causation, and foreseeable causation. This section takes these up in order.

Cause-in-Fact

The correct way to think about cause-in-fact is to avoid all complex questions of necessary and sufficient conditions, and to attack the question of causation by starting with the particular harm and working backward to its origins. Accordingly, the proof of causation in the case of fire starts with the very flames that consumed the house or fields, and then identifies the origin of the fire that caused them. It is a good defense in these circumstances to note that the defendant's fire was extinguished before it could reach the plaintiff's property, or that the harm came from some other source, either human or natural. In most clean cases, this is a routine fact question that is easily addressed.

Proximate Causation

Here is not the place to give an extensive overview of the subject (for my recent account, see Epstein 2010), but it is useful to pick up three strands in the overall debate. The first of these relates to questions of causal intervention, the second to questions of joint causation, and the third to the larger issue of the antecedent foreseeability of harm from the vantage point of the actor.

Causal Intervention

The question of proximate causation arises in two different guises. The first is when the harm to the plaintiff must be traced through some intermediate actions or events before they can be placed on the doorstep of the defendant. That issue was raised in the well-known case of *Vaughan v. Menlove* (132 Eng. Rep. 490 [C.P. 1837]), where the defendant did not set the fire, but rather built a hayrick that caught fire by spontaneous combustion, when heat from fermentation got trapped inside the structure. An initial cause-in-fact problem is introduced because the defendant can truthfully deny that he set the fire in the sense that he did not light the rick. But by the same token, it is clear beyond doubt that he did create the dangerous condition that led natural forces to generate the fire that did the harm. In every known legal system, therefore, the defendant's attempted defense fails. The case becomes more difficult if a third person in some way sets fire to the rick. Here the causation problem is that this particular action could easily have caused extensive damage if the same actions set aside loose stubble, so that it would be hard to attribute any *increased* risk of harm to the fire itself.

With *Vaughan*, therefore, we have the fire equivalent of a distinction between the writs of trespass for the direct application of force and the action on the case for indirect harms, which is similar to the distinction underlying damage by water, in which a defendant can either "send" water down into the plaintiff's land or allow water to "escape" after waterlogging the foundations in which the water was kept.[8] All these cases are not ones of remote damages but of indirect causation, for which the remoteness issue is a nonstarter for the defendant. The key question is whether, as the notion of causation shifts from direct to indirect, this should influence the standard of liability that is brought to bear in the particular case. The clear answer has long been that it should not, which leaves open the question of which way liability should run. In *Vaughan*, the court missed this issue and took advantage of the fact that the defendant had acted stupidly at best to avoid the question by noting at different points in time that his conduct was negligent or grossly negligent. But in general, on this question of proximate causation, there is no reason to deviate from the theory of strict liability as the length of the chain increases. The key issue therefore is just how far it can go.

On this last point, there is an ambiguity that needs correction. It is often said that deliberate actions by third persons that spread fire will eliminate the chain of causation. That seems to be true insofar as we have a person who takes a small fire and then puts bellows on it to expand. But once the fire is out of control, it probably does not matter if some third person did something to send it further on its way. But that particular point is fluid, to say the least. The key point is that once the fire is extinguished or controlled, the deliberate action of any third person to reset it shifts the liability away from the original party, in line with general theory.

Joint Causation

In all areas of tort law, the combination of two or more causes that result in a single harm is the source of logical difficulties and admits of no obvious solution. The issue, which has an important role to play in the law of fire, is initially best described by a simple illustration in which two individuals each administer a separate and independent blow to the plaintiff, which together are sufficient to cause some degree of harm. The question then arises how the responsibilities should be allocated between them. If one adopts the position of "but for" causation, each party might well be able to escape liability by showing that the action of the other party, standing alone, was sufficient to do the damage, which leads to the odd but indefensible position that neither party is liable in the case of dual causation. The system gets no easier when neither of the two forces is sufficient to cause the harm, but the combination of the two is. If the two blows are of equal strength, then an even division of responsibility seems to follow, but the allocation question is more difficult to answer when one of the blows is larger than the other but neither, taken alone, is sufficient to cause the harm in question. When precise measurement is possible, is an even division of responsibility proper because neither blow makes a difference without the other, or is the apportionment to be in accordance with the relative strength of the blows?

The second dimension to the problem arises when one of the defendants is present but the other is absent. At this point, does the one party who remains have to bear all or only some fraction of the loss? One variation on that question in turn asks what should happen if one of these blows is of natural, not human, origin. To which source, human or natural, does the priority of responsibility belong?

What can be said of two blows can also be said of two fires, transferring these allocation problems to another setting so long as at least one of the fires is attributable to human origin. In dealing with these questions, the usual answer is to impose a system of joint and several liability if both fires are of human origin, but to allow no recovery for the plaintiff if even one of the (two or more) fires is of natural origin, as in *Kingston v. Chicago & N.W. Ry. Co.* (211 N.W. 913 [Wis. 1927]). The difficulty of this approach is that it puts too much emphasis on the particulars of the given situation, when what is needed in these cases is a rule that makes the responsibility of one party invariant regardless of the other source (or sources) of danger. Here the simplest rule is one that proceeds as follows: first determine the number of fires (or forces) that are present, and then assign to each its proportional share. In most cases, the proper default rule is to treat the separate fires (and forces) of equal measure, and then allocate $1/n$ of the harm to each. At that point, the plaintiff bears the risk of all harms caused by natural events, and each defendant bears the fractional share of its own loss. If the fires are of unequal magnitude, it might be possible to alter the proportion of responsibility to reflect the relative sizes, except in those cases where the evidence does not allow for accurate determinations of those relative quantities.

Once these divisions are made, neither defendant should be responsible for the loss assigned to the other fire (or force). At this point, it is possible to avoid the odd conclusion that the liability of the first party depends on whether the second fire is of natural or human origin. It also avoids the situation where the plaintiff is better off when the fire is caused by both A and B than when it is caused by only one. Thus if all the damage were caused by A, and A was insolvent, the matter would come to an end. The relative simplicity of the basic allocation—each person is responsible for his or her pro rata share only—circumvents this difficulty, as it removes the further complications of trying to make sense of the logic of "necessary" and "sufficient" causes. These logical notions are hard to cash out in a theory of causation, because it is often wholly unclear where to draw the line between them. When there is no authoritative account of causation, the best approach is to pick a simple rule that works reasonably well in all situations, avoiding pointless refinements that do nothing to improve the incentives of any of the parties.

Antecedent Foresight

The last portion of the proximate cause debate deals not with the issue of intervention, but with the issue, broadly conceived, of foresight. Suffice it to say that for these purposes, the argument does not seek to trace the destruction of a fire back to its antecedents, but rather asks a very different question: What was the threshold probability from the ex ante perspective that the particular harm in question was likely to have occurred at the time of the defendant's action? The simplest answer is that any positive probability will do, in which case the whole question just disappears. That appears to have been the Roman approach, as *Justinian's Digest* says, "If someone wished to burn down my tenement building and the fire spread to my neighbor's block of flats, he will be liable to my neighbor too" (Watson 1998, 9.2.27.8). The limited intentions of the defendant did not limit the scope of the liability, nor does there appear to have been any restriction of consequence that is attached to the word "neighbor," which sounds as if it refers to any party located in the vicinity.

In general, this is the approach that has been taken in modern American law. The one notable early exception, *Ryan v. New York Central Railroad* (35 N.Y. 210 [1866]), involved the spread of a fire from the railroad's engines until it consumed the defendant's property some distance away. The court denied recovery by appealing to both notions of proximate causation. On the issue of causal intervention, it insisted that the harm was too remote. It thus wrote:

> The result, however, depends, not upon any necessity of a further com-
> munication of the fire, but upon a concurrence of accidental circumstances,
> such as the degree of the heat, the state of the atmosphere, the condition
> and materials of the adjoining structures and the direction of the wind. These
> are accidental and varying circumstances. The party has no control over them,
> and is not responsible for their effects.
>
> (35 N.Y. at 212)

It is hard to imagine a more crabbed account of the theory of proximate causation. If all these background factors are in play with properties that are located at some distance from the defendant's fire, they are also in play with those fires that are next door. This supposed test is at a notable variance from the requirement of a violent wind that drove the inquiry in *Tuberville* and for that reason is widely rejected today.

Unfortunately, on the foresight question, the court equally misfired by setting the antecedent probability far too high by noting that this fire did not fall within the class of "necessary or natural consequences, nor the results ordinarily to be anticipated from the negligence committed" (35 N.Y. at 211). These thresholds are far too high given the argument made above. And the decision further errs by making it appear that some negligence in the operation of the train is required, which, while often the case, need not always be the case if a strict liability theory is adopted.

Nor is this decision required by some odd notion that "[a] man may insure his own house or his own furniture, but he cannot insure his neighbor's building or furniture, for the reason that he has no interest in them" (35 N.Y. at 216). The question is not whether one can acquire property insurance, but whether one can acquire liability insurance, to which the answer is yes. It may well be that the fires will be ruinous financially, but that question is a matter of bankruptcy law, which should not be evaded by eliding the set of consequences in ways that no sound theory of proximate causation could allow. It is therefore no surprise that the narrow view of proximate causation adopted in *Ryan* has been widely rejected in both the United States and England,[9] in favor of a view that tracks the Roman position denying these nuances without making any distinctive appeal to a doctrine of proximate causation. Breaks in the causal chain make good sense. The elimination of liability for some low-probability events does not. Accordingly, on this topic at least, the law of fire should fold back into the general law of proximate cause, correctly understood.

Affirmative Defenses

The last of the great topics in tort law flips over from the issue of defendant's conduct to ask what, if anything, a plaintiff has done to forfeit or reduce the amount of recovery in a given case. In dealing with this question, it is important to distinguish between two forms of this argument. Under the first, the defendant insists that the plaintiff was the sole source of his or her own harm. This could arise by the simple observation that the plaintiff set the only fire that was responsible for the loss. That general denial, however, is not what is meant by an affirmative defense, which, consistent with standard use, requires that the defendant concede both the validity and truth of the prima facie case, only to show that even then the recovery should be removed or denied for some reason. In some instances, this argument is not all that difficult. Suppose, for example, that the defendant sets up a hayrick, which goes up in smoke when the plaintiff ignites it with sparks from his or her own land. At this point, the defense either reduces or eliminates the liability.

The far harder cases are those in which a fire set by a defendant spreads to the plaintiff's land, and the sole affirmative defense is that the plaintiff did not do enough to keep his or her land free of the material that allowed the fire to spread. At this point, the fire defense is a complex variation on the traditional view that holds that the defendant takes his victim as he finds him. Consider the cases where the defendant has struck a plaintiff with an "eggshell skull." The phrase "eggshell skull" refers to unusually sensitive individuals, where the legal rule is that the defendant takes that victim as he finds him. This principle applies in real property cases where flax is very flammable, such as *LeRoy Fibre Co. v. Chicago, Milwaukee & St. Paul Ry.* (232 U.S. 340 [1914]). It also applies in personal injuries cases, as when a defendant driver hits a plaintiff with serious antecedent psychological conditions that magnify the impact on any initial contact, such as *Steinhauser v. Hertz Corp.* (421 F.2d 1169 [2d Cir. 1970]).[10] In these cases, the law in effect adopts a strong and clear line in which all the risk of a mishap falls on the party who has engaged in the invasive conduct, and none on the party that has not taken steps for self-protection against that hazard. The same issue has arisen in connection with water, in the case of *Smith v. Kenrick* (137 Eng. Rep. 205 [C.P. 1849]), where the standard response is that each party is under a duty to take whatever steps it wants against a "common enemy," but none must take steps to protect another.

This overall approach sets the required level of victim precaution against harms inflicted by strangers at precisely zero. The stranger thus knows that he or she has to guard against the full range of potential injuries. In making that calculation, potential actors can also be confident that most persons with thin skulls will take some precautions against external harms because they fear physical injury from their own missteps, those of their family and friends, natural events, and total strangers without the resources to pay for any losses. The rule therefore has a huge ex post advantage in the cases that do make it into court of having a clean zero/one solution, which cuts down amply on administrative expenses.

In the land use context (in contrast to the personal injury case), this clear delineation of property rights could easily lead to efforts of parties to contract around the appropriate legal rule when it is cheaper for the owner of exposed property to take steps to avoid the harm than it is for the party that caused the harm to take other precautions. This possibility is explained by thinking of the matter in terms of a general single-owner test (see, generally, Epstein 1993). Thus, suppose that a single person owned both parcels of land, so that the only question he or she faced would be how to take those steps that minimize the total harm in question. The sole owner would not care two figs whether the effective precaution came from fixing one part of the parcel or the other. Since there are no transaction cost barriers to getting the right division of responsibility, he or she could adopt a strategy as simple as keeping a barrier in place to block water on one side and moving valuable objects out of harm's way on the other. Similarly, the rational single owner could attack the risk of fire by tamping down on a fire at the place of its origin and using some better insulation on the other. Two or more sets of precautions can be integrated into a cohesive plan.

But once the two (or more) parcels are placed in separate hands, only two possibilities remain. One is to keep with the hard zero/one allocation used for plaintiffs with eggshell skulls and hope that the needed steps are taken either by voluntary negotiation on the one hand or by state intervention on the other. The second is to guess what the efficient division of responsibility is in the joint care setting, and then to impose a liability rule that seems to meet the difficulties at hand by assigning the requisite tasks to each side.

Both of these solutions have serious drawbacks. One peculiar feature of both fire and water is their ability to spread, such that many plots of land could easily be at risk at the same time, which could block any voluntary efforts to achieve a better coordination of separate actions. At this point, the eminent domain solution actually has something to say for itself. In the standard case where sparks from a railroad destroy crops on many lands, one solution is for the state to condemn an easement over the abutting private land. The landowners receive some compensation that reflects the overall diminution in the value of the land, which might well be small, if the creation of the fire break is valuable for dealing not only with fires set by the defendant, but also with fires that are natural events. These charges could then be levied back on the owner of the railroad line, who could then pass the costs on to the various railroad companies that ran over the tracks. This achieves both an efficient allocation of resources and the correct distribution of the overall financial burden.

This approach may not be cheap to implement, especially if there is no uniform topography that allows for an accurate determination of the appropriate size of the fire break, or the even level of compensation needed to bring the landowner back to the antecedent state. The alternative solution is to generate out of whole cloth a straight joint care solution that imposes the appropriate affirmative duties on the landowners, wholly without regard to the niceties of compensation. One simple solution could require, for example, that farmers not "crowd" the railroad by setting back their crops a certain distance from the tracks. This solution could take into account variations in climatic conditions in the way that a once-and-for-all easement could not possibly do, requiring the parties to take higher levels of precautions during dry seasons than during wet ones.

Needless to say, on a legal matter of this difficulty, it is easy to find judicial endorsements of both positions. The most famous case on the subject, *LeRoy Fibre Co. v. Chicago, Milwaukee & St. Paul Ry.* (232 U.S. 340 [1914]), opted for what today we would call the corner solution: all the responsibility for the fire lay with the railroad whose conduct caused the harm in question. In *LeRoy Fibre*, this argument was made in the context of a negligence theory, where the allegations of negligence had a pro forma quality—no one much cared why the sparks were excessive relative to the condition. But the same issue arises in exactly the same form in a strict liability system. The language used to reach this conclusion had a somewhat archaic tone, when Justice McKenna wrote: "It upsets the presumptions of law and takes from him the assumption and the freedom which comes from the assumption, that the other will obey the law, not violate it. It casts upon him the duty of not only using his own property so as not to injure another, but so to use his own property that it may not be injured by the wrongs of another" (232 U.S. at 349).

In effect, the view is that the plaintiff is allowed at all times before the fire to act as if the defendant will take all the risk of liability on his or her own shoulders. To be sure, the plaintiff always has a duty to mitigate losses subsequent to the imposition of harm. But that position works in practice because the defendant is responsible for the costs of mitigation undertaken in good faith, whether or not he or she reduces the underlying harm. The difficulty from this perspective is that imposing the duty of care *prior* to the time of the wrong means that the defendant has to incur costs that will not be recoverable from anyone if the defendant does not start a fire, nor will he or she recover anything for those precautions even if they are effective in eliminating or reducing the damage from fire after the harm occurs. The result of Justice McKenna's effort is to prevent the tort system from working a redistribution of wealth from the passive to the active party, even in a case where the boundary line makes it clear which party turns out to be which.

What is striking in this case is that Holmes's dissent seeks to achieve the required joint care equilibrium by imposing a standard of care that maximizes, as we should say, joint welfare under the single-owner test articulated above. He writes:

> I should say that although of course he had a right to put his flax where he liked upon his own land, the liability of the railroad for a fire was absolutely conditioned upon the stacks being at a reasonably safe distance from the train.
> . . .
> If I am right so far, a very important element in determining the right to recover is whether the plaintiff's flax was so near to the track as to be in danger from even a prudently managed engine.

The upshot is that the plaintiff can store the flax wherever he or she wishes, but takes the risk if he or she stores it too close to the tracks. The reasonably safe distance is the distance that the single owner would choose to handle the situation to cover all cases. It is hard, for example, to determine the optimal level of spacing between buildings. Sometimes sufficient protection is obtained so long as no vegetation touches a building. In other cases, even vast distances offer scant protection from gusts of wind that can carry flames long distances, leapfrogging over one house before landing on another. Any determination of the optimal separation, however, is not made against the backdrop of a system of negligence liability, but is made, in all cases, so as to cover the "danger from even a prudently managed engine." It is an open question as to whether distance is the proper variable for measuring responsibility in these cases. It could well be that fires could jump any barrier in high winds, so that other types of more onerous precautions would be optimal, and it is uncertain just how far Holmes would have gone down that road, just as it is clear that McKenna would tolerate any location of the property no matter how manifest the gains from some simple precaution.

One reason for this toughness of mind is that railroads run adjacent to many plots of land, and the fear is that the joint care solution would not be uniform in all cases. This issue also arises in some nuisance cases with diffuse harms, where the benefits from setting sensible levels of victim precaution seem great enough to displace the thin skull rule. Thus the extrasensitive plaintiff may lose out, for example, when low levels of noise or pollution cause dislocation that are not suffered by others, such as in *Rogers v. Elliott* (15 N.E. 768 [Mass. 1888]). It is just too costly, so the standard theory goes, to let the legality of given conduct always be determined by the most sensitive person in the group, who, given the pervasive nature of noise and smoke, is always likely to be, as it were, in the line of fire.

On the other hand, in fire cases such as *Kansas Pacific Ry. Co. v. Brady* (17 Kan. 380 [Kan. 1877]), judges gravitate toward a joint care solution. They hold as a matter of law that there may be contributory negligence for failure to take steps for self-protection precisely because, "as the burning of said hay was the result of the acts and omissions of both the plaintiffs and the defendant, it would seem that the acts and omissions of both parties should have been submitted to the jury" (17 Kan. at 386), which is a position often taken by economics-oriented commentators (see Grady 1988). Note that the use of the phase "acts and omissions" bridges the divide that Justice McKenna thought dominated this case. Submitting both forms of conduct to the jury is, of course, the sure way to invite a divided verdict in those cases where both parties deviated from their optimal standard of conduct in the joint care situation.

These concerns are easily generalized into claims that the notion of causation generates a set of reciprocal duties on both parties (see *Svea Ins. Co. v. Vicksburg, S. & P. Ry.* (153 F. 774 [W.D. La. 1907])). This naturally leads to a neat tie-in with Coase's view of causation, in which that notion becomes useless as a decider of individual cases precisely because "to avoid the harm to B would inflict harm on A, the real question that has to be decided is: should A be allowed to harm B or should B be allowed to harm A?" (Coase 1960). At this point, however, it is critical to remember how deeply subversive Coase's influential account of causation is to ordinary notions of responsibility. For example, it becomes an open question whether A's face got in the way of B's fist or whether B's fist broke A's cheekbone. The Coasean account makes it appear that the notion of causation can be separated from the ordinary system of individual autonomy and property rights, which in most cases it cannot. Usually, the person who gets to a place first has the right to be there. That is why the thin skull rule has such power for ordinary interactions.

Yet more has to be done in cases where the collision risk is high. In those settings, the creation of a consistent set of rules that delineates rights-of-way, be it by the state or by a private owner, is the sensible way to address the property rights question. Once done, it is now possible to tell whether A had the right-of-way, for example, when he struck B. But one would not want to use that logic to ask which party should have done what if A's baseball beans B while B is sitting in her chair in her own backyard. In most cases, therefore, the rights structure is firm enough to make causation the second-tier issue. The physical invasion test dominates any notion that all forms of causation are perfectly reciprocal. (For cases of deviation, see Epstein 1979.)

In sum, in the fire cases, the badness of fit between the physical invasion rules and the model of optimal precautions can lead people to deviate from the corner solution. But it would be a mistake to generalize from these fire cases to a larger theory of causation that generates the kind of open-ended inquiries that Coase thought were an essential portion of any system of responsibility. It is far better to think of the fire cases as situations in which the inefficiency of the standard solution invites contractual, legislative, and judicial interventions. The correct way to think about the problem is to note the want of a good fit between the notions of causation and efficient behavior in the fire cases. It is not to treat the breakdown in this situation as evidence of the inability of an ideal causation theory to handle any case, when the notions work quite well for virtually all common interactions.

Conclusions

This brief tour of the common law rules for liability for fire is intended to show how the basic principles of tort liability carry over to a particular kind of activity that shares many, but not all, elements of the traditional torts that involve the ordinary use of force by one person against another. In this regard, the stakes with fire are very high, so that we should expect that even in a public choice universe, the rules in the long run would tend toward efficient outcomes. There is, quite simply, no interest group that stands to win from the adoption of an inferior set of liability rules. And in general, the shape of the law tends to confirm that hypothesis. At the minimum, nothing in the law of fire looks to be counterproductive, and many rules, such as those dealing with vicarious liability, seem to serve a useful function. In those cases, moreover, where there may be some deviation from the optimal solution, it should be chalked up not to interest group politics, but to a genuine difficulty understanding how to craft the optimal set of rules when, as with contributory negligence, different considerations tug in different directions.

The future of the law of fire probably lies not with the further evolution of common law rules, but with direct forms of regulation that could easily have some dramatic effect on the operation of these systems and with the private cooperative arrangements that pick up where the government regulations leave off. Thus the rules limiting the clearing of fields in the face of threats to endangered species could easily alter the standard practices of fire control, as could any rules that might limit the ability of landowners to clear dead wood from their property. These topics of land management under government regulation are areas in which political forces are likely to exert far greater, and more baleful, influences. It is not a story that one expects to see have a happy ending.

Acknowledgment

The author thanks Sharon Yecies of the Class of 2011 at the University of Chicago Law School for her usual excellent research assistance.

Notes

1. See the Restatement (Second) of Torts, § 363 (1965):

    Natural Conditions

    (1) Except as stated in Subsection (2), neither a possessor of land, nor a vendor, lessor, or other transferor, is liable for physical harm caused to others outside of the land by a natural condition of the land.

    The exception refers to the condition of trees near the highway. For a discussion of these issues, see Chapter 3.

2. For a discussion of this dimension, see Chapter 2, noting the extensive protection afforded to the government against liability for takings. For case law discussion, see also *United States v. Caltex, Inc.* (344 U.S. 149 [1952]), where the demolition of Caltex's terminal

facilities in Manila before the Japanese takeover did not generate a claim for compensation. The result there is particularly compelling, because if the United States had done nothing, the Japanese would have seized the facilities, only to destroy them before they could be retaken by American forces.

3. See, e.g., *Turner v. Lotts* (244 Va. 554, 557 [Va. 1992]): "A plaintiff who invokes that doctrine must present evidence which creates a factual issue whether the owner knew, or had reasonable cause to know, that he was entrusting his car to an unfit driver likely to cause injury to others. Furthermore, in order to impose liability upon the owner, the plaintiff must prove that the negligent entrustment of the motor vehicle to the tortfeasor was a proximate cause of the accident." Note that the doctrine easily generalizes from cars to other instrumentalities of danger.

4. See, e.g., *Powers v. Mass. Homeopathic Hosp.* (101 Fed. 896, 899 [C.C.D. Mass. 1899], *aff'd*, 109 Fed. 294 [1st Cir. 1901]). For different views on the role of charitable immunities, see Horwitz (2010) and Epstein (2010).

5. This privilege attaches to any government activity "based upon the exercise or performance or the failure to exercise or perform a discretionary function or duty on the part of a federal agency or an employee of the Government, whether or not the discretion involved be abused." See *Dalehite v. United States* (346 U.S. 15, 18 [1953]), using broad definition of policy judgments at the operational level.

6. See the discussion of *Mouse's Case* (66 Eng. Rep. 1341 [K.B. 1609]) in Epstein (2008). For more extended discussion, see Gilmore and Black (1975). See also Landes and Posner (1978).

7. See Restatement (Second) Torts § 519–520 (1965). The "ultrahazardous" language tended to be preferred in the first Restatement of Torts.

8. For a discussion of this point at the trial level, see *Fletcher v. Rylands* (3 H. & C. 774, 159 Eng. Rep. 737 [Ex. 1865], *rev'd*, 1 Ex. 265 [1866], *aff'd sub nom. Rylands v. Fletcher*, 3 H.L. 330 [1868]).

9. In the United States, *Pennsylvania R.R. Co. v. Kerr* (62 Pa. 353 [Pa. 1870]) and, in the Supreme Court, *Milwaukee & St. Paul Ry. Co. v. Kellogg* (94 U.S. 469 [1876]). In England, *Smith v. London & South Western Ry. Co.* (3 L.R. 6 C.P. 21 [1870]). ("What the defendants might reasonably anticipate is only material with reference to the question, whether the defendants were negligent or not, and cannot alter their liability if they were guilty of negligence.") Note that the disjunction disappears if liability for fire is treated as strict, which in some cases it is.

10. "[W]here the defendant has negligently struck a person whose skull is so fragile that it is broken by the comparatively slight blow, all courts are agreed that the defendant is liable for the wholly unexpected breaking. This is true not only with reference to physical harm but also other forms of harm" (Seavey 1939).

References

Arnold, Morris. 1979. Accident, Mistake, and Rules of Liability in the Fourteenth Century Law of Torts. *University of Pennsylvania Law Review* 128:361–378.

Bohlen, Francis H. 1926. Incomplete Privilege to Inflict Intentional Invasions of Interests of Property and Personality. *Harvard Law Review* 39:307–324.

Coase, Ronald H. 1960. The Problem of Social Cost. *Journal of Law and Economics* 3:1–44.

Dykes, Brett Michael. Yahoo News. 2010. Rural Tennessee Fire Sparks Conservative Ideological Debate. http://news.yahoo.com/s/yblog_upshot/20101005/pl_yblog_upshot/rural-tennessee-fire-sparks-conservative-ideological-debate Yahoo News (accessed April 21, 2011).

Epstein, Richard A. 1973. A Theory of Strict Liability. *Journal of Legal Studies* 2:151–204.

——. 1974. Defenses and Subsequent Pleas in a System of Strict Liability. *Journal of Legal Studies* 3:165–216.

———. 1979. Nuisance Law: Corrective Justice and Its Utilitarian Constraints. *Journal of Legal Studies* 8:49–102.

———. 1986. The Temporal Dimension in Tort Law. *University of Chicago Law Review* 53:1175–1218.

———. 1993. Holdouts, Externalities, and the Single Owner: One More Salute to Ronald Coase. *Journal of Law and Economics* 36:553–586.

———. 2008. *Cases and Materials on Torts.* New York: Aspen Publishers.

———. 2009. Medieval Libertarians. www.forbes.com/2009/08/23/bergen-norway-medieval-land-use-regulation-opinions-columnists-richard-a-epstein.html (accessed April 21, 2011).

———. 2010. Toward a General Theory of Tort Law: Strict Liability in Context. *Journal of Tort Law* 3 (1): article 6. www.bepress.com/jtl/vol3/iss1/art6 (accessed April 21, 2011).

Fifoot, Cecil H.S. 1949. *History and Sources of the Common Law.* New York: Greenwood Press.

Gilmore, G., and C. Black. 1975. *The Law of Admiralty.* Mineola, NY: Foundation Press.

Grady, Mark. 1988. Common Law Control of Strategic Behavior: Railroad Sparks and the Farmer. *Journal of Legal Studies* 17:15–42.

Gregory, Charles O. 1951. Gratuitous Undertakings and the Duty of Care. *DePaul Law Review* 1:30.

Horwitz, Jill R. 2010. The Multiple Common Law Roots of Charitable Immunity: An Essay in Honor of Richard Epstein's Contributions to Tort Law Scholarship. *Journal of Tort Law* 3 (1): article 44. www.bepress.com/jtl/vol3/iss1/art4/ (accessed April 21, 2011).

Klitzke, Ramon A. 1959. Roman Building Ordinances Relating to Fire Protection. *American Journal of Legal History* 3:173–187.

Landes, William M., and Richard A. Posner. 1978. Salvors, Finders, Good Samaritans, and Other Rescuers: An Economic Study of Law and Altruism. *Journal of Legal Studies* 7:83–128.

McChesney, Fred S. 1986. Government Prohibitions on Volunteer Fire Fighting in Nineteenth-Century America: A Property Rights Perspective. *Journal of Legal Studies* 15:69–92.

Seavey, Warren A. 1939. Mr. Justice Cardozo and the Law of Torts. *Columbia Law Review* 39:20–55; *Harvard Law Review* 52:372–407; *Yale Law Journal* 48:390–425.

Watson, Allen, ed. and trans. 1998. *The Digest of Justinian.* 4 vols. Philadelphia: University of Pennsylvania Press.

2

PROPERTY AND FIRE

Thomas W. Merrill

Fire has had a considerable impact on the scope of property rights. Historically speaking, the greatest impact has come from the danger of urban fires. For many centuries, catastrophic fires posed a very real danger to those living in cities. Much of London was wiped out by fire in 1666, Boston experienced repeated devastating fires in the eighteenth century, lower Manhattan was completely destroyed by fire in 1835, over one-third of Chicago was incinerated in 1871, and the greater part of San Francisco burned to the ground after the earthquake of 1906.[1] The problem was created by the close proximity of many easily combustible structures, combined with relatively primitive firefighting institutions and technology. Fire would break out in one building, would spread to adjacent structures, and if conditions were dry and windy, would soon pose a threat of general conflagration to the entire community.

Faced with a danger of cataclysmic proportions, it is not surprising that the threat of urban fire gave rise to some extreme qualifications of property rights. The most important qualifications were the following three: (1) the doctrine of overruling necessity, creating an exception to the law of trespass for those combating fires; (2) the expansion of the police power to include prophylactic measures designed to prevent fires as opposed to undoing presently existing harms; and (3) the conflagration rule, which denied compensation for official destruction of property to stop the spread of fire.

The degree to which these exceptions have been generalized beyond the problem of urban fire is mixed. The expansion of the police power to include prophylactic measures to reduce the risk of fire served as an important precedent for later social regulations such as temperance and narcotics laws. In contrast, the conflagration rule has been extended in only a limited fashion, primarily to destruction of property at risk of falling into enemy hands during time of war. Still, it is reasonable to anticipate that all three exceptions will be asserted, in the proper circumstances, in controversies over containment of wildfires.

The catastrophic fires that repeatedly plagued cities for centuries are now largely forgotten. This is undoubtedly due to a confluence of factors: the use of better building materials; a dramatic reduction in the use of open fires for heating and incineration of waste materials; the adoption of fire codes that regulate the design of buildings and water systems; incentives for better fire-prevention practices created by fire insurance companies; improvements in firefighting technology; and better trained and staffed professional fire departments (Tebeau 2003). This is a great success story, an example of property owners overcoming a daunting collective action problem with the help of government.[2] As we bemoan the many failures of government to solve the problems of the day—international terrorism, financial crises, runaway medical costs—it is worth pausing to consider the occasional triumph of government, in this case the success of local governments in ending the threat of devastating fire that haunted city dwellers for many centuries.

The contemporary danger posed by wildfire differs in many respects from the problem of urban fires. The threat of wildfire comes from outside urban areas rather than from within. The problem has been created, at least in part, by a newfound preference for leaving large tracts of land undeveloped, rather than by intensive development. The primary governmental actor in leading fire suppression activities is the federal government, acting through the U.S. Forest Service, rather than local governments. And property owners threatened by wildfire are more likely to complain of government inaction—for example, letting wildfires burn, failing to use controlled burns to limit the accumulation of natural fuels, or devoting inadequate resources to preventing or containing fires—than to challenge affirmative government acts such as pulling down structures to create a fire break. These differences mean that the exceptions to conventional property law developed in the context of urban fire do translate perfectly to the context of wildfires. Nevertheless, it is virtually certain that as wildfires proliferate and residents continue to build in close proximity to areas prone to wildfires, conflicts will emerge in which the property concepts developed in the context of urban fires will be tested.

In asking whether the qualifications to property rights recognized in the context of urban fires will carry over to wildfires, it is also important to consider some significant changes in the general organization of society that have occurred since the era of mass urban conflagrations ended about one hundred years ago. Four in particular strike me as important: the general growth in government and, in particular, the near-universal assumption today that government is responsible for preventing and controlling fires; the emergence of immunities for government officials including firefighters from actions in tort arising out of their official duties; the evisceration of sovereign immunity as a defense to claims against the government; and the growth and maturation of fire insurance as a general source of protection for property owners against the risk of fire. These institutional changes suggest that the exceptions to property law developed in the context of urban fires may need to be rethought in the context of wildfires. Nevertheless, I will argue that all three major qualifications of property rights should carry over to wildfires, including the exception to the just compensation requirement reflected in the conflagration rule.

Property Rights and Urban Conflagration

The great danger associated with catastrophic urban fires gave rise to three important exceptions to conventional property rights. Cumulatively, these exceptions amount to a near suspension of ordinary property rights of exclusion and managerial authority in the face of collective peril to all property.

First, under what has been called the doctrine of overruling necessity, a fire emergency creates a privilege of entry that overrides the ordinary right of owners to exclude others from their land. The privilege originally applied to public officials and private citizens alike. Indeed, because firefighting before the nineteenth century was largely in the hands of companies of volunteers, no sharp distinction between public and private actors could be maintained.

The privilege continues to exist today, although with firefighting now mostly performed by government agents, we have to translate it through the lens of Fourth Amendment law. As to entry into property where a fire has broken out, the doctrine of exigent circumstances applies: "No one questions the right of the firefighters to make a forceful, unannounced, nonconsensual, warrantless entry into a burning building" (*Michigan v. Clifford*, 464 U.S. 288, 299 [1984] (concurring opinion)). In contrast, the Fourth Amendment requires an administrative warrant for inspectors to ascertain whether a building complies with the fire code (*See v. City of Seattle*, 387 U.S. 523 [1967]). And it requires a search warrant if arson investigators seek to enter a building after a fire has been extinguished, there is no danger of a reignition, and all firefighters have left the scene (*Michigan v. Tyler*, 436 U.S. 499 [1978]; *Michigan v. Clifford*). Nevertheless, while the emergency lasts, no warrant or other process is required to do whatever it takes to extinguish the fire, including smashing in windows and doors, chopping holes in roofs and walls, and hurling personal belongings onto the street. Firefighters are allowed to disregard property rights, pursuing with ruthless single-mindedness the goal of extinguishing the fire before it gets out of hand. This is well understood and virtually never challenged.

The common law went further. Not only did it recognize a privilege of entry to extinguish fire, but it also recognized a much more draconian privilege to enter and destroy property that was not on fire in order to prevent the spread of fire. As the Supreme Court observed in 1880: "At the common law every one had the right to destroy real and personal property, in cases of actual necessity, to prevent the spreading of a fire, and there was no responsibility on the part of such destroyer, and no remedy for the owner" (*Bowditch v. Boston*, 101 U.S. 16, 18 [1880]). This privilege to "pluck down" buildings, as the English cases put it, was applied as recently as 1906, when the U.S. Army entered San Francisco to dynamite buildings in order to stop the spread of multiple fires that broke out from ruptured gas mains following an earthquake estimated to be 7.9 on the Richter scale.

Second, the risk of urban fire gave rise to an important expansion in public nuisance law, which in turn laid the foundation for a more general expansion of the police power. The classic example of a public nuisance was an actual interference with a right common to the general public, such as blocking a highway or a navigable river. Later this was extended to other actual interferences with public rights, such as overgrazing a commons or polluting a public water source. The risk of fire introduced the idea that potential harms to the general public could also be regulated as a public nuisance. One step in this direction was the enactment of statutes declaring the storage of gunpowder with the city limits to be a public nuisance (Novak 1996). Gunpowder was regarded as an inherently dangerous substance, because it was prone to accidental explosions, which could trigger a fire. Hence, gunpowder was ordered out of cities, as a purely prophylactic measure. Some legislatures went even further, banning the construction of wooden buildings in city centers (Novak 1996). There is nothing inherently dangerous about wooden buildings, but they are more prone to ignite when nearby buildings catch on fire than are buildings made of brick or stone. Ordinances banning wooden structures can be found as early as the late eighteenth century in cities like Philadelphia; New York; Boston; Charleston, South Carolina; and even Bangor, Maine.

One particularly interesting type of local regulation required every property owner to keep on hand water buckets, ladders, and hooks for the use of firefighters. The buckets and ladders are perhaps self-explanatory. But why hooks? These were evidently designed to be secured to the eaves in order to facilitate pulling the structure down (Novak 1996). In other words, local ordinances required owners of property to purchase instruments for use in the destruction of their own property.

Conceptually, there is no clear line of distinction between public nuisance law and what came to be known as the police power. The principal difference is that public nuisance law is enforced by the courts, whereas police measures are more likely to be enforced by administrative bodies (Merrill 2011). The expansion of public nuisance law to include prophylactic measures to prevent fires segued naturally into police regulations to prevent fires. In this fashion, the early measures designed to reduce the risk of urban fires led directly to modern fire codes, building codes, and zoning laws (Prentice 1894).

Third, the pervasive threat of urban fire led to what is known as the conflagration rule, which says that individuals are not entitled to just compensation when their property is destroyed at the direction of public officials in fighting a fire. The rule began as an application of the privilege of overruling necessity, which authorized individuals to enter burning structures without consent and even to pull down structures in the path of a fire. The privilege required that those who entered property for these purposes be immunized from later suits in tort seeking damages. The question whether the state was obligated to provide compensation to owners in these circumstances was analytically distinct. But as already indicated, the line between public and private actions in fighting fires was not sharp prior to the modern era. Moreover, during the era of major urban fires, the government was protected by sovereign immunity against any suit for compensation without its consent. So an individual tort suit against firefighters was the only realistic action to obtain compensation.

Interestingly, a number of jurisdictions, including both New York and Massachusetts, adopted statutes in the nineteenth century waiving their sovereign immunity by providing that under certain circumstances, owners whose buildings were pulled down to prevent the spread of fire should be compensated. These statutes might be regarded as a sign that "natural justice" requires compensation in these circumstances. Conceivably, the statutes could have been regarded as precedents evolving into a principle of constitutional law. Instead, courts interpreted the statutes narrowly, against a background rule that assumed no duty to compensate.

The path of legal evolution from the privilege of overruling necessity to the conflagration rule is interesting, but I cannot spell out all the details here. The first American decision to discuss the issue, *Respublica v. Sparhawk*, established a theme found in nearly all the decisions that followed. The court expressed concern that if compensation were required for property destroyed under conditions of necessity, this would create perverse incentives for public officials, who might hesitate before ordering destruction of property even when it was in the general interest to do so. The court drew the following lesson from the Great London Fire of 1666:

> We find, indeed, a memorable instance of folly recorded in the 3 Vol. of Clarendon's History, where it is mentioned, that the Lord Mayor of London, in 1666, when that city was on fire, would not give directions for, or consent to, the pulling down forty wooden houses, or to the removing of furniture, &c. belonging to the Lawyers of the Temple, then on the Circuit, for fear he should be answerable for a trespass; and in consequence of this conduct half that great city was burnt.
>
> *Respublica v. Sparhawk* (1 Dall. 357 [Pa. 1788])

This conflated the question of individual liability in tort with that of government liability under the Takings Clause—a conflation that was also a feature of many of the ensuing decisions.

After the New York City Fire of 1835, the New York courts decided a series of cases in which owners of personal property that had been destroyed sought compensation, even though the New York statute directing that compensation be paid applied by its terms only to real property. This gave rise to holdings that neither the New York statute nor the New York constitution required compensation for destruction of personal property (*Russell v. Mayor of New York*, 2 Denio 461 [N.Y. 1845]; *Stone v. Mayor of New York*, 25 Wend. 157 [N.Y. 1840]; *American Print Works v. Lawrence*, 21 N.J.L. 248 [N.J. 1847]). The U.S. Supreme Court reached a similar conclusion in 1880 when a bankrupt property owner sought compensation under the Massachusetts statute. The Court held that the statutory conditions had not been met, and it assumed no compensation was required outside the statute, i.e., by the Massachusetts Constitution (*Bowditch* 101 U.S. 16, 18).

Later, the constitutional principle was extended to property destroyed by order of military officers to prevent it from falling into enemy hands. The first such ruling came after the Mexican-American War; several more arose out of the Civil War (e.g., *United States v. Pacific Railroad Co.*, 120 U.S. 227 [1887]; *Mitchell v. Harmony*, 54 U.S. 115 [1851]). The Supreme Court held in *Caltex v. United States* in 1952 (344 U.S. 149) that the Takings Clause of the U.S. Constitution did not require compensation when the facilities of a U.S. firm in the Philippines were destroyed by the retreating U.S. military to prevent them from falling into the hands of the Japanese army. The Court expressly relied on the analogy to the destruction of buildings to prevent the spread of fire, which was treated as settled. Dicta in other Supreme Court cases, including *Lucas v. South Carolina Coastal Council* (505 U.S. 1003, 1029 n.16 [1992]), have also treated the conflagration rule as settled.

Intriguingly, there is no actual holding by the U.S. Supreme Court to the effect that the Takings Clause of the U.S. Constitution incorporates the conflagration rule. Nevertheless, given the state constitutional rulings, the parallel holdings involving military destruction of property, and the several approving references in dicta, it is unlikely that the rule would be repudiated at this point—at least, not in the context of an urban fire.

In sum, the eighteenth- and nineteenth-century experiences with catastrophic urban fire gave rise to three doctrines—overriding necessity, a greatly expanded police power, and the conflagration rule—that largely nullified conventional property rights. The threat to the collective was too great to stand in the way of ordinary rights of exclusion and owner sovereignty. As the threat of catastrophic fire has receded, these understandings are rarely revisited by courts today—although it is clear from their behavior that professional firefighters are taught to give no thought to property rights in combating a blaze. The interesting question is whether these understandings carry over to the context of wildfires and, in particular, whether the conflagration rule denying compensation for government destruction of property in fighting fire will be followed in a world much more accustomed to turning to governments for relief from disasters.

Property Rights and Wildfires: Recent Controversies

It will be useful to gain some sense of the types of situations in which these traditional modifications of property rights based on the danger of fire might be tested by wildfires. To this end, this section briefly describes the facts of three litigated cases in which takings claims have been brought against the U.S. government based on destruction of property by wildfires originating on National Forest lands.

In *Thune v. United States* (41 Fed. Cl. 49 [1998]), the Forest Service ignited a controlled burn aimed at enhancing elk habitat in the Bridger-Teton National Forest in Wyoming. Before igniting the fire, the Forest Service received a favorable weather forecast for the burn. Over the next two days, the wind changed direction, and the fire swept over a hunting camp owned by the plaintiff Thune. He was forced to evacuate before he could pack out all of his gear, which was destroyed. He sued the United States in the Court of Federal Claims, contending that the intentional setting of the fire was a taking of his personal property. The court held that Thune's property was destroyed by the change in the direction of the wind, not by an intentional action on the part of the Forest Service, and hence there was no taking.

In *Teegarden v. United States* (42 Fed. Cl. 252 [1998]), a large wildfire broke out in the Uinta Flats area in Utah. The Forest Service adopted a fire suppression plan that put first priority on firefighter safety, second priority on saving summer homes near Mammoth Creek, and third priority on saving commercial timber. The plaintiff owned a large tract of timberland in the path of fire. The Forest Service used a bulldozer to clear a fire break around the plaintiff's cabin, corral, and other buildings, which were spared. But by the time the fire burned out, nearly 8,000 acres of timber had been destroyed, including 612 acres owned by the plaintiff. Teegarden sued in the Court of Federal Claims, contending that the Forest Service had taken his timber when it intentionally decided to place a higher priority on saving the summer homes. The court found that the plaintiff's loss, even if partially attributable to the government's firefighting plan, was primarily due to natural causes, and there was no taking.

The most recent decision, *Cary v. United States* (552 F.3d 1373 [Fed. Cir. 2009]), involved one of the largest wildfires in California history, in the Cleveland National Forest near San Diego. The fire claimed the lives of 15 people, consumed nearly 275,000 acres of land, and destroyed 2,232 residences. The fire started when a deer hunter who was lost in the forest set a fire to aid his rescue. The plaintiffs claimed that the Forest Service was responsible, because it had adopted a policy of nearly complete suppression of all fires in the area, which allowed the vegetation to accumulate into unnaturally thick stands of trees and underbrush. Thus, they argued, the Forest Service took a calculated risk that its land management policies would result in a taking of the plaintiffs' property. The court held that there was no taking, because the government had no intention of starting a fire. The court warned, however, that if the Forest Service did have a plan to increase fuel loads in the forest, this would be sufficient to establish causation, because ignition of the fire, whether caused by a hunter or a lightning strike, was foreseeable.

In each of these cases, the takings claim was rejected on the ground that the government's action or inaction was not the proximate cause of the plaintiff's injury; some other event of nature or of a third party was an intervening cause of the destruction. It is not difficult, however, to imagine a case where this defense will not be available. Suppose, for example, that the Forest Service starts a controlled burn on the plaintiff's land in order to stop the progress of a wildfire. Such an action would be directly analogous to the plucking down of a building to stop an urban fire, the phenomenon that gave rise to the conflagration rule. In such a situation, it would be necessary to decide whether to extend the conflagration rule to the context of wildfires.

The three cases also open a window onto some of the ways in which the institutional backdrop has changed from the era of urban fires to the wildfire problem we confront today.

First, there is the simple fact of the growth of the state. It is difficult for those living today to imagine what it was like to live in London when it burned in 1666 or even in Chicago when it burned in 1871, in terms of the limited scope of government. There was nothing remotely equivalent to picking up a cell phone, dialing 911, and getting a quick response from an emergency response center. People were largely left on their own. Nowhere is the difference between then and now more evident than with respect to the emergence of modern professional fire departments (Tebeau 2003). Up to the final decades of the nineteenth century, firefighting was an amateur affair. Fires were fought by volunteer companies, whose primary form of compensation was "camaraderie" (McChesney 1986). Equipment was donated by wealthy patrons or insurance companies. Today, nearly everyone, whether he or she lives in a city, a small town, or a canyon next to a National Forest, expects some kind of governmental response from professional emergency responders when a major fire threatens his or her property.

The growth of government bears on the question of the continued validity of the exceptions to standard rules of property law in at least two respects. First, the fuzzy, if not indistinguishable, line between public and private responses to fires that prevailed during the era of urban fires has been sharply resolved. Those who respond to fire emergencies today are understood to be acting as government agents, or at least to be acting under the direction of government agents. Firefighting today is unambiguously state action. Second, the growth of government has given rise to the expectation that government will be successful in controlling fires. This expectation, in turn, makes it more likely, as a matter of political science if not law, that government will be held responsible for casualty losses associated with large fires.

Another change is the emergence of doctrines of official immunity shielding government officials, including firefighters, from actions in tort. In the eighteenth and nineteenth centuries, someone whose house was "plucked down" at the orders of a city official because it was in the path of a raging fire could file an action for trespass against the official; the official would defend by claiming overriding necessity; and the court would decide whether the defense was good, that is, whether it was reasonable to believe that a fire break was needed to protect other property from destruction. Today, statutes like the Westfall Act (28 U.S.C. § 2679(b)) make federal officials acting in the course of their official duties immune from tort actions. State law is more variable but has generally followed the same course.

The fact that individual responders today are immune from tort liability clearly diminishes the concern, expressed in decisions from *Sparhawk* to *Caltex*, that imposing liability for destruction of property to stop the spread of fire would deter officials from taking action necessary to protect the public. It does not eliminate this concern completely. If the federal government were required to pay just compensation for the value of any property intentionally destroyed by the Forest

Service in fighting a wildfire, one can readily envision that the Forest Service would adopt measures to reduce the likelihood of destruction. For example, it might promulgate guidelines requiring local fire crews to obtain prior approval from headquarters before undertaking any act of deliberate destruction. Thus, the concern about incentives on the ground is still relevant, although of diminished force.

A third change is the emergence of general waivers of sovereign immunity reflected in statutes like the Tucker Act (28 U.S.C. § 1491) and the Federal Torts Claims Act (28 U.S.C. § 2674 et seq.) and their state analogues. During the era of the great urban fires, it would have been impossible to sue the government for actions taken in fighting fires; an individual tort action against officials or private citizens doing the firefighting was the only possible remedy. Not surprisingly, courts sought to immunize these individual responders from the threat of tort liability by creating a broad privilege of overruling necessity. Today, individual government actors enjoy statutory immunity from suit, and suing the government is a more promising avenue of redress, given general waivers of sovereign immunity to sue the government in tort or for takings of property.

Here again, we can see that institutional change has made it more likely that the government will be held liable for just compensation. As the three decisions previously summarized suggest, the path to the Court of Federal Claims is a familiar one to lawyers, and the Judgment Fund stands ready to be tapped when the Court of Federal Claims or the Federal Circuit concludes tapping is appropriate. As is well known, both courts have tended to be more sympathetic to takings claims than have most other courts in the United States. So here again, institutional change suggests, as a predictive matter, that liability for takings will more likely be recognized in the context of wildfires than it was during the era of catastrophic urban fires.

For all these reasons, one cannot predict with confidence that the traditional exceptions to property rights that emerged in the context of urban conflagrations will necessarily be extended to private property destroyed by wildfires. The potential for doctrinal change is probably most acute with respect to the issue of government compensation for property losses attributable to government action or inaction in controlling wildfires. It is not inevitable that the historically sanctioned conflagration rule will be applied when a case arising out of wildfire calls that rule into question—which is surely only a matter of time. To gain a better sense of the possibility of doctrinal change here, we need to probe more deeply into the rationale for the traditional rule.

Takings Theory and the Conflagration Rule

Broadly speaking, there are three theories that support requiring the government, as a matter of constitutional law, to pay just compensation for takings of property. The first theory is grounded in distributive justice. Takings on this view are an unjust burden imposed on one or a small number of owners for the benefit of the general public. Compensation is required to eliminate or at least mitigate this disparity in treatment. The second theory is grounded in the need to preserve the transaction structure for the acquisition of resources. Takings on this view are forced exchanges of property rights that ordinarily would be acquired through negotiated exchange. Compensation is required on this view whenever the government acquires property rights that ordinarily would be purchased. The third theory is that compensation is required because private insurance markets are unlikely to function when property is taken as a result of deliberate government action. Insurance markets work best when insured parties have no ability to predict or control the occurrence of insurable events. When this condition is not satisfied, compulsory government insurance may be the only way to eliminate undue risk.

There are some circumstances in which these theories point to different results in terms of takings doctrine. Insofar as the conflagration rule is concerned, however, there is no conflict. Each theory suggests that the conflagration rule is a proper interpretation of the Takings Clause.

The Armstrong Principle

The distributive justice conception of the just compensation requirement is the one favored by most academics. It draws inspiration from the statement in *Armstrong v. United States* (364 U.S. 40, 49 [1960]) that the government should not "forc[e] some people alone to bear public burdens which, in all fairness and justice, should be borne by the public as a whole."[3] Of course, different people have different ideas about what makes for unjust distribution. Richard Epstein believes that all government redistribution is problematic, including progressive income taxes and welfare benefits (Epstein 1985). More commonly, the kind of troublesome distribution associated with the Takings Clause is what has been called "singling out"—government action that imposes high costs on a relatively small number of persons through no fault of their own (Levmore 1991). The classic example would be a taking of land for a new public road.

On first impression, one might think that the deliberate destruction of property to halt the spread of fire would easily satisfy the general criterion of unfair singling out. The government deliberately destroys one person's property in order to save many other persons' property. The individual whose property was singled out for this fate has done nothing to warrant such a severe imposition. He or she has committed no crime or no nuisance. Quite likely this property was targeted more or less by accident—it was fated for destruction based on how far the fire had spread when the firefighters arrived, and whether they concluded there was no other way to contain the blaze. Had the firefighters arrived a few moments earlier, some other property would have been chosen for destruction, and this person's property would have been spared. The government's decision to destroy the property, in other words, was basically a random act—far more random than the typical choice of which land to take for a road or bridgehead, which will be significantly affected by geography. These kinds of freakish sacrifices of one person's property for the benefit of many others are the precise type of situation in which compensation is required in order to prevent government action from imposing unfair burdens on isolated individuals.

On closer examination, however, the notion that the conflagration rule entails an unjust distribution of burdens from government action dissolves. One problem with the argument can be expressed in terms of causation. Suppose the government did not order the destruction of the claimant's property? Very likely it would have been consumed by flames moments later and would have been destroyed in any event. Thus, although government action is the proximate cause of the destruction of the property, this has not placed the claimant in a worse position than if the government had stayed its hand. There may be unusual cases where a careful ex post analysis reveals that the claimant's property would have survived the fire, had it not been destroyed by the government. But this kind of close empirical inquiry is not open to firefighters busy reacting to an emergency situation. The general rule—that the destruction caused no harm—will be true in the vast majority of cases, and a general rule that provides guidance to emergency responders is what we need here.

Another problem with condemning the conflagration rule under the *Armstrong* principle is that property owners almost certainly obtain implicit in-kind compensation from the rule (Epstein 1985). The practice of allowing the government to destroy buildings in the path of fire significantly reduces the total amount of destruction caused by catastrophic fires. Ex ante, the expected cost of fires goes down for all property owners if such destruction is allowed. The simplest way property owners can cash in on this reduced cost is by purchasing fire insurance—which will be cheaper if destruction is allowed than if it is not (more on insurance momentarily).

The matter is more complicated if we assume the relevant comparison is between destruction without compensation (the conflagration rule) and destruction with compensation. If ex post compensation has no incentive effects on firefighters, and the costs of processing insurance claims and processing compensation claims are the same, then the two rules are equivalent. But it seems plausible that some negative incentive effects will result from compensation: firefighters will hesitate to destroy property or will have to call headquarters to get advance approval before destroying property. It also seems plausible that compensation claims—which require formalities like a complaint being filed, a hearing, and often one or more appraisals—will be more expensive to process than insurance claims. If so, then owners will be better off purchasing private insurance than they would be with a rule of government compensation. Either way, however, there is no unfair distribution from the conflagration rule once in-kind compensation is factored into the picture. Consequently, there is no reason to condemn the rule under the *Armstrong* principle.

Preserving the Transaction Structure

An alternative understanding of the just compensation requirement is grounded in the need to preserve the transaction structure and, in particular, to preserve the understanding that property rights are ordinarily acquired through a voluntary exchange of rights, rather than through government coercion. The Takings Clause, on this view, implicitly permits the government to engage in forced exchange in circumstances where voluntary exchange would encounter high transaction costs, for example, due to some form of bilateral monopoly. The burden of these high transaction costs is unacceptable when the government is attempting to secure property rights for a "public use." Nevertheless, government must pay just compensation when it exercises this power, in order to preserve a rough equivalence between free exchange and forced exchange. Otherwise, the temptation would be too great to use the police power to acquire property rights without any payment of compensation at all. This would encourage overuse of the police power and undermine the security of property rights. The decision most closely identified with this perspective is *Pennsylvania Coal v. Mahon* (260 U.S. 393 [1922]), where the Court noted that an exercise of the police power that looks too much like a forced exchange of property rights will be enjoined unless and until the government uses the power of eminent domain to acquire the rights.

The transaction structure perspective cashes out into an inquiry, which is largely grounded in historical understandings, between the types of actions that fall within the police power and the types of actions that require an exercise of eminent domain. The regulatory takings doctrine, on this view, is designed to preserve the boundary between these two powers (Dana and Merrill 2002). In other words, it is necessary to develop a doctrine that requires the government to use eminent domain, rather than police regulation, in circumstances where ordinarily one would expect the legislature to use eminent domain to acquire the relevant rights. This, is turn, corresponds to circumstances where nongovernmental actors would be expected to engage in market transactions.

The transaction structure idea does not require that we develop a general theory of distributive justice (Merrill 2010). It does require that we have in mind ideal typical situations when eminent domain should be used, as well as ideal typical situations governed by the police power. For example, seizing possession of land might be regarded as a paradigmatic exercise of eminent domain, whereas ordering a landowner to stop discharging pollution on neighboring property might be regarded as a paradigmatic exercise of the police power. Armed with these ideal typical situations, we can then seek to decide disputed cases—such as whether ordering a landowner not to fill a wetland on his or her property requires the exercise of eminent domain or can be justified as a police regulation—by attempting to determine whether the challenged action falls closer to the eminent domain or the police power end of the spectrum.

Approaching the problem from this perspective, the relevant question is whether one would expect the government to either purchase or use the power of eminent domain to acquire land before engaging in destruction of buildings to stop a fire. The question answers itself. The situation is an emergency, and there is simply no time to engage in any kind of land transaction, whether by negotiation or eminent domain, before the structures are pulled down. Because one would not expect the government to use eminent domain in this situation, there is no reason to insist on just compensation in order to preserve the transaction structure.

Another way to make the point is that there are two different kinds of transactions costs that can prevent the government from acquiring property by voluntary negotiation. One kind of transaction cost is associated with bilateral monopoly. Say, for example, the government needs a specific plot of land to complete a right-of-way for a highway, and there is only one buyer and one seller. The seller is in a position to hold out, drive up the acquisition price, or delay the project for an unreasonable time. An institutional solution to this kind of transaction cost problem is eminent domain. When it invokes the power of eminent domain, the government is allowed to engage in a forced transaction, provided it pays the owner the judicially determined fair market value of the land.

Another type of transaction cost is associated with emergency situations. The government must acquire a resource immediately. The government, say, needs to requisition an airplane to evacuate soldiers from a collapsing battlefield. There is no time to contemplate what kinds of airplane would be most appropriate, let alone to negotiate a purchase or lease or to go through the formalities of eminent domain. Here, one would expect the government to take the asset using its police power, because the transaction costs prohibit using any kind of exchange, free or forced.[4] Because the government is not violating the transaction structure, there is no call to impose a requirement of just compensation in order to deter the government from proceeding in this fashion. In short, if we conceptualize the regulatory takings doctrine as a device for maintaining the transaction structure, the conflagration rule also appears to be an appropriate exception to the doctrine.

Insurance

The compensation requirement for takings has also been described as a form of mandatory public insurance. Because private insurance is available for many risks—including fire—this has led to a debate about why certain kinds of risks must be covered by mandatory public insurance, as opposed to private insurance (Fischel and Shapiro 1988; Kaplow 1986). The explanations that have been advanced all involve opportunistic or strategic behavior. Private insurance against government takings would be afflicted by adverse selection, as property owners would have superior information about the probability of a taking, and hence only relative poor takings risks would seek insurance. Private insurance would also be under-mined by moral hazard, since owners with insurance would be less inclined to resist government takings of their property. Finally, private insurance would create an incentive for government to engage in excessive takings activity, because the costs would be borne by private insurance carriers, not by taxpayers. Mandatory government insurance in the form of the just compensation requirement is thought to be less susceptible to these incentives for opportunistic behavior.

The arguments for takings liability as a substitute for private insurance suggest that there is no need, as a general matter, to extend takings liability to government action in fighting fires. This is because private fire insurance is widely available, and, more importantly, private insurance appears to cover the risks associated with government destruction of property in the course of fighting fires.

Fire insurance was first developed in London after the Great Fire of 1666. It was primarily a local institution for some time thereafter, which meant it was available in some cities but not in others. The local nature of insurance also created a risk of incomplete compensation due to the insolvency of insurance carriers. For example, the Great New York Fire of 1835 destroyed nearly every local fire insurance company, along with most of their assets (Wall 1936). Twenty-three of twenty-six local New York insurance companies failed, leaving many property owners destitute (Tebeau 2003).

The inadequacies of the early insurance industry magnified the risk from fire, which in turn created greater pressure for government intervention and qualification of property rights. The causation runs in the other direction as well. As government regulation and improved technology gradually brought the risk of catastrophic fire under control, fire insurance became increasingly available and affordable. Today, nearly all residential and business structures are covered by fire insurance. Certainly, any structure subject to a mortgage is required to carry fire insurance.

The universal availability of fire insurance means there is no need to require the government to pay just compensation when it orders the destruction of a structure as part of the effort to contain a fire. Owners can purchase private insurance to cover this risk. A standard homeowner's fire insurance policy excludes from coverage "the destruction, confiscation or seizure of property . . . by order of any governmental or public authority" (Abraham 2005, 186). But it immediately qualifies this as follows: "This exclusion does not apply to such acts ordered by any governmental or public authority that are taken at the time of a fire to prevent its spread, if the loss caused by the fire would be covered under this policy." It thus appears that standard fire insurance policies specifically *include* coverage for losses that are not compensated by the government because of the conflagration rule. Public compensation is not necessary, because private compensation is available to cover this loss.

The reason private insurance encompasses government destruction of property to combat fire is that this kind of government behavior is largely immune from the usual concerns about strategic behavior. Accidental fires are unplanned and uncontrollable events. That is why they can be covered by private insurance. Since no one can know in advance when fire will strike, or when it will threaten to become catastrophic, government destruction of property to contain a fire is also an unplanned and uncontrollable event. Consequently, it too can be covered by private insurance. Government destruction of property in fighting fires is thus different from other types of deliberate government takings. Being unplanned and uncontrollable, it is not subject to strategic manipulation. Consequently, there is no need to discipline such acts by imposing a right to compensation as a matter of constitutional law. In short, there is little justification for holding that the government must compensate owners for destroying their property in fighting fire, given that nearly every property owner can obtain insurance against this risk.

Are Wildfires Different?

As we have seen, the risk of catastrophic urban fire gave rise to three important modifications of conventional property rights: the rule of overriding necessity, the expanded conception of the police power as a prophylactic against future harms, and the conflagration rule denying compensation for government activity in combating fire. To what extent are these three qualifications of rights likely to carry over to the wildfire context?

The first two qualifications should extend to wildfires with little controversy. I have no doubt that National Forest Service firefighters battling a wildfire can enter private land without the consent of the owner, provided some reasonable basis exists for believing that this is an appropriate measure for combating a fire that involves federal land. Wildfires pose a grave danger to human life, wildlife, and public and private property. The courts would have no difficulty finding that government agents can make a forcible entry onto private property to fight a wildfire no less than an urban fire, under the overriding necessity exception to the law of trespass and the exigent circumstances exception to the Fourth Amendment. Forest Service firefighters would also be allowed to destroy private property to block the spread of fire, if this is deemed to be necessary, and individual firefighters will be immune from any action in tort for such actions under the Westfall Act.

The Forest Service will also be found to have very broad powers to adopt regulations, plans, and procedures for dealing with the risk of fire in accordance with the Multiple Use, Sustained Yield Act (16 U.S.C. § 528 et seq.) and the National Forest Management Act (16 U.S.C. § 1600 et seq.). This includes balancing fire suppression policies and actions against other values, including habitat protection. One question is how far the Forest Service or other federal agencies can go in adopting regulations that apply to private property located outside federal lands, in order to minimize the risk of fire. The Property Clause of Article IV has been held to permit some kinds of regulations of activities outside federal lands, when this is necessary in order to protect federal lands, including regulations designed to protect against fire (*United States v. Alford*, 274 U.S. 264 [1927]). As the Supreme Court has observed: "The danger depends on the nearness of the fire, not upon the ownership of the land where it is built. . . . Congress may prohibit the doing of acts upon privately owned lands that imperil the publicly owned forests" (274 U.S. 267). I will not pursue the interesting question of whether this might permit the federal government to adopt a code of land use regulations that would apply outside federal lands, in the interest of providing more effective fire management on federal lands.

Although the matter is slightly more complicated, I also think that there is little justification for requiring the government to compensate owners for losses to property caused by wildfires. Insofar as the issue involves structures torn down to form a fire break, there would seem to be little reason to distinguish wildfires from urban fires. In both instances, the government is acting in response to an emergency; there is little time for deliberation (or for opportunistic calculation); and private insurance is available for structures destroyed by wildfire (Kovacs 2001). Based on the cases reviewed earlier in this chapter, as well as in Chapters 3 and 4 of this volume, I take it that pulling down structures to break the spread of wildfire is not the issue of controversy. To the contrary, the government makes the protection of residential structures on the urban-wilderness boundary a top priority once fire breaks out. The point of contention, rather, is the government's failure to adopt policies that would do more to minimize the risk or severity of wildfires, and in particular, its failure to act more aggressively to limit the accumulation of biomass fuels.

Whether the government should be required to pay compensation to owners for losses caused (in whole or part) by excessive biomass accumulation presents a question not addressed by the classic conflagration rule. It is tempting to think that if the government were forced to internalize the costs to property owners of its defective fuel accumulation policies, the government would rethink its policies. But the lawyer's instinctive response is that this is not going to happen—at least, not as a matter of judicial interpretation of the Takings Clause. In terms of the urban analogy, the proposition is akin to saying the government should be held liable for having a water system with inadequate pressure, or fire hoses that are too short, or firefighters who are badly trained. As a rule, the government cannot be held liable for adopting defective policies, even if they are causally linked to individual losses. This is true both under the Torts Claims Act, with its exception for "discretionary functions" (*United States v. Varig Airlines*, 467 U.S. 797 [1984]), and under the Due Process Clause (*DeShaney v. Winnebago County*, 489 U.S. 189 [1989]). The judges who heard the cases described earlier had a similar reaction about liability under the Takings Clause, although they described the result in terms of causation rather than liability for adopting bad policies.

The reasons for denying government liability for adopting bad policies are not clearly spelled out in the cases. So few attempts have been made to challenge the principle that its rationale has not been thoroughly explored. Concerns about foreseeability, about hindsight bias, about potentially large government liabilities, and about the asymmetry of imposing liability for losses without any capacity to recover gains are all undoubtedly relevant. One can also question whether government agents would respond to a Pigouvian tax designed to internalize the costs of defective policies in a predictable manner (Levinson 2000). In any event, given the larger pattern of the law, it is unlikely that courts will require the government to compensate owners for losses caused by government biomass accumulation policies.

Conclusions

The danger of fire, especially on a catastrophic scale, has been responsible for some dramatic limitations on ordinary property rights. The right to exclude disappears, the government's power to regulate soars, and no one is entitled to compensation even for intentional government destructions of his or her property. One could almost say that when a large fire breaks out, property rights go up in smoke—at least until the fire is put out. There is every reason to think that these understandings will carry over to wildfires. Government may adopt good or bad policies for minimizing the risks presented by wildfires. But solicitude for property rights cannot be cited as a barrier to effective government action in this context. If the government performs poorly in controlling the risk of wildfire, it is not because private property rights are standing in the way.

Notes

1. For accounts of dramatic urban fires in the eighteenth and nineteenth centuries, see Fowler (1873) and Goodspeed (1871).
2. Firefighting was performed by volunteer companies until the latter half of the nineteenth century, when a general movement toward full-time municipal fire departments occurred in large cities. As McChesney (1986, 85, 88–90) recounts, the standard explanation for municipalization was the desire to eliminate violence among volunteer companies, stimulated by their racing to obtain bonuses paid by insurance companies. He offers an alternative hypothesis, based on opportunistic behavior by firefighters (who previously served without pay), politicians, and insurance companies. His account overlooks the coordination benefits of municipalization, especially important in fighting potentially catastrophic fires, as well as the advantages of drawing upon the municipal tax base to pay for new technologies like steam-powered pumping engines. In any event, the development of professional full-time fire departments was followed by the demise of catastrophic urban fires, and it is unlikely that these phenomena were not related.
3. As Treanor (1997) notes, this quotation is so popular that it has been given its own name, the "*Armstrong* principle."
4. Another way to put the problem is to ask whether compensation is constitutionally required in cases where trespass is justified by the doctrine of necessity. At common law, some decisions require compensation (e.g., *Vincent v. Lake Erie Transp. Co.*, 124 N.W. 221 [Minn. 1910]), but others do not (e.g., *Ploof v. Putnam*, 71 A. 188 [Vt. 1908]). This suggests that the matter is best left to legislative discretion, rather than being something to be decided as a matter of constitutional law.

References

Abraham, Kenneth S. 2005. *Insurance Law and Regulation: Cases and Materials*. 4th ed. New York: Foundation Press.
Dana, David A., and Thomas W. Merrill. 2002. *Property: Takings*. New York: Foundation Press.
Epstein, Richard A. 1985. *Takings: Private Property and the Power of Eminent Domain*. Cambridge, MA: Harvard University Press.
Fischel, William A., and Perry Shapiro. 1988. Takings, Insurance, and Michelman: Comments on Economic Interpretation of "Just Compensation" Law. *Journal of Legal Studies* 17:269–293.

Fowler, William. 1873. *Fighting Fire: The Great Fires of History*. Hartford, CT: Dustin, Gilman.

Goodspeed, E. J. 1871. *History of the Great Fires in Chicago and the West*. New York: H. S. Goodspeed & Co.

Kaplow, Louis. 1986. An Economic Analysis of Legal Transitions. *Harvard Law Review* 99:509–617.

Kovacs, Paul. 2001. *Wildfires and Insurance*. ICLR Research Paper No. 11. Toronto, ON: Institute for Catastrophic Loss.

Levinson, Daryl J. 2000. Making Government Pay: Markets, Politics, and the Allocation of Constitutional Costs. *University of Chicago Law Review* 67:345–420.

Levmore, Saul. 1991. Takings, Torts, and Special Interests. *Virginia Law Review* 77:1333–1368.

McChesney, Fred S. 1986. Government Prohibitions on Volunteer Fire Fighting in Nineteenth-Century America: A Property Rights Perspective. *Journal of Legal Studies* 15:69–92.

Merrill, Thomas W. 2010. Why *Lingle* Is Half Right. *Vermont Journal of Environmental Law* 11:421–435.

———. 2011. Private Property and Public Rights. In *Research Handbook on the Economics of Property Law*, edited by Kenneth Ayotte and Henry E. Smith. Cheltenham, UK: Edward Elgar, 75–103.

Novak, William J. 1996. *The People's Welfare: Law and Regulation in Nineteenth-Century America*. Chapel Hill: University of North Carolina Press.

Prentice, W. P. 1894. *Police Powers Arising under Law of Overruling Necessity*. New York: Banks & Brothers.

Tebeau, Mark. 2003. *Eating Smoke: Fire in Urban America, 1800–1950*. Baltimore: Johns Hopkins University Press.

Treanor, William Michael. 1997. The *Armstrong* Principle, the Narratives of Takings, and Compensation Statutes. *William and Mary Law Review* 38 (3):1151–1176.

Wall, Alexander J., Jr. 1936. The Great Fire of 1835. *New York Historical Society Quarterly Bulletin* 20:3–22.

3

FUEL FOR THE FIRE

Liability and the Economics of Wildfire Risk

Jonathan Yoder

A couple of decades ago in California, a fire ignited by accident on a property and spread quickly, racing through trees and grass onto adjacent property and beyond, destroying the home of the next neighbor over. Property in this section of the woods is highly valued in part for its natural amenities, and the fire was fueled solely by natural vegetation until it reached the house on the third property. Public firefighting agencies ultimately suppressed the fire, and insurance companies and the courts thereafter became involved to begin the process of assigning culpability and financial responsibility for damage and suppression costs.

This actual wildfire incident illustrates that land management practices, precaution regarding fire use, and wildfire suppression are all important determinants of wildfire outcomes. And each has a long history in the common law pertaining to wildfire losses and costs. If the landowner had carelessly ignited the fire or could have stopped it from spreading but failed to take action, he would likely have been found negligent, been liable for damages, and might even have been required to pay for subsequent public fire suppression. If the landowner had stockpiled flammable man-made materials or let buildings deteriorate so as to create a fire hazard, he might have been held liable for this also. But this fire spread through natural fuels, and landowners in rural areas are generally immune to liability solely due to natural conditions on their land.

The central argument of this chapter is that existing liability law along with property insurance and public wildfire suppression provide weak incentives for ex ante management of natural fuel loads for wildfire risk management. The likely consequence is excessive natural fuel loads that contribute to high aggregate resource losses from wildfires and excessive suppression costs.

This chapter examines the structure of incentives for private investment in three interrelated activities: (a) efforts to mitigate wildfire hazards, (b) efforts to control intentional fires, and (c) suppression efforts once a fire has escaped. The primary focus is on the structure and implications of liability on wildfire risk mitigation, with ancillary discussions of two other important factors that affect ex ante wildfire risk: the structure of standard property insurance and characteristics of public wildfire suppression. The next section provides a synopsis of liability law in the United States. An economic model is then developed and applied to illustrate the implications of liability law and other factors on incentives. This is followed by discussion of the economic foundations of liability law and the development of public policy alternatives.

Liability Law over Wildfire Risk

Wildfire risk and damage from wildfires is addressed in various ways via joint use of liability law, property law, and regulation. Chapter 1 gave a historical overview of the breadth of legal doctrine applicable to wildfire, and Chapter 2 provided a detailed examination of property rights as applied to fire.[1] Despite some diversity in law surrounding wildfire throughout history and in statutory law, the common law of the United States has largely adhered to negligence standards in regard to liability for the spread of fires, with or without intentional ignition (ALR 1994a, 1994b; M. 1929; Sun 2007a; Yoder 2008; Yoder et al. 2003).[2] This chapter therefore focuses on simple negligence rules over wildfire, with particular emphasis on mitigating risk prior to fires, the occurrence of wildfires, and precaution for intentional use of fire. Incentives for wildfire suppression are covered in more detail in Chapter 4.

Precaution: Ignition and Escape

This section provides a legal context surrounding wildfire risk, with some examples of typical case outcome for two general classes of fires: those that were set unintentionally and those that were set intentionally for some "legitimate" productive purpose. This synopsis relies on two summaries of court cases pertaining to fire liability published in *American Law Reports* (ALR), one focusing on liability for spread of accidental (unintentional) fires (ALR 1994b), and the other focusing on liability for spread of intentionally set, non-arson fires (ALR 1994a).

Liability for Spread of Accidental Fire

ALR (1994b) provides a representative review of case law pertaining to liability for damage due to the spread of accidental fires of known or unknown origin. There have been numerous cases in which courts have found landowners or their employees liable (but generally not tenants or invitees) for accidental ignitions from negligent machinery operation, failure to repair machinery or structures, and other similar activities or omissions. In *Roddiscraft, Inc. v. Skelton Logging Co.* ([1963, 1st Dist] 212 Cal App 2d 784,28 Cal Rptr 277), Roddiscraft, Inc., was found negligent and liable for fire damage to timber that followed from operating a Caterpillar tractor without a spark arrester amid flammable material. In contrast, in *Collins v. George* ([1904] 102 Va 509, 46 SE 684), the owner of a stationary sawmill engine without a spark arrester was found not negligent, because the level of danger is lower and more easily managed in a stationary setting than on moving engines, and because spark arresters impede the power of engines. Note in this latter case the explicit concern over the net benefits of precaution, which are perceived by the court to be low in this case. The review also contains a large body of case law over fires originating from the trains along rail lines (ALR 1994b), which is a notable category of case law not only for its impact on subsequent wildfire liability cases, but also for its place in the economics and law literature, from Pigou (1932) through Coase (1960) and beyond.

An important component of negligence and liability for the spread of fire relates to the duty to take prompt and reasonable measures to prevent a fire from spreading to neighboring property. Several cases in ALR (1994b) find landowners liable for a fire that they had initially thought was extinguished but later spread. In several other cases, property owners were found negligent for not having firefighting apparatuses on hand where it would be prudent to have them. The scope of economic costs from escaped fires includes not only the value of damaged property, but also the costs of suppressing a fire. ALR (1994b) contains examples of cases where landowners were found under statutory law to be liable for suppression costs incurred by the state for negligent spread of fire.

Much of the variation in the outcomes of these cases revolves around ownership, causation, the capacity of a defendant to possess information about a potential hazard, the capacity for control of the spread of a fire, and the contribution of the plaintiff to damage. It is clear from this case law that actions and omissions contributing to the spread of fire onto another property are subject to negligence standards of due care, and that these standards are assessed largely on a case-by-case basis subject to preexisting conditions of the property from which a fire spread, the manner in which the fire was ignited, and the actions of the defendant after the fire started.

Liability over Intentional Ignition and Escape

ALR (1994a) provides an extensive review of case law pertaining to liability for escaped fires "intentionally set for legitimate purpose." This includes fires that were started for the purpose of clearing land or otherwise burning trees, forest debris, grass, and so forth; burning rubbish and refuse; campfires; and backfires to control the spread of existing wildfires. It is clear from this case law that the activity of intentionally starting a fire is another dimension that broadly opens individuals to liability under tort law and is generally predicated on negligence and trespass.

General conditions of the environment at ignition often play a crucial role in these decisions. Setting a fire in excessively dry conditions has been the basis for a negligence ruling. Setting a fire with knowledge of a likelihood of high winds is also taken to be an important intervening factor as support for a negligence ruling, but an unpredictable change in wind patterns for the worse after otherwise critical decisions have been made are generally not taken to imply negligence.

Prescribed fire, also known as broadcast burning, is among the more complex and potentially risky uses of fire. As mentioned above, simple negligence applied to ignition and spread of fire has been the norm, but statutory law has codified the application of strict liability and gross negligence in some cases, as well as a menu of related regulatory restrictions. Yoder et al. (2003) and Sun (2007b) provide synopses of these laws. Yoder (2008) provides an empirical analysis of the relationships between liability law and the incidence and severity of escaped prescribed fires, and finds that stringent statutory liability laws and regulations tend to reduce the number and severity of escaped prescribed fires on private land but not on federal land, where state liability laws do not directly apply.

Prior Condition of Land

The Second Restatement of Torts (ALI 1965) § 364 states:

> A possessor of land is subject to liability of others outside of the land for physical harm caused by a structure or other artificial condition on the land, which the possessor realizes or should realize will involve an unreasonable risk of such harm, if (a) the possessor has created the condition, or (b) the condition is created by a third person with the possessor's consent or acquiescence while the land is in his possession, or (c) the condition is created by a third person without the possessor's consent or acquiescence, but reasonable care is not taken to make the conditions safe after the possessor knows or should know of it.

So, landowners may be found liable for harm due solely to physical conditions that lead to injury. ALR (1994b) provides numerous examples of court decisions pertaining to the spread of fire whose primary cause was found to be one of myriad flammable materials on a property, including flammable liquids and fumes, dust and lint, wood structures and products, and others. The decisions of these cases are consistently predicated on negligence over artificial conditions of the land when the landowners have had or should have had knowledge and control over those conditions.

Importantly, however, the Second Restatement of Torts § 363 indicates an exception for "natural conditions":

> Except as stated in subsection (2), neither a possessor of land, nor a vendor, lessor, or other transferor, is liable for physical harm caused to others outside of the land by a natural condition of the land. (2) A possessor of land in an

urban area is subject to liability to persons using a public highway for physical harm resulting from his failure to exercise reasonable care to prevent an unreasonable risk of harm arising from the condition of trees on the land near the highway.

The "natural condition of land" is defined to mean that "the land has not been changed by any act of a human being." It includes "the natural growth of trees, weeds, and other vegetation upon land not artificially made receptive to them."[3] The definition of natural fuels is quite vague in the law, however. For example, Noel (1943) infers that it might apply to grass and weed growth even if the land had previously been cultivated. However, heavy vegetation due to irrigation may be considered beyond the definition of unnatural. Based on a reading of the case law, nothing suggests that heavy fuel loads have been, or necessarily would be, considered as "unnatural" due solely to fire exclusion through active suppression.

The implication of this passage is that rural landowners are immune to liability for injury due to natural fuels, except insofar as fuel contributes to damage when landowners are found negligent over other activities. Based on a review of prior and subsequent case law, the exception for natural conditions in § 363 clearly reflects prior case law, and it is consistent with and has even been cited in subsequent cases. Case law cited in the legal literature on liability over natural conditions causing damage beyond property boundaries include occurrences such as the spread of noxious weeds, blowing sand, rolling rocks, and the spreading of surface water (Burns 1974; Noel 1943).[4] The role of natural fuels in wildfire cases does not seem to have been central to the development of tort law over natural conditions of land. Nonetheless, the principle has been explicitly applied to liability for damage by the spread of wildfire (Burns 1974).

ALR (1994b) subsection V § 22 provides summaries of nine cases in which a landowner was found liable for excessive natural fuel accumulation, but in each case the finding of negligence was based in part on other actions that increased the likelihood of ignition. In one case, *Dealer Service & Supply Co. v. St. Louis Nat. Stockyards Co.* (1987, 5th Dist), the court found that the stockyards had an independent duty to prevent the accumulation of flammable materials such as weeds on the premises. The court explicitly noted § 363 of the Second Restatement of Torts, but found that conditions at the stockyard were not natural, in part because the property owner had allowed dumping of additional flammable materials on the premises. The stockyard therefore had a duty to mitigate risk of damage by cutting weeds and/or creating a fire break and was found negligent of this duty.

In another case, an energy utility company was found liable for damage from a brush fire that started when tree limbs fell on power lines. The utility was found negligent for allowing a tree to stand in close proximity to a power line *and* for allowing grass and brush to accumulate in the same location. In two cases, timber companies that owned land on which timber slash was left over from logging operations (again, not in a "natural" state) were found liable for damage due to fires that spread from those landholdings.

These examples are consistent with case law broadly, and the case law is generally consistent with the Second Restatement of Torts § 364: landowners and/or their agents may be found liable for wildfire spread from land that had been actively managed or for which there were intervening actions that increased the risk of ignition or escape. However, the natural accumulation of biomass fuels generally has not been sufficient as a basis for landowner liability (consistent with ALI 1965, § 363). The implication is that heavy fuel loads can contribute to a finding of negligent human activity, but by itself, excessive or dangerous "natural" fuel is not the object of a negligence standard per se.

A Model of Wildfire Management Trade-offs

In this section, a model of environmental management for risk mitigation, precaution, and suppression is developed that characterizes the basic landowner incentives for investing in three activities that affect wildfire risk for the landowner and neighbors. It combines and extends a widely used model of wildfire cost minimization (Donovan and Brown 2005; Sparhawk 1925) and a model of precaution against harm in the tradition of John Brown (Brown 1973).[5] This model is first applied to show incentives for input substitution, and then is applied to help understand the structure of tort law.

The Landowner's Problem

Consider a landholding on which there is potential for wildfire within a fireshed that spans numerous landholdings (see Chapters 4 and 8). Three types of actions can affect wildfire outcomes: ex ante risk mitigation m, precaution p, and suppression effort s. Each of these three categories may include multiple types of activities and so can be interpreted as vectors of activities.

Mitigation (m) is defined to include any land management activity pursued for any purpose, and is defined such that an increase in m provides general pre-fire wildfire risk reduction as one of its outcomes. This might include, for example, commercial and/or pre-commercial forest thinning, thinning and fuels reduction specifically for wildfire risk mitigation, or even wildland-urban interface development strategies designed to reduce wildfire risk to structures.[6]

Precaution (p) represents the effort to keep a given fire or set of existing fires from escaping a landholding.[7] This includes the decision about whether, when, where, and how to ignite a fire if the fire is intentional. Among many other intentional uses of fire, it can include forest fuel control via prescribed fire for wildfire risk mitigation.[8]

Suppression (s) is the effort of reducing damage imposed by a wildfire after escape or unintentional ignition.

It is useful to recognize that these three inputs are in large part sequential in application. Mitigation occurs prior to a fire and not in relation to any particular planned fire; precaution relates to control of a fire; and suppression takes place thereafter if necessary.

Wildfire risk over a period of time comprises the probability or rate of ignition and escape and the potential damage given ignition and escape. The probability or rate of ignition and escape for a given a period of time from landholding i to j is dependent on mitigation and precaution applied to landholding i: $\pi_i^j(m_i, p_i)$.[9] Damage given escape to property j is $d^j(m_j, s_j)$ and is affected by mitigation and suppression on property j.[10] Both the rate of escape and potential damage decline at a decreasing rate in their inputs, and all inputs are assumed to be technical substitutes.[11] Escape risk and damage are assumed conditionally independent, and expected damage to landholding j is $\pi_i^j(m_i, p_i)\, d^j(m_j, s_j)$.

If suppression occurs subsequent to escape, mitigation and precaution choice would be based on an expectation of subsequent suppression. Public funding and direct public involvement in fire suppression can be viewed as a response to nonexclusive benefits associated with fire suppression, the difficulties with private contracting over fire suppression, and to some degree the extent of public land management. Incentives surrounding suppression effort are complex and covered elsewhere (see Chapters 4 and 8). Suppression effort is here assumed to be exogenously determined from the landowner's perspective.

Consider two neighboring landowners, 1 and 2. Suppose that m, p are applied to landholdings 1 and 2 to maximize the aggregate value of land in an environment with wildfire risk subject to expected suppression. Assume a land use with positive value $r^i(m_i)$ is affected either positively or negatively by mitigation m_i. This function might include private positive land management values from prescribed fire and/or mechanical thinning, or any other land management activities.

Optimal mitigation and precaution by each landowner would fully account for both their own private benefits and expected damage to the neighbor. This is equivalent to maximizing the net value of effort on both landholdings conditional on $s = (s_1, s_2)$:

$$\lim_{m,p} V(\mathbf{s},\mathbf{c}) = \sum_{i=1}^{2}\left(r^i(m_i) - (c^m m_i + c^p p_i) - \sum_{j \neq 1}\left(\pi_i^j(m_1, p_1)d^j(m_2, s_2)\right)\right), \tag{3.1}$$

where c^k is the constant marginal input cost for input $k \in (m, p)$. Assuming an interior maximum, efficient input use, landowner 1 would satisfy first-order conditions

$$\frac{\partial r^1}{\partial m_1} - \left(\frac{\partial \pi_1^2}{\partial m_1}d^2 + \pi_1^2\frac{\partial d^1}{\partial m_1}\right) = c^m$$

$$-\frac{\partial \pi_1^2}{\partial p_1}d^2 = c^p\,, \tag{3.2}$$

and landowner 2 would satisfy analogous conditions. If suppression were expected to be applied to each landholding efficiently, then the solution (m_i^*, p_i^*, s_i^*) would be jointly efficient for all landholdings.[12] Figure 3.1 illustrates three activity

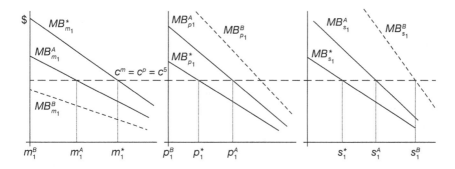

FIGURE 3.1 Landowner incentives and input investment choice

Notes: Superscript * indicates socially optimal effort levels; superscript A indicates non-contingent insurance but accounting for contribution to neighbors' risk; and superscript B indicates non-contingent insurance and failure to account for contribution to neighbors' risk.

outcomes under three different incentive structures, each of which will be discussed in turn. The full social marginal benefit of each landowner 1 input is represented in each respective panel by MB_x^*. The solution based on these social marginal benefit functions is (m_1^*, p_1^*, s_1^*), shown on the horizontal axes.

In this formulation, high wildfire risk can arise as a result of high values at risk or high probability of damage to these values. Residential construction in forestland and biomass growth due in part to a century of active fire suppression are examples of how wildfire risks might change over time. In this static model, optimal mitigation and precaution would tend to increase as expected damage increases and decrease as expected suppression increases.[13]

Incentives, Actions, and Outcomes

There are at least three major reasons that landowners may have weak incentives for the provision of mitigation and precaution. First, property insurance indemnification for wildfire damage has historically been provided without contingencies for private risk mitigation. This will reduce the incentive for self-protection from wildfire (Collins 2009; Holmes et al. 2007; Kovacs 2001; Lankoande et al. 2005; Talberth et al. 2006). Second, landowners have weak incentives to reduce natural fuel loads that contribute to their neighbors' wildfire risk. Third, it is often claimed that public wildfire suppression management agencies have poor incentives to limit suppression expenditures while in the process of suppressing fires, and therefore have an incentive to overinvest in suppression efforts (Donovan et al. 2008). Suppression and property insurance are covered elsewhere in this volume (e.g., Chapters 1 and 2; see also Lankoande et al. 2005) and are not a central focus here, but these issues are important determinants of the economic costs of wildfires and provide illustrations of the interactions among the three risk management activities.

Consider the effect of exogenous differences in suppression effort once a fire has escaped. Suppose that public suppression agents have weak incentives to limit suppression costs once a fire has started, and therefore choose to invest too heavily in suppression such that $s_i > s_i^*$ (see Chapter 4). Because inputs are substitutes, the marginal productivity of mitigation and precaution will decline, and landowners would have an incentive to underinvest in both mitigation and precaution, leading to both a higher incidence of wildfires and a larger sum of damage and suppression costs per fire.

Now consider the impact of insurance and landowner immunity from liability over natural fuels, conditional on expected suppression. In spite of the discussion of suppression directly above, assume for the sake of focus that suppression is applied optimally conditional on m and p. Unconditional insurance coverage over wildfire damage will reduce the incentive for self-protection, thereby reducing the private marginal productivity of mitigation m_i on $d^i(m_i, s_i)$. That is, $\partial r^i / \partial m_i$ in equation (3.2) approaches zero, and in Figure 3.1, the marginal benefit to landowners of m shifts down to $MB_{m_1}^A$.[14] Because precaution and suppression are substitutes for m, the marginal benefit functions for these two inputs shift up to $MB_{p_1}^A$ and $MB_{p_1}^A$, respectively.[15] The consequence is lower mitigation levels and higher precaution and suppression levels, $(m_1^A < m_1^*, p_1^A > p_1^*, s_1^A > s_1^*)$.

If a landowner with insurance coverage is also immune to liability over natural fuels, landowner 1 would have de facto rights to impose damage on landowner 2 without bearing the costs of damage. Assume for clarity one mitigation input that applies to natural fuels. Landowner 1 would ignore the marginal value of mitigation to the neighbor, $(\partial \pi_1^2 / \partial m_1) d^2$ in equation (3.2). The marginal benefit of mitigation to landowner 1 would then shift down to $MB_{m_1}^B$ in Figure 3.1, and as shown in this illustration, landowner 1 would then choose $m_i^B = 0$. Further, there would be no incentive at all for landowner i to invest in precaution p.[16] Precaution is therefore shown as $p_i^B = 0$ (though $MB_{p_1}^B$ is shown for completeness). Suppression effort chosen optimally but conditional on no prior mitigation and precaution would then be much higher, at s_i^B. Further, if the suppression agent has weak incentives for cost management while fighting fires, suppression costs would be larger still, and the overall costs of wildfires would climb even higher because of weak incentives for mitigation and precaution.

Suppose now a negligence standard $(\bar{m}_1, \bar{p}_1)$ is imposed for liability over damage. Such a standard would induce landowner 1 to exactly meet the standard, thereby avoiding liability at minimum cost. Because landowner 1 avoids liability, the damage to neighboring property from the fire is borne by the neighbor. If neighbors understand this incentive, they then *expect* to bear the damage from wildfire moving onto their properties and have an incentive to mitigate risk from wildfires (Brown 1973; Yoder et al. 2003).[17] If the standard applies to all dimensions of mitigation and precaution, an effectively placed and implemented negligence standard can in principle induce efficient precaution by both parties.[18] For later discussion, note that corner solutions are possible with optimal mitigation of zero and if the marginal costs of mitigation everywhere outweigh the marginal benefits.

The model implies that if $(\bar{m}_1, \bar{p}_1)$ are set at the (joint) social optimum for each landowner (conditional on suppression), and information is complete across all economic parties, then the negligence standard would induce conditionally optimal mitigation and precaution by all landowners. Further, if suppression were set at s_i^*, a negligence standard $(\bar{m}_1 = m_1^*, \bar{p}_1 = p_1^*)$ would induce unconditional efficient levels of mitigation and precaution by each landowner. The above statement assumes that the negligence standard internalizes self-protection even if insurance coverage does not require landowner mitigation for indemnification. However, if insurance coverage is also contingent on efficient self-protection, then efficient input allocation will follow.

In summary, non-contingent insurance and immunity from liability over natural fuels jointly weaken these incentives, potentially leading to underinvestment in risk mitigation and precaution, and potentially very high suppression costs and property damage from wildfires. Total costs of wildfire are further increased if the suppression agent tends to overinvest in suppression. The next section examines potential reasons for this liability structure and is followed by developments in regulation, insurance markets that in some cases can be interpreted as attempts to bolster incentives for management of natural fuels.

Information and the Structure of Liability over Fire

Why are natural conditions treated differently in liability law than other contributing factors to risk? Burns (1974, quoting Prosser (1971)) writes that legal doctrine over natural conditions "reflects the dichotomy drawn between liability based on misfeasance as opposed to non-feasance, and is thought to have originated 'in an early day when much land, in fact most, was unsettled or uncultivated, and the burden of inspecting it and putting it in safe condition would have been not only unduly onerous, but out of all proportion to any harm likely to result.'"

To help understand this statement, two dichotomies will help approach this question: the choice between *rules* and *standards* in law, and a *risk-benefit asymmetry* as examined by Gilles (1992a). Gilles defines "standard-based negligence" as one extreme that relies solely on case-by-case determinations of optimal care. The other extreme is "rule-based negligence" that relies on a proxy for optimal care applied to all cases to which that proxy is pertinent. Merrill's terms "mechanical entitlement-determination rules" versus "judgmental entitlement-determination rules" (1985) are approximately analogous to Gilles' concepts of judicial rules versus standards, respectively.

It seems clear that a negligence *standard* has evolved vis-à-vis wildfire such that due care is defined ex post depending on the specifics of a case. In contrast, case law over natural conditions has evolved in a *rule* that implies immunity of landowners from liability over natural fuels.[19] This outcome leads to two questions. First, why would mechanical rule-based negligence hold for natural land characteristics, while standards-based negligence evolves for other characteristics and activities that affect wildfire risk? Second, given a rule, why would or should the neighbor rather than the source landowner bear the risk contributed by the land characteristics at the source? There are several possible explanations.

First, imposing a negligence standard for natural fuels on the source landowner may be more costly than it is worth. Gilles (1992b, 357) argues that the costs of making fine-tuned private cost-benefit calculations concerning everyday activities, such as whether or not to drive a car in a given instance, are too high relative to the benefits of doing so, and therefore economically unwarranted. In the context of wildfire escape, Gilles' argument is that it would be too costly relative to the potential efficiency gains to require landowners to monitor the contribution of natural fuels to the (external) risk of damage to neighbors. First, while land modifications and accumulation of other types of fuels require human activity, natural fuel accumulates on its own, so that human action is not required for marginal increases in wildfire risk. Actively created risk is therefore likely to be associated with low-cost risk assessment relative to natural risk accumulation. Second, the marginal contributions of risk via incremental natural fuel growth (on own and/or neighboring land) may be relatively small, making the cost-benefit comparison required by a *due care* standard more costly than it is worth. This is essentially the high assessment cost/low benefit argument of Gilles (1992b), indicating an optimal negligence standard of $\bar{m}_1 = 0$, which is consistent with the negligence standard imposed on natural fuels.

This same characteristic of "creeping" natural fuel accumulation may also lead to evidentiary and judicial uncertainty that makes case-by-case determinations of fault and due care under a standard prohibitively costly (Kaplow and Shavell 1996). A case in point is *Cary v. United States* (552 F.3d 1373 [Fed. Cir. 2009]) (also discussed in Chapter 2 of this volume). Plaintiffs claimed that the U.S. Forest Service was responsible for property damage on adjacent land because fuels had been allowed to accumulate. Part of the court's justification for favoring the defendant in this case was that fuel load accumulation was not an explicit policy, that it was the consequence of a "long sequence of decisions . . . spread over decades," and that no identifiable causal act or decision by the U.S. Forest Service could be identified as the cause.

Now to the next question: given a rule over natural fuels rather than a standard, why does the law impose risk of spread from natural fuels on the owner of adjacent land instead of the owner at the origin of the fire? For example, why would such an outcome not be considered akin to trespass on the part of the source land-owner, as it is sometimes characterized for other dimensions of precaution against the spread of fire?[20] One potential reason stems from the costs of assessing damage ex post. Given that a negligence standard is not applied, if damage assessment and associated court costs are high, these can be avoided entirely by the court if the source is immune and the neighbor bears the damage costs to the property.[21] Under a negligence standard, these costs would be incurred on a regular basis.

A second reason relates to ex ante landowner assessments of risk and damage. Given a mechanical liability rule, a second-best outcome would be for liability to fall on the *cheapest cost avoider* (Calabresi and Hirschoff 1972; Diamond and Mirrlees 1975; Gilles 1992a). The conception of Calabresi and Hirschoff is that the cheapest cost avoider is the party "in the best position to make the cost-benefit analysis between accident costs and accident avoidance cost and to act on that decision once that decision is made" (1972). In the case of damage to a neighbor's property, even though the fire originates elsewhere, the owner of the fire destination would be in the best position to assess appropriate mitigation activities on that landholding and is thus best suited for bearing the liability under an absolute liability setting.

A similar argument can be made for differences in productivity between the risk of escape and damage given escape, assuming that transaction costs generally preclude contracting among landowners over ex ante risk. Equation (3.1) provides some specificity. Potential damage is affected in the model by mitigation by the destination landowner, but the probability of spread is defined by mitigation and precaution at the source of the fire. If the destination landowner is more productive at both assessing and reducing potential damage than the source is at assessing and reducing risk of damage, then each landowner should remain liable for damage from incoming fires.

Regulation, Voluntary Incentive Programs, and Contingent Insurance

Several developing contractual approaches to risk mitigation can be interpreted as responses to weak incentives for managing natural fuels. First is the development of public programs to promote fuel management on private land. Second are statutory developments in several fire-prone Southeastern states that ostensibly reduce liability standards and precaution costs for the application of prescribed fire for fuel management. Third is a discussion of recent changes in insurance policies in some fire-prone environments.

Public-Private Fuel Management Programs

Many communities in wildfire-prone areas have adopted local ordinances, often based on national- and state-level risk mitigation standards, that require developers to implement vegetation management plans and satisfy other zoning requirements. Standard requirements have also been developed and adopted for building design specifically for mitigating wildfire risk. As of 2005, California and Oregon had also adopted legislation that requires private landowners in high-risk areas to manage vegetation to mitigate risk (Haines et al. 2008).

There has also been substantial development of publicly funded local- and state-level educational programs and voluntary cost-share arrangements for fuel removal and management (Haines et al. 2008; McKee et al. 2004; Reams et al. 2005). A cost-share (subsidy) program could be interpreted as a Pigouvian instrument to bolster weak private incentives for fuel management (Butry and Donovan 2008;

Shafran 2008). For a program to be consistent with this perspective, it would have to be targeted to reduce the risk of wildfires moving across properties. However, many of these cost-share programs seem to be focused on creating defensible space around homes rather than, for example, fuel breaks around property boundaries (USDA 2010). As such, these programs seem to be primarily addressing incentives for self-protection potentially related to standard insurance coverage, rather than being contributions to cross-boundary risk (externalities among neighbors).

Developments That Bolster Fuel Reduction Incentives

A liability structure with immunity over natural fuels but a negligence standard over precaution over the use of fires would have the effect of reducing the number of intentional fires, because expected costs of escape (including damage, precaution, and suppression costs) will be more likely to outweigh benefits (private or otherwise) of intentional fire use. Prescribed fire has long been used for vegetation management and wildfire risk mitigation (Prichard et al. 2010; Yoder 2004). Fire has played an especially important ecological role in the Southeastern U.S., which is reflected in a history of fire use unique in the U.S. (Brenner and Wade 2003; Crow 1973; Shea 1940; Wade et al. 2006). Beginning with Florida in 1990, several Southeastern states have adopted extensive legislation explicitly to promote careful prescribed burning. In 1999, Florida modified its legislation to change its simple negligence standard to a gross negligence standard for certified prescribed burn managers who follow a substantial set of additional regulatory standards. Other states have followed suit (Sun 2007b; Yoder et al. 2003).

If not for the risk of escape, prescribed fire would likely be *the* low-cost method of wildfire risk reduction under most situations (Yoder 2004).[22] However, the risk of escape is critical, and virtually all prescribed fire application costs are incurred for controlling the fire. As with other intentional fires, negligence rules generally apply to prescribed fire escapes, though there are some statutory exceptions (Yoder 2008; Yoder et al. 2003). The landowner faces weaker liability risk for fuel accumulation, thereby making prescribed fire relatively more costly than allowing fuel and wildfire risk to accumulate (Yoder 2004), and dampening the incentive to use prescribed fire for wildfire risk mitigation.

As argued in some detail in Yoder (2008), the application of a gross negligence standard conditional on satisfying an extended set of regulatory standards likely reduces both uncertainty and expected costs of using prescribed fire.[23] If there were no uncertainty about either the judicial standard or the regulatory standard, this arrangement reduces the precaution costs for burners because the gross negligence standard is satisfied with less precaution. If the burner faces uncertainty about the ex post liability standard but not the ex ante regulatory standard, replacing liability with regulation over a subset of precautionary activities also is likely to reduce expected costs to burners of an escape. Therefore, the shift toward more substantive regulation and reduced liability standards will tend to reduce the costs to burners.

As is clearly the hope of the drafters of the "right to burn" laws in the Southeast, this cost reduction will in principle increase prescribed fire use in these states.

Contingent Insurance

As is evident from the model and discussion earlier in this chapter, insurance coverage for wildfire damage can reduce the incentive for physical self-protection from wildfire damage. Among the most important developments in this arena is the implementation by State Farm Insurance Company of mitigation-contingent property insurance policies in wildfire-prone areas of Colorado, Arizona, and New Mexico. In high-risk areas, State Farm has begun to require compliance to wildfire risk mitigation standards. If these standards are not met, property owners face potential nonrenewal (Haines et al. 2008). A California state insurance program called the FAIR Plan has a similar wildfire risk policy, but instead of nonrenewal, it imposes a surcharge for noncompliance to management standards (CFP 2010). Thus, landowner incentives for self-protection are bolstered by such policies.

Potential Changes in Liability over Natural Fuels

Will the liability law evolve toward a negligence standard over natural fuels? Bakken suggests that the law of California, which is a hotbed of conflict over wildfire, by 1995 had been moving toward imposing a negligence standard on landowners for natural fuel, and he feels that the inertia continues today (Bakken 1995, 2010).[24] He cites a California case in which the state Supreme Court found that the "progression of the law in California mirrors what appears to be a general trend toward rejecting the common law distinction between natural and artificial conditions. Instead, the courts are increasingly using ordinary negligence principles to determine a possessor's liability for harm caused by a condition of the land."

Since then, there have been limited developments along these lines in relation to wildfire risk due to natural conditions. *Huebner v. State of California* (2000) was brought in response to the wildfire incident that opens this chapter. The plaintiffs argued that the state was negligent in allowing a dangerous condition in the form of wildfire fuels in a public park (the source of the fire) adjacent to private property.[25] This is one of the few cases in which no other contributing risk factors on the source land were blamed on the defendant(s). (The source of ignition was a third-party criminal act that was posted as prohibited within the park.) The Superior Court of California, Los Angeles, found, based strictly (and explicitly) on existing statutory law, that the state is absolutely immune from liability due to natural conditions. However, there was a five-acre private holding between the state park and the plaintiff's property, and apparently the court found the owner to be contributorily negligent on the basis of excessive fuel loads. The owner was required to pay 30% of damages, with the remaining 70% absorbed by the plaintiff (Bakken 2010). This may be the only case to date in which fuel loads are the sole basis of a negligence ruling, but the case has not been ruled on by an appellate court.[26]

Florida is another hotbed for wildfire risk and is the origin of the prescribed burning laws discussed above designed to promote prescribed fire in part for wildfire risk mitigation. Based on several cases, Varner et al. (2001) find no evidence that landowners have a legal duty to reduce fuel loads via the use of prescribed fire or any other means.

Conclusions

This chapter develops the argument that liability law over natural fuels and traditional real estate insurance induce too little ex ante fuel management, which in turn leads to excessive precaution costs for intentional fires and suppression costs for wildfires. Recent evidence suggests that the aggregate resource and property losses and suppression costs from wildfires are increasing. Substantial growth and complexity of the wildland-urban interface intensify the risk to high-value property (McKee et al. 2004; Radeloff et al. 2005), and the wildfire science literature is full of claims that fuel loads have been growing and becoming increasingly incendiary in many fire-prone areas, due at least in part to a century of active fire suppression. Taken together, this means that today in high-risk areas with heavy fuel loads, the marginal productivity of fuel management is high, and therefore the economic losses from weak incentives for fuel load management are also likely to be high.[27] If baseline natural wildfire risks are higher and values at risk are higher, it is likely that poorly aligned incentives for risk management will become increasingly costly.

Ostensibly in response to these developments, public fuel management programs for private landowners have developed substantially over the last decade, insurance companies are beginning to address moral hazard in wildfire risk mitigation, and statutory law pertaining to prescribed fire has changed considerably in many Southeastern states. It remains unclear how landowner immunity from liability over natural fuels will evolve. Nonetheless, the notion of natural conditions for natural fuels seems to be increasingly stretched by heavy fuel accumulations due to fire exclusion by active fire suppression. It is not yet clear under what conditions fuel loads will be interpreted by the courts to be unnatural, but it is clear that this would alter the legal landscape surrounding liability over wildfire risk mitigation.

Notes

1. Damage and nuisance from smoke are also a substantive issue that has a long history in case law and is the focus of substantial regulatory attention at all levels of government (EPA 1998; Haines et al. 2008; Hauenstein and Siegal 1981; Morrissey 1971) but will receive little attention here.
2. By "ancient common law," anyone who kindled a fire that subsequently escaped was "absolutely liable" regardless of the extent of precaution, meaning that strict liability applied to spread of fire after intentional ignition. English common law imposed strict liability for spread of intentional fires as of 1929 (M. 1929), but the law has apparently

migrated toward negligence rules (Sun 2007a). It should also be noted that a limited number of states at various points in time have imposed strict liability rules by statute in the U.S. (M. 1929; Sun 2007b; Yoder 2008). Because of the emphasis in the U.S. on negligence rules, however, strict liability will not be discussed further. Some rulings have concluded that escape be taken as prima facie evidence of negligence, effectively placing the burden of proof of no negligence on the defendant (Sun 2007a; Yoder et al. 2003). This distinction also will not be pursued further here.

3. Further, subsection (2) of § 363 does not necessarily pertain to rural areas, as the language suggests.

4. Finally, a "tentative draft" of the Third Restatement of Torts (ALI 2009, 155) upholds this exemption from liability over natural conditions on rural property (also citing Prosser 1941), even though there is an apparent general movement toward negligence relative to the Second Restatement of Torts (ALI 1965).

5. Donovan and Brown (2005) examine fire manager incentives for managing effort across suppression and "presuppression" efforts. Rideout et al. (2008) develop a model that similarly focuses on suppression and fuel management, but they incorporate a budget constraint into the problem. For our purposes, an additional precaution input is important to examine the pertinent liability, whereas a budget constraint is of little use for present purposes.

6. The term *prevention* is often used in the context of wildfire management, but its connotation of prevention of escape and/or proximate unintentional ignition is too narrow for the purposes of this chapter.

7. The term *control* is often used in the context of wildfire to represent the control of fire from escape or the act of bringing an escaped fire back under control. *Precaution* as used here is a broader concept that includes decisions surrounding the act of lighting a fire. Smoke and associated smoke damage can also fall into the escape and damage category to the extent that smoke from an intentional fire imposes damage on others, whether it be expected or due to unexpected smoke behavior.

8. This last example illustrates a subtle distinction between mitigation input m and the precaution input p in the model formulation here. When prescribed fire is being used for wildfire risk mitigation, it requires precaution. The application of a prescribed fire may be used to mitigate future fire risk and therefore be counted as m, but precaution during the application of particular prescribed fire would be in p. A similar distinction applies to backfires lit as a wildfire suppression tactic.

9. It is more common to think of $\pi_j(m_i, p_i)$ as the probability of a single event. However, the present characterization of probability of escape over a given time period allows for multiple ignitions (whether intentional or not) and thereby largely sidesteps the distinction between *levels of care* and *levels of activity* that are often recognized as implicit in these models (Gilles 1992b; Shavell 2007). This has consequences for interpretation that will be discussed in a specific light later.

10. Precaution in ignition and pre-escape control could be defined more broadly so that it affects damage from an escape as well, but these types of activities, for modeling purposes, can be thought of as a component of m. This formulation is cleaner and suffices for present purposes.

11. Values at risk for a given escaped fire can be interpreted as $d^i(m_i, 0)$, which is the damage that would occur if a fire escaped the landholding and no suppression efforts were exerted.

12. In the case of several inputs in each category m, p, and s, there would be one equimarginal condition for each input.

13. A dynamic version of this model that explicitly incorporates biomass growth over time would provide a richer environment to examine optimal suppression. Accounting for the effect of current suppression on future wildfire risk would generally indicate less suppression effort than a myopic objective that ignores these relationships. See Yoder (2004) for a dynamic model of prescribed fire use that provides a useful framework for considering this issue.

14. Insurance coverage will likely not cover all costs, so the marginal benefit of self-protection likely will not be zero (Talberth et al. 2006).
15. Even if suppression were not produced optimally, but tended to be overapplied conditional on m and p, substitution effects would still lead to an increase in the marginal benefit of suppression.
16. For an experimental examination of the interaction between the incentives of one landowner and another in the context of wildfire risk that fleshes out this problem further and from a slightly different perspective, see Prante et al. 2010.
17. Shavell (2007, Section 4A.3) finds that an efficient negligence standard will also induce efficient *prior precaution*, which could be interpreted as activities much like mitigation that are performed prior to a specific incident. However, this result follows because Shavell assumes damage is solely a function of an analogue to p, but not prior effort. Rather, prior precaution in his model is useful only to reduce the marginal cost of precaution. This approach is likely to be overly restrictive for the present set of problems, and indeed, Shavell's result does not hold for this model.
18. A negligence rule that imposes a standard over negligent escape given prior ignition, but does not impose a standard of care over the decision to ignite a fire, will tend to induce intentionally set fires with too much risk even at the optimal level of precaution over escape (Shavell 1980; Yoder et al. 2003). For more general examinations of efficiency in liability rules, see Jain (2009); Jain and Singh (2002); and Kim (2004).
19. Kaplow (1992, 611) discusses the transformation of standards into rules by precedent.
20. Indeed, there seems to be a trend in case law to treat negligent spread of fire as trespass. See, for example, *Kelly v. CB&I Constructors, Inc.* (Cal App 4th 442). See Chapter 1 of this volume for related discussion.
21. One might also wonder whether damage assessment costs might be a reason why a mechanical liability rule in favor of the source landowner is chosen over a negligence standard based on the types of transaction cost arguments that Merrill (1985) finds to underlie the differences between trespass and nuisance, such as contracting costs among small versus large groups. However, it is not clear how this line of reasoning alone would distinguish natural fuels as a risk factor from other types of risk factors. These costs might, however, be one factor of several that would support a mechanical rule, to paraphrase Merrill.
22. The literature on the effectiveness of prescribed fire suggests, though, that its usefulness and efficacy are, not surprisingly, environment-dependent (Fernandes and Botelho 2003). The primary alternative fuel reduction method is mechanical thinning and removal, which is a relatively costly activity and has substantially different impacts on vegetation ecology (Omi and Martinson 2004).
23. See Schmitz (2000), Rose-Ackerman (1991), Kolstad et al. (1990), and Shavell (1984) for examinations of the joint use of regulation and liability.
24. The frame of reference for Bakken (1995) was the overarching tension between public land managers' mission of effectively managing natural environments, of which natural vegetation plays a central role, and the substantial costs that liability associated with natural fuels would impose on public land management agencies.
25. I thank Stephen Bakken for bringing this case to my attention.
26. Despite attempts to obtain the court records, I was able to gain access only to a defendant trial brief.
27. One might wonder if weak incentives for fuel management amount to much in economic costs relative to the strong incentives to oversuppress. The answer is not clear, but imagine if landowners were responsible for paying for damage to neighboring property and for fire suppression expenditures (as negligent defendants often are) just because they have allowed fuels to accumulate on their land. This could be a game changer in terms of land management for a lot of landowners in fire-prone areas, and aggregate suppression expenditures might well decline.

References

ALI (American Law Institute). 1965. *Restatement of the Law Second, Torts.* Vol. 2. St. Paul: American Law Institute Publishers.

——. 2009. Restatement of the Law Third, Torts: Liability for Physical and Emotional Harm. Chapter 9, Duty of Land Possessors. Tentative Draft No. 6. St. Paul: American Law Institute.

ALR (*American Law Reports*). 1994a. Liability for Spread of Fire Intentionally Set for Legitimate Purpose. *American Law Reports* (5th ed.) 25:391–567.

——. 1994b. Liability of Property Owner for Damages from Spread of Accidental Fire Originating on His Property. *American Law Reports* (5th ed.) 17:547–652.

Bakken, Stephen R. 1995. The Liability and Environmental Consequences of Not Burning in California. In *Proceedings of the Environmental Regulation & Prescribed Fire Conference: Legal and Social Challenges,* edited by Dana C. Bryan. Tallahassee, FL: Center for Professional Development, Florida State University.

——. 2010. Personal communication with the author, October.

Brenner, J., and D. Wade. 2003. Florida's Revised Prescribed Fire Law: Protection for Responsible Burners. In *Proceedings of Fire Conference 2000: The First National Congress on Fire Ecology, Prevention, and Management,* edited by K. E. M. Galley, R. C. Klinger, and N. G. Sugihara. Miscellaneous Publication No. 13. Tallahassee, FL: Tall Timbers Research Station, 132–136. www.srs.fs.usda.gov/pubs/ja/ja_brenner001.pdf (accessed April 22, 2011).

Brown, John. 1973. Toward an Economic Theory of Liability. *Journal of Legal Studies* 2 (2): 323–349.

Burns, P. 1974. Liability for Blowing Thistle Down and Seed: A Thorny Problem Resolved. *Modern Law Review* 37 (6): 702–705.

Butry, David, and Geoffrey Donovan. 2008. Protect Thy Neighbor: Investigating the Spatial Externalities of Community Wildfire Hazard Mitigation. *Forest Science* 54 (4):417–428.

Calabresi, Guido, and Jon Hirschoff. 1972. Toward a Test for Strict Liability in Torts. *Yale Law Journal* 81 (6):1055–1085.

CFP (California FAIR Plan Association). 2010. Brush/Wildfire Information. www.cfpnet.com/BrushWildfireInfo.html (accessed April 22, 2011).

Coase, Ronald. 1960. The Problem of Social Cost. *Journal of Law and Economics* 3:1–44.

Collins, Timothy. 2009. Influences on Wildfire Hazard Exposure in Arizona's High Country. *Society and Natural Resources* 22:211–229.

Crow, A. B. 1973. Use of Fire in Southern Forests. *Journal of Forestry* 71 (October): 629–632.

Diamond, Peter, and James Mirrlees. 1975. On the Assignment of Liability: The Uniform Case. *Bell Journal of Economics* 6 (2):487–516.

Donovan, Geoffrey, and Thomas Brown. 2005. An Alternative Incentive Structure for Wildfire Management on National Forest Land. *Forest Science* 51 (5):387–395.

Donovan, Geoffrey, Thomas Brown, and Lisa Dale. 2008. Incentives for Wildfire Management in the United States. In *The Economics of Forest Disturbances: Wildfires, Storms, and Invasive Species,* edited by T. P. Holmes, Jeffrey P. Prestemon, and Karen L. Abt. Dordrecht, Netherlands: Springer-Verlag, 323–340.

EPA (U.S. Environmental Protection Agency). 1998. Interim Air Quality Policy on Wildland and Prescribed Fires. www.epa.gov/ttncaaa1/t1/memoranda/firefnl.pdf (accessed April 22, 2011).

Fernandes, P. M., and H. S. Botelho. 2003. A Review of Prescribed Burning Effectiveness in Fire Hazard Reduction. *International Journal of Wildland Fire* 12 (2):117–128.

Gilles, Stephen G. 1992a. Negligence, Strict Liability, and the Cheapest Cost Avoider. *Virginia Law Review* 78 (6):1291–1375.

——— . 1992b. Rule-Based Negligence and the Regulation of Activity Levels. *Journal of Legal Studies* 21 (2):319–363.

Haines, Terry, Cheryl Renner, and Margaret Reams. 2008. A Review of State and Local Regulation for Wildfire Mitigation. In *The Economics of Forest Disturbances: Wildfires, Storms, and Invasive Species*, edited by Thomas P. Holmes, Jeffrey P. Prestemon, and Karen L. Abt. Dordrecht, Netherlands: Springer-Verlag, 273–293.

Hauenstein, Eric, and William Siegal. 1981. Air Quality Laws in the Southern States: Effects on Prescribed Burning. *Southern Journal of Applied Forestry* 5(3):132–145.

Holmes, Thomas, Karen Abt, Robert Huggett, Jr., and Jeffrey Prestemon. 2007. Efficient and Equitable Design of Wildfire Mitigation Programs. In *People, Fire, and Forests: A Synthesis of Wildfire Social Science*, edited by T. C. Daniels, M. S. Carroll, C. Moseley, and C. Raish. Corvallis: Oregon State University Press, 143–156.

Jain, Satish. 2009. Efficiency of Liability Rules with Multiple Treatments. *Pacific Economic Review* 14:119–134.

Jain, Satish, and Ram Singh. 2002. Efficient Liability Rules: Complete Characterization. *Journal of Economics* 75 (2):105–124.

Kaplow, Louis. 1992. Rules versus Standards: An Economic Analysis. *Duke Law Journal* 42 (3):557–629.

Kaplow, Louis, and Steven Shavell. 1996. Property Rules versus Liability Rules: An Economic Analysis. *Harvard Law Review* 109 (4):713–790.

Kim, Jeonghyun. 2004. A Complete Characterization of Efficient Liability Rules: Comment. *Journal of Economics* 81 (1):61–75.

Kolstad, Charles, Thomas Ulen, and Gary Johnson. 1990. Ex Post Liability for Harm vs. Ex Ante Safety Regulation: Substitutes or Complements? *American Economic Review* 80:888–901.

Kovacs, Paul. 2001. Wildfires and Insurance. ICLR Research Paper Series No. 11. www.iclr.org/images/Wildfires_and_insurance.pdf (accessed April 22, 2011).

Lankoande, Mariam, Jonathan Yoder, and Philip Wandschneider. 2005. Optimal Wildfire Insurance in the Wildland-Urban Interface in the Presence of a Government Subsidy for Fire Risk Mitigation. Working paper WP 2005-9. Pullman: Washington State University. www.ses.wsu.edu/PDFFiles/WorkingPapers/Yoder/LankoandeEtAl_InsuranceSubsidies Wildfire_2005.pdf (accessed April 22, 2011).

M., J. E. 1929. Torts. Fault and Liability. Liability for the Escape of Fire. *Virginia Law Review* 16 (2):174–182.

McKee, Michael, Robert Berrens, Michael Jones, Ryan Helton, and John Talberth. 2004. Using Experimental Economics to Examine Wildfire Insurance and Averting Decisions in the Wildland-Urban Interface. *Society and Natural Resources* 17:491–507.

Merrill, Thomas. 1985. Trespass, Nuisance, and the Costs of Determining Property Rights. *Journal of Legal Studies* 14 (1):13–48.

Morrissey, Francis. 1971. Private Nuisance: A Remedy against Air Pollution. *Insurance Council Journal* 38:367

Noel, Dix W. 1943. Nuisance from Land in Its Natural Condition. *Harvard Law Review* 56 (5):772–798.

Omi, Philip, and Erik Martinson. 2004. Effectiveness of Thinning and Prescribed Fire in Reducing Wildfire Severity. USDA Forest Service Gen. Tech. Rep. PSW-GTR-193. www.fs.fed.us/psw/publications/documents/psw_gtr193/psw_gtr193_2a_04_Omi_Martinson. pdf (accessed April 22, 2011).

Pigou, Arthur. 1932. *The Economics of Welfare*. 4th ed. London: Macmillan.

Prante, Tyler, Joseph Little, Michael Jones, Michael McKee, and Robert Berrens. 2010. Inducing Private Wildfire Risk Mitigation: Experimental of Measures on Adjacent Public Lands. Working paper 10-10. Boone, NC: Appalachian State University Department of Economics. http://econ.appstate.edu/RePEc/pdf/wp1010.pdf (accessed April 22, 2011).

Prichard, Susan, David Peterson, and Kyle Jacobson. 2010. Fuel Treatments Reduce the Severity of Wildfire Effects in Dry Mixed Conifer Forest, Washington, USA. *Canadian Journal of Forest Resources* 40:1615–1626.

Radeloff, V. C., R. B. Hammer, S. I. Sterwart, J. S. Fried, S. Holcomb, and J. F. McKeefry. 2005. The Wildland-Urban Interface in the United States. *Ecological Applications* 15 (3): 799–805.

Reams, Margaret, Terry Haines, Cheryl Renner, Michael Wascom, and Harish Kingre. 2005. Goals, Obstacles, and Effective Strategies of Wildfire Mitigation Programs in the Wildland-Urban Interface. *Forest Policy and Economics* 7:818–826.

Rideout, Douglas, Yu Wei, Andrew Kirsch, and Stephen Botti. 2008. Toward a Unified Economic Theory of Fire Program Analysis with Strategies for Empirical Modeling. In *The Economics of Forest Disturbances: Wildfires, Storms, and Invasive Species*, edited by Thomas P. Holmes, Jeffrey P. Prestemon, and Karen L. Abt. Dordrecht, Netherlands: Springer-Verlag, 361–380.

Rose-Ackerman, Susan. 1991. Regulation and the Law of Torts. *American Economic Review: Papers and Proceedings* 81 (2):54–58.

Schmitz, Patrick. 2000. On the Joint Use of Liability and Safety Regulation. *International Review of Law and Economics* 20:371–382.

Shafran, Aric P. 2008. Risk Externalities and the Problem of Wildfire Risk. *Journal of Urban Economics* 64:488–495.

Shavell, Steven. 1980. Strict Liability versus Negligence. *Journal of Legal Studies* 9 (1):1–25.

———. 1984. A Model of the Optimal Use of Liability and Safety Regulation. *Rand Journal of Economics* 15 (2):271–280.

———. 2007. *Economic Analysis of Accident Law*. Cambridge, MA: Harvard University Press.

Shea, J. P. 1940. Our Pappies Burned the Woods and Set a Pattern of Human Behavior in the Southern Forests That Calls for New Methods of Fire Prevention. *American Forests* 46:159–162.

Sparhawk, W. N. 1925. Use of Liability Ratings in Forest Protection. *Journal of Agricultural Research* 30:693–792.

Sun, Changyou. 2007a. Common Law Liability for Landowners When Using Prescribed Fires on Private Land in the Southern United States. *Forest Science* 53 (5):562–570.

———. 2007b. State Statutory Reforms and Retention of Prescribed Fire Liability Laws on U.S. Forest Land. *Forest Policy and Economics* 9:392–402.

Talberth, John, Robert Barrens, Michael McKee, and Michael Jones. 2006. Averting and Insurance Decisions in the Wildland-Urban Interface: Implications of Survey and Experimental Data for Wildfire Risk Reduction Policy. *Contemporary Economic Policy* 24 (2):203–223.

USDA (U.S. Department of Agriculture). 2010. National Database of State and Local Wildfire Hazard Mitigation Programs. www.wildfireprograms.usda.gov/index.html (accessed April 22, 2011).

Varner, J. Morgan, David Steinau, Thomas Ankersen, and F. E. Putz. 2001. Wildfire in Florida: Issues of Law and Forestry Practices. A Report to the City of Waldo, Florida. www.law.ufl.edu/conservation/pdf/firepaper.pdf (accessed April 22, 2011).

Wade, Dale, Steven Miller, Johnny Stowe, and James Brenner. 2006. Rx Fire Laws: Tools to Protect Fire: The "Ecological Imperative." In *Fire in Eastern Oak Forests: Delivering Science to Land Managers, Proceedings of a Conference*, edited by Matthew B. Dickinson. November 2005, Columbus, OH. Gen. Tech. Rep. NRS-P-1. Newtown Square, PA: U.S. Department of Agriculture, Forest Service, Northern Research Station, 233–262. www.treesearch.fs.fed.us/pubs/18452 (accessed April 22, 2011).

Yoder, Jonathan. 2004. Playing with Fire: Endogenous Risk in Resource Management. *American Journal of Agricultural Economics* 86 (4):933–948.

——— . 2008. Liability, Regulation, and Endogenous Risk: Incidence and Severity of Escaped Prescribed Fires in the United States. *Journal of Law and Economics* 51 (2):297–325.

Yoder, Jonathan, Marcia Tilley, David Engle, and Samuel Fuhlendorf. 2003. Economics and Prescribed Fire Law in the United States. *Review of Agricultural Economics* 25:218–233.

4

ECONOMICS AND THE ORGANIZATION OF WILDFIRE SUPPRESSION

Dean Lueck

Every summer for a hundred years running, the U.S. government has made war in America's wildlands under the pretense of "fighting" fires. Under the command of the Forest Service and other federal land management agencies, tens of thousands of young people are sent into the forests of the West to suppress wildfires at a cost to taxpayers of more than a billion dollars a year. Organized with military structure and discipline, and supplemented with an armada of firefighting vehicles, heavy equipment, and aircraft, Uncle Sam's firefighting army is unrivaled in size and expense in the world.

(Ingalsbee 2005, 223)

The use of wildfires (also called wildland fires) is one of the earliest coordinated activities of humankind and has been chronicled by scholars in great detail (Pyne 2001). Fires have been set for cooking, for forging metals, for chasing game, and for clearing forests. Yet for all the benefits of fire, there are costs as well, and humans often have needed to limit or eliminate fires. Suppression, putting out an unwanted fire, is just one part of our longtime relationship with fire. Suppression efforts can be simple, as when individuals and families put out (or try to put out) fires when they threaten homes, crops, and livestock. But as the opening quote suggests, the organization of modern wildfire suppression is complicated.

More prominent and important are the large wildland fires that burn across property and political boundaries. In the United States there are roughly 70,000 wildland fires annually, burning about 6 million acres, and federal suppression expenditures have averaged over $1 billion since 2000.[1] For those fires exceeding 100,000 acres, the organization can become exceedingly complex. On such fires, the large fire organization (LFO) resembles a military-style hierarchical organization with a temporary encampment near the fire in which leaders and administrators coordinate and deploy firefighters and equipment. The size of these temporary organizations can be staggering. For example, the Biscuit Fire burned nearly half a million acres in Oregon in 2004. It began on July 13, and at its zenith on July 31, there were over 2,000 firefighting personnel, 21 helicopters, and 40 bulldozers assigned to the fire. Even so, it was not completely suppressed until December 2002 and cost more than $150 million. The Biscuit Fire destroyed four homes and ten other structures, forced the evacuation of 15,000 people, and destroyed or damaged thousands of acres of valuable timber (GAO Report 2004; the salvage logging that followed the fire became controversial as well).

Large and often devastating fires have occurred throughout the history of the United States, long before the documented history that began with the arrival of Europeans. Table 4.1 shows some important fires, most of which are very large, and some are discussed at several points in this chapter. (Note that this chapter focuses on the United States; see Chapter 8 for an analysis of fire suppression in Australia.)

Although we now routinely think of large fires as western phenomena, there were many large fires in the east and Great Lakes states in the 19th century. For example, the Peshtigo Fire burned 3.7 million acres in Michigan and Wisconsin in 1871, and the Lower Michigan Fire burned 2.5 million acres in 1881. In combination, nearly 2,000 people died in these great fires.

The Great Burn of 1910 in Idaho and Montana, however, is much more famous in fire history and lore. The 1910 Burn was indeed large and devastating—3 million acres, 85 lives, and destruction of buildings and towns—but it was more or less of the same scale as the 19th-century fires. Nevertheless, the 1910 Burn became a focal point for political action that dramatically affected wildfire suppression throughout the 20th century. The Peshtigo and Lower Michigan Fires had no such similar effects.

The goal of this chapter is to explain the basic economic history of wildfire suppression, in terms of both its organization and its effectiveness. Many questions emerge: What does economic theory imply about the structure of wildfire suppression organization and the allocation of resources by these organizations? Does the history—the spatial and temporal variation in wildfire suppression organizations—comport with this theory? For example, prior to the Great 1910 Burn, there were many large, even larger, fires (see Table 4.1), but there were no large-scale fire suppression organizations. Why not? It is easy to see that there may be gains from collective action across landowners and the creation of large specialized organizations, but what are the costs? What have been the effects of the development of these legal and political institutions?

This chapter first provides an economic framework for analyzing optimal organization of fire suppression, focusing on how various organizations can gain control or ownership of a wildfire in the larger context of land management. This is followed by an examination of the economic history of wildfire suppression in the United States. The chapter then looks at some of the prominent features of the spatial and temporal variation in the organization of wildfire suppression.

TABLE 4.1 Important and large wildfires in the United States

Date	Name	Location	Acres	Impacts
1825	Miramichi and Maine Fires	New Brunswick and Maine	3,000,000	160 lives lost
1871	Peshtigo	Wisconsin and Michigan	3,780,000	1,500 lives lost
1881	Lower Michigan	Michigan	2,500,000	169 lives lost; 3,000 structures destroyed
1898	Series of South Carolina fires	South Carolina	3,000,000	14 lives lost (unconfirmed); numerous structures destroyed
1902	Yacoult	Washington and Oregon	1,000,000+	38 lives lost
1903	Adirondack	New York	637,000	
1910	Great Idaho	Idaho and Montana	3,000,000	85 lives lost
1918	Cloquet–Moose Lake	Minnesota	1,200,000	450 lives lost; 38 communities destroyed
1933	Tillamook	Oregon	311,000	1 life lost
1947	Maine	Maine	205,678	16 lives lost
1949	Mann Gulch	Montana	4,339	13 smokejumpers killed; fire safety rules developed
1953	Rattlesnake	California	Unknown	15 lives lost
1970	Laguna	California	175,425	382 structures destroyed
1988	Yellowstone	Montana and Idaho	1,585,000	Large amount of acreage burned; limited "let burn" policies
1994	South Canyon	Colorado	1,856	14 lives lost
2000	Cerro Grande (escaped prescribed fire)	New Mexico	47,650	235 structures destroyed; Los Alamos National Laboratory damaged
2002	Biscuit	Oregon	500,000	100,000+ acres in backfire burnout
2006	East Amarillo Complex	Texas	907,245	12 lives lost; 80 structures destroyed
2009	Station	California	160,000	2 lives lost; 89 homes destroyed just outside LA

Source: Based on NIFC (2011b).

An Economic Framework for Wildfire Suppression Organization

> Whether attacked by two smokechasers with hand tools or by dozens of organized crews with sophisticated equipment, every fire requires a certain degree of organization. Certain functions must be performed, and it is a truism that, in some form, all these functions must be done on all fires. Not only do fires require a division of labor, an organization by function; they need an integration of that division, an organization by complexity.
>
> (Pyne 1984, 372)

Wildfire is an unusual resource or asset for economists to study.[2] It is an ephemeral biochemical phenomenon that requires fuel (i.e., vegetation), oxygen, and heat. It is influenced by the management of land by owners and users, but it is not otherwise constrained by the boundaries of property. Its size and shape are uncertain, but it can be described and explained with mathematical models (see, e.g., Agee 1993). In some ecosystems (e.g., ponderosa pine), the "fire regime" is quite regular; in others, it is more variable and even chaotic over time and space.

This chapter develops an economic framework for analyzing the organization of wildfire suppression by asking a few simple questions: Who owns the fire? Who bears the cost of it? And who will benefit from it? This approach is unique to the rather small body of literature on wildfire but can illuminate the economic history of wildfire suppression and also clarify the incentives and choices for wildland fire policy. The existing economic literature on wildfire has historically focused on the costs of suppression and, more recently, examined the widely acknowledged benefits of wildfire.[3] This literature, however, has largely taken the institutional structure as a given rather than attempted to explain its structure and evolution. The approach in this chapter is to examine the question of ownership of the fire in the context of land management and show how the realities of fire and landownership affect the organization of wildfire suppression.

The Baseline Case: Sole Ownership of the Fireshed

Fire can be considered an input in a land value function, say $V = v(q(l,n), f(l,n))$, where q is a market output (or a composite output) from the land such as timber or crops, f is fire, n is a random composite of natural parameters such as climate and topography, and l is a composite of land management decisions. Land management decisions influence the amount and type of fire, which in turn affect the value of output. Fire can impose costs by damaging other inputs or reducing output, but it can also generate benefits in many forms directly and indirectly (Agee 1993). For example, fire can generate benefits directly by increasing forage and timber production and indirectly by reducing the severity of expected future damages from fires. This implies that some fire is generally optimal. Because fire depends on both natural and human inputs (n, l), and because n is random, fire has an uncertain outcome.[4]

The optimal amount (and type) of land management required to maximize the expected value of the land requires simply that the (expected) net marginal value of a unit of land management must be equal in its impact on the market output and the fire output. (The problem becomes more complicated in a dynamic framework where, for example, fuel buildup depends on past fire activity.) By putting structure on this model, one could easily derive comparative statics predictions for the optimal level (and type) of land management (l^*).

Consider, first, the case of a single owner of land (e.g., forest, range, or other fire-prone habitat) who is optimally managing for some market output as in the problem above. To this simple land management problem is added the idea of a "fireshed," a well-defined area of land that will, on a regular basis, carry a natural fire.[5] In the simplest case, the fireshed has a fixed acreage and this acreage is burned once per year. It can be viewed as a wholly contained natural resource stock like a groundwater basin or an oil reservoir, or perhaps more like a watershed. In reality, a fireshed will not have a fixed acreage, but rather a distribution of size and shape depending on the habitat, topography, weather, climate, and land use. Furthermore, the fireshed will not contain an active fire continuously, nor will the frequency of the fire generally be consistent, though in some cases (as with ponderosa pine, for example), it can be quite regular and predictable. Fire ecologists have long recognized the variability in size, shape, and frequency of fires (e.g., Agee 1993).

Figure 4.1 shows the simplest scenario, in which a single landowner has a plot of fire-prone land that wholly contains a fireshed. The parcel is a rectangular piece of flat land for simplification, and the fireshed is an ellipse. The fire ecology and fire science literature (e.g., Agee 1993; Anderson 1983) indicates that on a flat landscape, fire will tend to burn in an ellipse. In more rugged terrain, fire shape

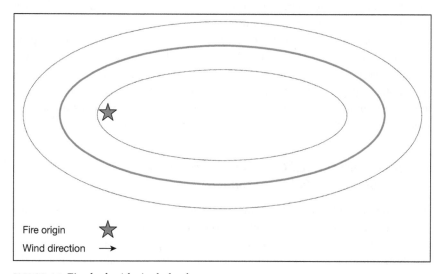

FIGURE 4.1 Fireshed with single landowner

Note: Dotted lines represent 95 percent confidence interval for fire perimeter.

and size are more variable, but the fire is often likely to be a V-shape going up a drainage (on both sides), getting larger at the higher elevation.

The fire management component of the land management decision (l) can be broken down into three choices: prevention (p), control (c), and suppression (s), all of which influence the size, intensity, and frequency of a fire.[6] Prevention can include logging and clearing. Control includes various methods of intentional or prescribed burning. The private landowner will maximize the expected value of the land by allocating resources so that the marginal expected values of prevention, control, and suppression are equated at the optimum. This generally implies some positive amount of all three fire management actions. The landowner fully "owns" the fireshed and fully internalizes the costs and benefits of fire in a manner noted by Coase (1960). In the simplest case, the landowner is also a specialized fire manager, so there is no need to contract for expertise and then monitor that contract.

The decision to choose suppression efforts comes after the start ("ignition") and detection of a wildfire. To simplify, let's assume that the choice of prevention and control are optimal and focus on the choice of suppression effort, which can be thought of as a decision to allocate resources over time, from the "initial attack" until the point at which the fire is declared to be out and the resources are demobilized from the fire.

From an economic perspective, the question is how to allocate suppression resources over the potential lifespan of the fire to maximize the net gains from suppression. The gains from suppression are simply the reduction in expected damages from the fire. The costs include the costs of the suppression resources (human resources and equipment) and the benefits of fire. (The fire suppression problem is essentially an optimal control problem with a finite but endogenous time horizon.) In simple terms, the optimal level of fire suppression effort implies that the marginal reduction in fire damages must be equal to the combined costs of suppression and forgone fire benefits. The optimal level of suppression will depend on natural forces, such as habitat and weather, and economic forces, such as the cost of suppression resources. In principle, optimal suppression effort can range from nothing (e.g., a "let burn" policy) to a vigorous effort to suppress immediately after detection (e.g., the "10 a.m. rule"). Consideration of how actual suppression compares to this economic baseline appears later in the chapter.

Complications: Divided Ownership, Uncertainty, Specialization, and Political Economy

This section considers several potential and realistic complications from the baseline case of a single landowner who wholly controls that fireshed and thus has incentives for optimal wildfire management. Fire management can be sophisticated purely because of the complex forces that affect fire and a fireshed, but in the baseline case of a single owner, the incentives and thus the organization of wildfire suppression are simple. Four additional complicating issues are examined in this section: 1) firesheds that comprise acreage of multiple landowners; 2) uncertainty due to variability in the occurrence and characteristics of the fireshed; 3) gains from specialized suppression resources; and 4) political economy and interest group forces. With each of these issues, a more complex organizational structure is likely to occur, and with such an organization come complicated and often seemingly perverse incentives.

Divided Ownership of the Fireshed

The first important consideration is that the large scale of a wildfire, or fireshed, might be well beyond the acreage of a single landowner. Indeed, the Great 1910 Burn, for example, covered 3 million acres of private and public land. The private land included large tracts of forest land as well as small rural plots and town lots. Figure 4.2 shows a more realistic scenario where the fireshed crosses property boundaries.

Optimal suppression effort, and generally optimal fire management, now requires coordinated effort across the properties. This simple addition to the fire model generates a rationale for either large-scale ownership of fire-prone lands or coordinated activity among the landowners. Coordination could come through contract or legal and policy constraints, such as contracting among landowners,

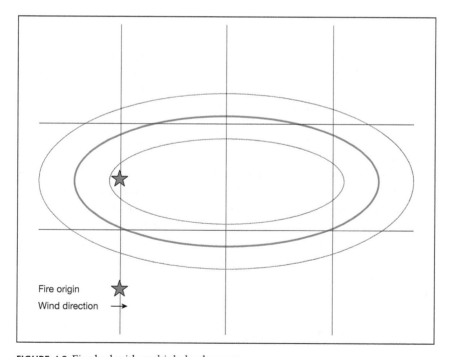

FIGURE 4.2 Fireshed with multiple landowners

Note: Dotted lines represent 95 percent confidence interval for fire perimeter.

consolidated ownership, political organizations that have jurisdictional control over fire management, or legal rules that mandate landowner management decisions. Landowner contracting is more likely when landowners are few and homogenous (Libecap 1989). Large-scale landownership can consolidate fire management interests, and this could occur with private or public ownership (e.g., national forests).

Fireshed Uncertainty and Natural Forces

Uncertainty surrounding the characteristics of the fireshed is a second important consideration. Uncertainty exists over several dimensions of a fireshed, including the fire's size, location, intensity and speed, frequency, and duration. Fireshed uncertainty is affected by topography, weather, and climate. Land use changes can also affect the fireshed and its variability by changing fuel loads and types. Even in relatively simple cases such as landscapes dominated by fire-adapted species as ponderosa pine, where fires occur frequently and regularly, there is still substantial variation in fireshed characteristics. Returning to Figure 4.2 and noting the 95 percent confidence interval for the border of the fireshed makes the point. If there is no uncertainty, the fireshed border is clear and, with good information, known to all parties.

Uncertainty further increases the costs of contracting for ownership of the fireshed. Uncertainty will increase the costs of contracting among private parties and thus more likely lead to government control through administrative agencies. Similarly, when fireshed uncertainty is lower, it is more likely that private contracting will emerge. In addition to uncertainty about the size of the fireshed, uncertainty about the speed and path of the fire will also raise the costs of contracting for control and increase the gains from an administrative or rule-bound response. This feature of wildfire, and fire generally, was noted in Chapter 2 as generating dramatic limitations on private property rights for fire control in the common law.[7]

The 1910 Burn is an extreme example of fireshed uncertainty, both in its border and in its frequency and intensity. Such a fire is an event that occurs perhaps once in two or three centuries, and its "border" is likely so variable that the term *fireshed* is stretched to the limit of its application as a well-defined asset. Contracting for ownership and control of such a fire would obviously be a costly and complicated contingent-laden arrangement, though liability law (discussed in Chapter 1) would influence the contracting environment and could, in principle, lower the costs of contracting.

Specialization in Wildfire Suppression

The potential gains from specialization in wildfire suppression are another important consideration. If there are large gains from specialized fire managers who have different skills than the landowners, who may be interested in timber, minerals, or agriculture, then there exists an additional rationale for coordination across landowners and perhaps even across fire regimes or habitat types. Landowners in fire-prone areas are unlikely to be trained and equipped to take suppression action on more than the smallest fires generally. The organized involvement of landowners in the Australian bush is a case where they do attain a degree of specialization (see Chapter 8). Modern wildfire suppression involves specialized crews for initial attack, fire detection, fire prevention, mop-up, and so on. Specialized resources include not only manpower, but also equipment such as chainsaws, pumps, hand tools, trucks, bulldozers, helicopters, and fixed-wing aircraft. If fires are spread over space and time, it may be optimal to have specialized resources that are highly mobile to meet needs across the landscapes and firesheds.[8] In this setting, there can be gains from creating a network of suppression specialists who are available to travel across large regions to work on fires as they occur.[9]

Political Economy of the Fireshed

A final important consideration is political economy. The combination of divided landownership, fireshed uncertainty, and highly specialized suppression resources creates a demand for a highly bureaucratic organization, and thus the economic analysis of bureaucracy will be useful. The creation of a specialized crew is likely to require a bureaucratic regime because of the importance of teamwork and coordination (Williamson 1999) in a fire suppression effort where decisions and actions must be taken quickly, so that decentralized contracting is likely to be too costly to be effective. The questions of optimal crew size and of organization and coordination are important as well. For example, should the crews have a rigid, military-style hierarchy, such as in the U.S. Army, or a more flexible organization in which individuals have more authority and autonomy, like a special forces unit? A key feature of the economics of bureaucracy is the recognition that low-powered incentives tend to dominate the organization in which ownership is inherently weak. Rule-based constraints tend to emerge in bureaucracies to counter the effects of these low-powered incentives. As noted in Chapter 2, the common law of fire, which allows suppression organizations to work quickly, also causes incentives of the landowners to get muted.

In addition to the economics of bureaucracy, the economics of politics and law are likely to be relevant. The interest groups (e.g., landowners) that are present during early stages of the formation of an organization are expected to shape wildfire suppression organization, and the interest groups that form in response to suppression organization will in turn exert influence. These interest group forces not only may create organizations, but also may lead to path dependency in wildfire suppression organization.

A Brief Economic History of Wildfire Suppression

> Since 1910, much of the history of the Forest Service can be translated into a succession of efforts to get firefighters on fires as soon as possible—the sooner, the smaller the fire. If a campfire left burning can be caught soon enough, a man with a shovel can bury it.
>
> (Maclean 1989, 23)

This section briefly examines the history of wildfire suppression in the United States to see how it comports with the framework developed in the previous section. The focus is primarily on the 20th century, though both the 19th-century precursors and recent changes in the 21st century are also discussed. Table 4.2 is a reference for this analysis and shows the history of fire policy and law. This section first summarizes the history, and then links it to the economic framework above and examines some of the incentives and issues surrounding modern suppression policy.

TABLE 4.2 Important wildfire law and policies

Date	Law or Policy	Impact
1891	Forest Reserve Act	Allowed president to reserve forests from public domain
1905	Transfer Act	Forest reserves moved to Bureau of Forestry (later USFS)
1907	Midnight reserves	16,000,000 acres added to national forest system
1908	Forest Fire Emergency Act	Created "blank check" policy for suppression
1911	Weeks Act	USFS gets authority to buy forests in south and east
1924	Clarke-McNary Act	Created cooperative fire control system, USFS at center
1934	National Fire Danger Rating System	
1935	10 a.m. rule	Emphasis on initial attack
1940	Smokejumpers established in USFS	Emphasis on initial attack
1944	Smokey the Bear born in New Mexico	National anti-fire campaign launched
1960	Specialized interregional (IR) fire suppression crews established	Creation of a suppression network
1964	Wilderness Act	Limited fire suppression
1965	National Interagency Fire Center (NIFC) created	USFS loses authority to coordinating agency
1978	USFS Manual eliminates 10 a.m. rule for suppression	Allows fires to burn under some prescriptions
1995	1995 Federal Wildland Fire Management Policy rules	Reinforces suppression and increases budget authority

Suppression Organization

In the United States, the organization of wildfire suppression has varied from haphazardly organized crews of volunteers and the conscripted to a centralized, military-style hierarchy of highly specialized crews, managers, and equipment operators. Prior to the 20th century, suppression was undertaken by local volunteers and fledgling fire protective associations. In the early days of the U.S. Forest Service (USFS), before the 1910 Burn, national forest rangers organized crews as needed, using combinations of itinerant unskilled labor and prison crews (Pyne 1984). Egan (2009) describes how, during the 1910 Burn, rangers went to bars and prisons to round up men to fight the fire. Many of these men had never been in the woods and were not familiar with the use of axes and shovels in firefighting.

Major organizational changes occurred in the first few decades of the 20th century. In 1908, the so-called blank check policy of federal suppression funding emerged. In 1911, in the wake of the 1910 Burn, the Forest Service and its supporters were able to get authority to buy forests in the southeast, which aided in the dramatic expansion of the national forest system from its early days in the late 1800s (Egan 2009). The blank check budgeting continued more or less unchecked until the 1980s, when budgetary limits were imposed, but it was reestablished soon after the 1988 Yellowstone Fires and remains more or less intact today. The national forest system grew during the early 20th century, as did the fire suppression organization within the Forest Service (Pyne 1984).

During the 1930s and 1940s, specialized fire crews and smokejumpers emerged within the Forest Service. In 1924, the Clarke-McNary Act created the cooperative fire control system, which links Forest Service fire suppression to state and other organizations; all 50 states ultimately joined this system. The 10 a.m. rule was established in 1935, with the goal that all fires be suppressed by 10 o'clock the morning following detection.[10] During this period, there were also large programs to build roads, lay telephone lines, and establish fire lookouts throughout the national forests. This effort was the beginning of the establishment of a vast network for fire control, from reporting fires to communicating with resources during suppression.

By the 1960s, the current military-style organization was more or less established. This regime began to emerge in the post-World War II era and was influence by the Mann Gulch Fire. At Mann Gulch, an extreme fire event called a "blowup" killed 13 firefighters, including 12 members of the fledgling smokejumper unit based in Missoula, Montana.[11] This period also saw the emergence of fire science within the Forest Service, which ultimately led to the establishment of the Missoula Fire Sciences Laboratory in 1960.

Important changes during this period were the establishment of 20-man "hotshot" crews, which were deployable throughout the west, and the increased use of aircraft. Details of modern suppression organization and policy can be found in NWCG (2004) and BLM (2011). Interestingly, the term "fire boss" emerged

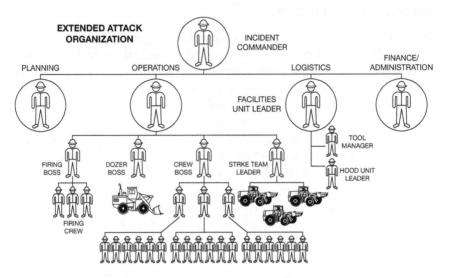

FIGURE 4.3 Large fire organization in the Incident Command System

Source: NWCG (2004, 112).

early to refer to the person in charge of the fire with the authority to declare it contained and controlled and the authority to order resources. The term implies ownership of the fire, once ignited, but not of the fireshed itself. Every fire has a fire boss, even if there are just two firefighters working the initial attack on a small fire. When fire suppression organization became integrated into the Incident Command System, the fire boss became the incident commander. The term "fire boss" should not be confused with the terms "firing boss" and "firing crew" (see Figure 4.3), which refer to those in charge of implementing backfires and burnouts (smaller fires that remove fuel) for the purpose of suppressing the larger wildfire. Figure 4.3 shows the structure of modern large fire organizations (LFOs), which is the same general structure also used for crews dealing with natural disasters such as floods and hurricanes.

The National Interagency Fire Center (NIFC) now coordinates wildfires suppression efforts throughout the United States.[12] In the last two decades, periods in which there have been relatively more and larger fires than during prior decades, policies and organizations have changed. (See Chapter 9 for evidence on large fire trends.) Many of the changes stemmed from reaction to the large fires in the Yellowstone region in 1988 (see Table 4.1). In 1995, the United States developed its first nationwide fire management policy that further centralized fire suppression organization and put renewed emphasis on aggressive initial attack as well as on fuels management, including reintroducing fire to certain ecosystems. NWCG (n.d.) has a good summary of the 1995 policy and subsequent 2001 policy.

The Peculiar Incentives of Wildfire Suppression

Many observers, including economists, have noted that the current suppression regime has unusual incentives that may generate waste, perhaps substantial waste, in the allocation and timing of suppression resources. Any organization that deviates from complete ownership of the fireshed will create imperfect incentives for decision-makers, because no one faces the full net benefits of their actions (Coase 1960). In the complex organization of modern fire suppression, there are such incentives for both suppression crews and their leaders, and for landowners both public and private. These incentives come from the large rule-based bureaucratic structure of suppression organizations, the emergency status of fire suppression in law (Bradshaw 2011) and policy (e.g., blank check funding), and the extremely divided ownership of the fireshed. These incentives naturally raise questions about the overall efficiency of fire suppression and how different organizational structures might improve incentives.

In this volume, other authors have shown how interest groups shape the allocation of fire management resources (Chapter 6) and how the large-scale organization of suppression implicitly subsidizes private landowners and encourages them to develop in fire-prone areas (Chapter 10). Not only are there low-powered incentives generally for bureaucrats (Williamson 1999), but there are also other features unique to wildfire suppression organization. First, during an active fire, there is no liability for damages during suppression. Bradshaw (2011) argues that this has led to an overuse of backfires on large fires and the significant destruction of valuable commercial timber. Second, given the blank check budgeting, the fire boss faces almost a zero marginal cost of resources up to the supply constraint of contract.[13] This creates an implicit incentive to let large fires get even larger, both to increase current salaries and also for overhead teams to gain large fire experience, which will lead to increased returns in the future. Consider the following admission by a senior member of a firefighting team on the Flicker Creek Fire in Idaho in 1989:

> "We're a little overstaffed because the fire didn't do what we expected," he admitted. . . . "What did you expect the fire to do?" I asked. "Well . . . The guys don't want to see the forests burn, but on the other hand, they want to have a good, productive summer. They like to have two to three weeks on a fire and then move on to another one. In that sense, it's disappointing to have the fire lay down so fast."
>
> (Junger 2002, 14)

The quote above is anecdotal, but the incentives are corroborated by Canton-Thompson et al. (2008), in a case study of incident management team incentives and culture, and by Kennedy et al. (2005), who interviewed Forest Service personnel. A more extreme case is when firefighters deliberately set fires, and there are cases in which such individuals have been apprehended and prosecuted as criminals.

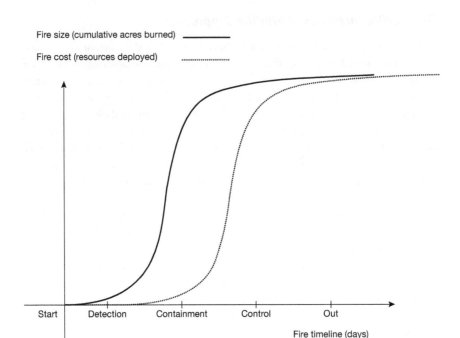

FIGURE 4.4 Timeline of fire activity and resource deployment

Figure 4.4 shows what many have argued is a typical situation on large fires (e.g., those over 1,000 acres): that is, the rather late buildup of resources after the fire has burned to near its maximum extent. The solid line in the figure shows the cumulative acreage of the fire from the time of ignition. The dotted line shows the cumulative buildup of resources (measured in $) beginning with detection. This figure shows the case in which the fire had mostly completed its natural progression before the majority of suppression resources arrived. This can occur because of the costs of mobilizing a large suppression effort. The phenomenon in Figure 4.4 is consistent with some evidence that in many cases, suppression action on large fires (especially crown fires) has little effect on the outcome of the fire. In turn, it is possible that fire suppression costs can exceed the value of the fire damages.[14]

The strongest critics of the current military-style organization, such as Ingalsbee (2005) and others, also have suggested that too many resources are spent on suppression, and that suppression is often ineffective as well as damaging to the natural environment. (Ingalsbee is a particularly harsh critic, especially on the environmental effects of fire suppression, and uses the metaphor of the "fire-industrial complex.") Indeed, the 1978 end of the 10 a.m. policy recognized that short-term suppression efforts may increase long-term fire danger and fire suppression costs.

There are well-known cases in which the suppression resources spent dramatically exceeded the value of the potential (and sometimes realized) damages.[15]

Conclusions

> It is clear that the government has powers which might enable it to get things done at a lower cost than a private organization. ... But the governmental administrative machine is not itself costless. It can, in fact, on occasion be extremely costly.
>
> (Coase 1960, 18)

This chapter has conducted a preliminary examination of the economic history of wildfire suppression in the United States. It presents an economic framework that focuses on the question of who owns the fire or the *fireshed*—the expected area over which wildfire burns in a given location. Because of the ephemeral and large-scale nature of fire, a rationale exists for widespread government intervention in what is basically a land management question. The large scale of most firesheds suggests that large-scale landownership or landscape-level organizations are optimal for wildfire suppression. In this regard, wildfire suppression is similar to the governance of groundwater, oil and gas, and wildlife. To further understand wildfire suppression, the chapter has also stressed the economics of uncertainty about the dimensions (spatial and temporal) of the fireshed and the political economy of bureaucracy.

In economic terms, the optimal level of wildfire suppression should maximize the expected net benefits of this rather unique land management effort. Optimal wildfire suppression must mitigate the losses from wildfire and capture its benefits as well. Yet the observed structure and the incentives it generates suggest waste in the form of excessive suppression resources and perhaps overdevelopment of fire-prone areas. In some cases, the incentives appear to lead fire suppression commanders to commit resources on suppression far in excess of potential fire damages and with scant evidence of effectiveness. Little work, however, has been done to systematically quantify the costs of the existing suppression organization, so no strong overall conclusions can be made. Indeed, because the suppression of wildfire is an exceedingly complex organizational enterprise, it is possible that the best feasible solution may appear at first glance to be wildly wasteful.

Acknowledgments

The author is grateful for the assistance of Dave Calkin, Mark Finney, and other researchers at the USFS Rocky Mountain Research Station FireLab in Missoula, Montana. Thanks also to Jon Yoder and other participants in the Wildfire Symposium for their helpful comments.

Notes

1. USFS fire suppression costs have been over $1 billion on average for the last decade, but average total expenditures (federal, state, and private) exceed $3 billion. The 10-year average at the end of 2010 was 70,363 fires and 6,317,714 acres (NIFC 2010). For more information on wildfire statistics, see NIFC (2011a). NIFC is the National Interagency Fire Center in Boise, Idaho, which coordinates fire suppression efforts among agencies.

2. The discussion in this chapter ignores controlled or industrial fire, such as in an internal combustion engine or a coal-fired power plant. In such cases, there is a clear owner of the fire for the process at hand, and uncertainty is relatively small. For a nice overview, see Wikipedia, s.v. "Wildfire," http://en.wikipedia.org/wiki/Wildfire (accessed May 3, 2011), which defines the term as "an uncontrolled fire in combustible vegetation that occurs in the countryside or a wilderness area."

3. Much of this literature has been published as USDA Forest Service technical reports, although there is a recent literature on some of the economic effects of wildfire (e.g., Loomis et al. 2002). For overviews, see Donovan and Brown (2005) and Donovan and Rideout (2003). For a good survey of Forest Service fire management and suppression, see Mills and Bratten (1988).

4. Nature will vary across fire regimes, and this will influence fire uncertainty. For example, one technical report shows that for ponderosa pine, 73 percent of the fires are surface fires with a mean interval of 13 years, whereas for lodgepole pine, 78 percent are replacement fires with a mean interval of 125 years (USFS n.d.).

5. This term is not well defined in the literature on fire ecology (Agee 1993). Watersheds, airsheds, and viewsheds are similar concepts used in environmental policy discussions. The term *floodplain* is also similar, and Swetnam (2011) indicates that "fire plain" has been used by some fire scientists recently.

6. In the notation above, fire depends on these choices and nature, so that $f = f(p, s, c; n)$. Chapter 3 uses a similar distinction among types of fire management (i.e., land management) decisions referring to mitigation, precaution, and suppression.

7. A private agreement for wildfire suppression could in principle include rule-based prescriptions for suppression, and this too would increase the cost of the agreement and suggest a bureaucratic solution (Williamson 1999).

8. The seasonal aspect of fire, which creates a longer-term demand for specialized suppression efforts, is similar to the seasonality in certain parts of American agriculture (Allen and Lueck 2003). In the Great Plains, for example, custom (specialized) harvest firms travel for several months, harvesting wheat from Texas to Saskatchewan. For fires in Australia, this seasonality is well known; see Geoscience Australia (2011). Calkin et al. (2005a, Table 1) discuss fire seasonality for large regions of the United States.

9. The gains from such a network do not by themselves suggest public provision of suppression services, but they do suggest the creation of a network that may be more easily created as a public entity. Suppression services themselves might be provided by a variety of public or private entities.

10. The 10 a.m. rule was official abolished by the USFS in 1978 in order to allow fires to burn under certain prescriptions, but after the 1998 Yellowstone Fires, it once again became the norm, if not the official policy. Chapter 9 examines how this policy has impacted large fire frequency in the western states.

11. Maclean (1992) made the story of Mann Gulch an American legend. Smokejumpers are organized differently from other fire crews in that they do not have a fixed group with a set leader, but rather a loose hierarchy in which groups are formed from an initial random draw and then on the basis of fire demand.

12. NIFC coordinates the following resources: National Area Command Teams, Type 1 Incident Management Teams, Type 1 Interagency Hotshot Crews, Smokejumpers, Smokejumper Aircraft, Type 1 & 2 Helicopters, Airtankers, Infrared Aircraft, Leadplane

Aircraft, Large Transport Aircraft, Modular Airborne Firefighting Systems (MAFFS), National Mobile Food Units, National Mobile Shower Units National Commissary Units, NIRSC Communication Components, Fire Weather RAWS Systems, and Critical Cache Items. According to NIFC (2011c), more than 15,000 trained firefighting personnel are available during the main summer fire season, and more than 100 helicopters and 40 to 50 air tankers are under contract each season and available for use.

13. The blank check budgeting is somewhat puzzling but may serve to relax resource constraints for actions such as fire suppression that require relatively rapid response to be effective at all. The fact that wildfire suppression is strongly linked to public land agencies (historically the Forest Service) is another reason for such funding.

14. Snider et al. (2006) argue that suppression costs are large relative to presuppression treatment in southwestern forests. Ingalsbee (2005) suggests that environmental costs of suppression can be large relative to fire damages and suppression costs. Calkin et al. (2005b) show cases in which the net benefits of suppression are negative.

15. The empirical evidence is, however, quite limited. Calkin et al. (2003) examine cases in which fire suppression costs vastly exceeded the potential property damage. Liang et al. (2008) use data from the Northern Rockies to estimate the determinants of fire-specific suppression expenditures and find only fire size and the presence of private land to be statistically important.

References

Agee, James K. 1993. *Fire Ecology of the Pacific Northwest Forests*. Washington, DC: Island Press.

Allen, Douglas W., and Dean Lueck. 2003. *The Nature of the Farm*. Cambridge, MA: MIT Press.

Anderson, Hal E. 1983. Predicting Wind-Driven Wildland Fire Size and Shape. Research paper INT-305. Ogden, UT: USDA Forest Service, Intermountain Forest and Range Experiment Station.

BLM (Bureau of Land Management). 2011. BLM Fire Training Unit. www.blm.gov/nifc/st/en/prog/fire/training/fire_training.html (accessed May 3, 2011).

Bradshaw, Karen. 2011. Backfire: Distorted Incentives in Wildfire Suppression Techiniques. *Utah Environmental Law Journal* 31:155–179.

Calkin, David, Krista Gebert, Greg Jones, and Ronald Nelson. 2005a. Forest Service Large Fire Area Burned and Suppression Expenditure Trends, 1970–2002. *Journal of Forestry* 103 (4):179–183.

Calkin, David, Kevin Hyde, Krista Gebert, and Greg Jones. 2005b. Comparing Resource Values at Risk from Wildfire with Forest Service Fire Suppression Expenditures: Examples from 2003 Western Montana Wildfire Season. Research Note RMRS-RN-24WWW. Fort Collins, CO: USDA Forest Service.

Canton-Thompson, Janie, Krista Gebert, Brooke Thompson, Greg Jones, David Calkin, and Geoff Donovan. 2008. External Human Factors in Incident Management Team Decision Making and Their Effect on Large Fire Suppression Expenditures. *Journal of Forestry* 106 (8):416–424.

Coase, Ronald H. 1960. The Problem of Social Cost. *Journal of Law and Economics* 3:1–44.

Donovan, Geoffrey, and Thomas C. Brown. 2005. An Alternative Incentive Structure for Wildfire Management on National Forest Land. *Forest Science* 51:387–395.

Donovan, Geoffrey H., and Douglas B. Rideout. 2003. A Reformulation of the Cost plus Net Value Change Model of Wildfire Economics. *Forest Science* 49:318–323.

Egan, Timothy. 2009. *The Big Burn: Teddy Roosevelt and the Fire That Saved America*. NY: Houghton Mifflin Harcourt.

GAO (U.S. General Accounting Office). 2004. *Biscuit Fire: Analysis of Fire Response, Resource Availability, and Personnel Certification Standards.* GAO Report 04-426. Washington DC: GAO.

Geoscience Australia. 2011. Where Do Bushfires Occur? www.ga.gov.au/hazards/bushfire/bushfire-basics/where.html (accessed April 28, 2011).

Ingalsbee, Timothy. 2005. The War on Wildfire. In *Wildfire: A Century of Failed Forest Policy*, edited by George Wuerthner. Island Press, 223–231.

Junger, Sebastian. 2002. *Fire.* New York: Harper Perennial.

Kennedy, James J., Richard W. Haynes, and Xiaoping Zhou. 2005. Line Officers' Views on Slated USDA Forest Service Values and the Agency Reward System. USFS PNW-GTR-632. www.fs.fed.us/pnw/pubs/pnw_gtr632.pdf (accessed May 3, 2011).

Liang, Jingjing, David E. Calkin, Krista M Gebert, Tyron J. Venn, and Robin P. Silverstein. 2008. Factors Influencing Large Wildland Fire Suppression Expenditures. *International Journal of Wildland Fire* 17:650–659.

Libecap, Gary D. 1989. *Contracting for Property Rights.* New York: Cambridge University Press.

Loomis, John, Dana Griffin, Ellen Wu, and Armando González-Cabán. 2002. Estimating the Economic Value of Big Game Habitat Production from Prescribed Fire Using a Time Series Approach. *Journal of Forest Economics* 8:119–129.

Maclean, Norman. 1989. *Young Men and Fire.* Chicago: University of Chicago Press.

Mills, Thomas J., and Frederick W. Bratten. 1988. Economic Efficiency and Risk Character of Fire Management Programs, Northern Rocky Mountains. USFS Research Paper PSW-RP-192. www.treesearch.fs.fed.us/pubs/29125 (accessed May 3, 2011).

NIFC (National Interagency Fire Center). 2010. Fire Information: National Fire News: 10-Year Average. www.nifc.gov/fire_info/nfn.htm (accessed November 7, 2010).

——. 2011a. Fire Information: Wildland Fire Statistics. www.nifc.gov/fire_info/fire_stats.htm (accessed May 3, 2011).

——. 2011b. Historically Significant Wildland Fires. www.nifc.gov/fire_info/historical_stats.htm (accessed May 3, 2011).

——. 2011c. National Interagency Fire Center home page. www.nifc.gov/index.html (accessed May 3, 2011).

NWCG (National Wildfire Coordinating Group). 2004. Fireline Handbook. www.nwcg.gov/pms/pubs/410-1/410-1.pdf (accessed May 3, 2011).

——. No date. Fire Policy. www.nwcg.gov/branches/ppm/fpc/archives/fire_policy/index.htm (accessed April 30, 2011).

Pyne, Stephen J. 1984. *Introduction to Wildland Fire: Fire Management in the United States.* New York: John Wiley and Sons.

——. 2001. *Fire: A Brief History.* Seattle and London: University of Washington Press and British Museum.

Snider, Gary, P. J. Daugherty, and D. Wood. 2006. The Irrationality of Continued Fire Suppression: An Avoided Cost Analysis of Fire Hazard Reduction Treatments versus No Treatment. *Journal of Forestry* 104 (8):431–437.

Swetnam, Tom. 2011. Personal communication with the author, November 13.

USFS (USDA Forest Service). No date. Expanded Fire Regime Table. www.fs.fed.us/database/feis/fire_regime_table/fire_regime_table.html (accessed May 3, 2011).

Williamson, Oliver E. 1999. Public and Private Bureaucracies: A Transaction Cost Economics Perspective. *Journal of Law, Economics and Organization* 15:306–342.

Yoder, J. 2008. Liability, Regulation, and Endogenous Risk: The Incidence of and Severity of Escaped Prescribed Fires in the United States. *Journal of Law and Economics* 51:297–325.

5

NORMS OF FIRE SUPPRESSION AMONG PUBLIC AND PRIVATE LANDOWNERS

Karen M. Bradshaw

Private commercial landowners hold the majority of American timberlands. Government land managers, represented by various agencies, collectively control the second largest proportion of timberlands. Interactions between private and public landowners have changed dramatically over the past 120 years; the once-collaborative relationship is increasingly adversarial as the goals of adjacent land-owners conflict. This shift is especially evident in the norms followed, and practices used, to address wildfire. As public land management objectives changed in response to environmental pressures, the core competency of government land management agencies similarly shifted from forestry to firefighting. Accordingly, government firefighting agencies' objectives for firefighting are sharply divergent from—and sometimes directly opposed to—the interests of private landowners.

This chapter presents an ethnographic study of the extralegal norms governing fire suppression among private landowners. The ethnographic component of this chapter is based upon a dozen interviews conducted between 2007 and 2010 with institutional private landowners, registered professional foresters, an attorney specializing in wildfire litigation, and California Department of Forestry and Fire Protection employees. The norms revealed in the interviews are premised upon the closely knit nature of the group, which anticipates future ongoing inter-actions, as well as benefits from the reduced cost of extralegal dispute resolution. Historically, when the government acted primarily as a land manager, it shared in these norms. Collaborations between government firefighting agencies and private landowners under exigent circumstances provided efficiencies in resource allocation and communication of institutional knowledge. But, as government agencies reduced their land management capacities, sharing norms with private land managers became less desirable; the groups were no longer composed of foresters with similar backgrounds; and the need for repeated interactions on day-to-day land management issues decreased, as did the related need for an inexpensive, relationship-preserving method of conflict resolution. Without the backdrop relationship of cooperation in land management, the use of norms in wildfire suppression efforts similarly declined. Although restoration of shared norms is infeasible given the current policy objectives of government land management agencies, this chapter does propose that a more collaborative, less adversarial approach to fire suppression is normatively desirable.

There is a conundrum in wildfire that would make a fitting question on the final exam of a public choice course:

> Historically, a government agency competed against private industry in selling trees to sawmills. As a secondary function, the agency fought wildfires that damaged its trees and also those on private lands. In response to environmental pressure, the agency stopped selling trees and instead allocates its resources toward fighting fires that endanger the trees of private industry. The agency budget for protecting trees increases sharply over a ten year period. Private industry is angered by the shift and wishes to return to the old model. Explain this reaction.

This question captures a scenario in which the beneficiaries of a public service—which protects their assets without charging for the protection—are complaining that the agency protecting it is expanding to focus more fully on providing protection. This is analogous to parents complaining that their children's school received increased funding or neighborhood residents complaining that their community received increased policing; it seems quite illogical. So, why do private commercial timberland owners (landowners) complain that government land management and fire agencies (GFAs) are expanding their fire suppression efforts?[1] Explaining this conundrum requires tracing the history of government land management agencies and commercial timber operations, which emerged at roughly the same time but developed in different directions.

Wildfire profoundly affects a diverse group of stakeholders: conservationists, wildland-urban interface homeowners, landowners, government firefighters, private firefighters, and taxpayers. The relationship among stakeholders in wildfire suppression is a vital component to the strategy and efficacy of suppression efforts. Unfortunately, the perspectives and contributions of various stakeholders are seldom studied or intentionally engaged. GFAs retain absolute authority to fight wildfires; they unilaterally decide which methods to use, how to allocate resources among various fires burning simultaneously, and whether to pursue cost recovery for suppression efforts. Ex post, GFA actions are subject to review and criticism by stakeholders. Sharp criticisms of the methods used and decisions made abound, ranging from environmental groups claiming the chemicals used for fire suppression endanger animal life to Native American tribes reporting deleterious health consequences caused by the smoke of unsuppressed fire. But GFAs are virtually never liable for decisions made in their firefighting capacity, due to sovereign immunity and the discretionary function exception to the Federal Tort Claims Act.

Landowners—roughly conceived here as owners of 5,000 acres or more of timberland, who use their land for commercial timberland operations—are especially critical of GFA firefighting efforts. Historically, there was considerable cooperation between landowners and GFAs. Landowners viewed the services provided by GFAs as valuable and sought to aid in suppression efforts by providing GFAs with free use of their private roads, equipment, manpower, and institutional knowledge. But, as the core competency of GFAs shifted away from managing timberlands like a landowner, the norms that once bound the groups dissipated. Lessened interactions led to decreased reliance on landowner norms by GFAs, which resulted in enhanced reliance on formal conflict resolution and firefighting methodologies that levy losses on private landowners that cannot be recouped. Today, fires are managed by GFA leaders from across the country, who may be indifferent to local norms and have little incentive to protect the resources of private landowners, with whom the incident commanders have no preexisting relationship and no expectation of future transactions. GFAs instead pursue objectives such as vegetative management or training exercises, which are antithetical to the interest of protecting private timberland. GFAs' increasing use of backfire, cost recovery, and let-burn policies impose high costs on private landowners, who have virtually no ex post recourse.

This shift can be explained through exploring the historic and present uses of norms for wildfire suppression between landowners and GFAs. Norms are informal social rules governing behavior, which are premised upon social attitudes of approval and disapproval.[2] Law and economics theorists suggest that the use of norms to resolve conflict is cost efficient and preserves relationships relative to undertaking litigation or other legalized means of resolutions. Norms typically arise among closely knit groups who expect to engage in ongoing transactions over a prolonged period of time. Some suggest that the government uses norms to achieve policy objectives. Norms and laws interact in a variety of ways: (1) sometimes norms control individual behavior to the exclusion of law, (2) sometimes norms and law together influence behavior, and (3) sometimes norms and law influence each other.

The customs governing extralegal interactions among wildfire stakeholders have received little attention. This chapter seeks to begin the inquiry of the effect of norms on wildfire by starting with the particularized group of landowners. This group is important given its size: private industrial landowners conducting timberland operations own more than 60 percent of all timberlands. Moreover, the land managers of privately held timberland are a closely knit group who, given their fixed and adjacent properties, must regularly interact over time. In other words, they are likely to have—and indeed do have—a well-established system of norms including, but also extending well beyond, wildfire suppression.

This chapter begins by describing the historic development of relationships between landowners and GFAs. It goes on to describe a shift in the goals and policies of GFAs, which resulted in a move away from their use of landowner norms in fire suppression. The chapter concludes by finding that although the shifts have been necessary to meet the policy objectives, the loss of collaboration in institutional knowledge and resources produces undesirable losses in efficiency, safety, and firefighting efficacy when suppression is attempted.

The Relationship between GFAs and Landowners

The relationship between GFAs and landowners has waxed and waned over the past 120 years. Early GFAs began with the twin aims of discouraging the clear-cutting of land by timber barons and increasing the supply of timber as a resource for the growing nation. Thus, at their inception, GFAs focused upon the long-term yield of timberland holdings had a greater interest in protecting timberlands from forest fire than did private forestry operations, which focused upon clear-cutting practice rather than growing new generations of trees. Later, from approximately 1920 to 1970, the forest management goals of GFAs and landowners aligned well. Both groups sought to produce sustainable-yield forests, which necessitated fire protection. In the present period, from roughly 1970 to 2010, GFAs have dramatically reduced their commercial timber operations and therefore no longer require suppression of wildfire to preserve economic values in timber. The core competencies of GFAs have, however, shifted from forestry to fire suppression. Accordingly, the continued success of GFAs is predicated upon attracting resources for their wildfire suppression efforts, which, paradoxically, is best achieved through allowing some fires to grow quite large. In contrast, landowners continue to operate sustainable-yield forests. Their profit is yielded through the harvest of mature timber, which requires fire suppression.

1862–1920: The Early GFAs

The history of GFAs begins with the establishment of the Department of Agriculture in 1862 (USDA 1992). By 1881, the agency appointed Dr. Franklin B. Houghs as the chief of the Division of Forestry, based upon his study of the national forests and belief that the government should manage (harvest) timberlands. In 1891, Congress enacted the Forest Reserve Act, which empowered the President to set aside forest reserves out of public lands. Government conservation agencies were established in part to respond to the wide-scale destruction of natural resources at the hands of timber barons. The worst of these practices included clear-cutting land without reforestation efforts, leaving barren swaths of cut-over land. Notably, these were logging operations, not forestry operations—distinct concepts often conflated. Foresters at the time had the goal of sustained yield, or continuous supply over time, focused on human intervention to maintain and increase the supply of natural resources.

Formal forestry education in the United States began in the 1870s. The increased interest in conservation and a scientific approach to forestry led botanists and European forestry experts to begin teaching the topic in American universities. Forestry lectures began at universities in 1873, and formal forestry programs emerged in 1886. There was a strong linkage between the forestry schools and

GFAs, which persisted for many years thereafter. Consequently, public and private foresters had virtually identical college educations and internships for the first eighty years of forestry in the United States.

Public sector forestry employment expanded in response to the 1897 Organic Act. The Act established management of the public forest lands for "continuous timber supply." Early GFA managers believed that showing a profit while practicing sustained-yield management would encourage private landowners to take similarly sustainable approaches.[3] In addition to permitting the Secretary of the Interior to permit the sale of timber, the Organic Act also required GFA directors to provide for fire protection.

Practitioners of scientific forestry regarded fire protection as a "fundamental mission" of their profession. The rationale for this position, although simple, is vital to understanding the past and current views on the importance of fire suppression by entities engaged in sustained-yield forestry. Unlike most crops, under sustained-yield forestry, timberlands were required to be populated by several generations of trees. Every decade or so, the most mature trees were cut, leaving behind several generations of trees ranging in age and size. Seedlings were planted to compensate for the mature trees that were cut. Accordingly, the forest had an ongoing supply of timber, and the landscape always reflected multiple generations of trees. This multigenerational timber stand represented a considerable investment on the part of the landowner, who had borne the cost of planting and maintaining the landscape over several decades.

The value of the timber stand is, therefore, the net present value of the trees on the lot, discounted to reflect the time to their maturity. A stand of timber's value cannot be accurately calculated based upon the investments made or present value, but is instead dependent upon the future value of the trees. Realization of the value is dependent upon the trees reaching maturity—a process interrupted by wildfire. For these reasons, early GFA officers, proponents of scientific management, believed that wildfire must be suppressed.[4]

In 1911, the Weeks Act added firefighting work to the Forest Service mission and authorized matching funds for state forest protection agencies that met government standards. This legislation was accompanied by public support garnered through several devastating, fatal wildfires that captured the national attention. Political pressure for wildfire suppression mounted. Public sentiment reflected near unanimity that fire was a threatening evil to be fought and suppressed at any cost. Nationalistic pride was associated with the ability of humankind to prevail over fire; early efforts to establish forest federations dedicated to timber harvest and fire suppression were even viewed as part of the war effort. Printed material of the time, such as a booklet published in 1900 by the Forest Service and the California Division of Forestry, captures the forest-fire-fighting fever that swept the nation:

> We have inherited a tremendous responsibility: the priceless treasures of natural resources of this Nation have been entrusted to our care. As Nature's abundance sustained our forefathers, it sustains us; that abundance will and must

be available for our children and their children. To keep these natural riches abundant, we must zealously guard them from all destructive agents. The foremost among these agents is fire—man's best servant but worst enemy!

(CDF/USFS 1900)

Members of the general public without direct economic interests in a forest economy were encouraged to personally, directly fight fire. The same booklet suggested that "all forces of church, school, civic clubs, industry, labor, and government be organized and trained to prevent and suppress wildfire" (CDF/USFS 1900). This was a model similar to the largely volunteer firefighting forces described in Chapter 8.

Public forestry proliferated during this period, expanding from a virtually unknown science to the overseer of much-watched fire suppression efforts. In contrast, landowners were slower to engage in sustained-yield forestry operations and thus valued fire suppression less than government firefighters. As foresters entered the private sector and brought with them ideas of conservation and sustained yield to supplant previous clear-cutting practices, the private sector too began to embrace the need for wildfire suppression.

1920–1970: Aligned Goals among Public and Private Landowners

In the fifty-year period between 1920 and 1970, GFAs and landowners largely shared the common goal of sustained-yield forestry, which necessitated fire protection. To facilitate landowner fire suppression efforts, GFAs actively sought to engage landowners and to learn and follow local customs.

In 1924, Congress enacted the Clarke-McNary Act, which required the federal government to assume some responsibility for protecting private timberland. Wildfires were seen as a public problem analogous to floods or dust storms, over which individual landowners had no control and inadequate resources or capability to cope with the problem (Folweiler and Brown 1946). Further, the coordinated effort to suppress wildfires was needed because they affected diverse groups, such as farmers whose water, transported several hundred miles, could be diminished by wildfire. The Act created a shared system of responsibility among private, state, and federal entities by requiring that the amount spent by the federal government could not exceed the combined funds spent by state and private entities. This led to the so-called 25-25-50 ratio, in which it was expected that private owners and states would each bear 25 percent of suppression costs and the federal government would bear 50 percent. The rationale for state expenditures was premised upon its stake in fire control: "[The state] can pass legislation which will be an aid to protection; it levies and collects tax assessments which encourage or discourage the practice of forestry; it has police powers which the landowner cannot possibly exercise; it should be interested in any activity which will build up its own wealth and resources" (Folweiler and Brown 1946, 171). This formula proved problematic because the contributions by states and private owners differed considerably among states.

In this period, foresters entered the private sector and began to transition from clear-cutting to sustainable-yield harvesting. Accordingly, they developed similar economic motivation to prevent and suppress fire. The commercial viability of private industrial landownership is predicated upon the ability to detect and suppress wildfire. Simply put, fire destroys the cash crop of timberlands—rendering trees far less valuable and imposing constraints on harvests. "No private owner, once he has committed himself to the task of investing capital in timber growing, is willing to jeopardize his investment by permitting fire to destroy it. Fires, because of their destructive nature, are intolerable to this type of owner and he generally takes steps to control their inception on his own land" (Folweiler and Brown 1946, 171). To protect their resources, private landowners formed cooperative fire associations. *Oregon v. Gourely* (306 P.2d 1117, 1117–19 [Or. 1956]), for example, describes the Douglas Forest Protect Association, a private firefighting organization operated by landowners but contracted out to the government.

By the 1950s, GFAs had widespread public appeal. A cover story about the Forest Service in *Newsweek* magazine in 1952 said, "No one can deny that the Forest Service is one of Uncle Sam's soundest and most businesslike investments. It is the only major government branch showing a cash profit." At the time, the majority of Forest Service timber harvest operations were selective cutting, which harvests mature timber but leaves younger trees behind. Accordingly, the forest looked natural, although it was producing a profit.

This was a period of cooperation between GFAs and private landowners. The groups had similar goals and often operated as adjacent landowners rather than being in an authoritarian relationship. For example, the GFAs and private landowners entered into bilateral road-sharing agreements that permitted each to use the other's roads under prescribed conditions to haul timber. Such cooperation was common among landowners and extended easily to GFAs, who acted primarily as just another profit-maximizing timber producer.

But the objectives of the GFAs were beginning to shift away from forestry. In 1960, the Multiple-Use Sustained-Yield Act was passed, which directed the Forest Service to give equal consideration to outdoor recreation, range, timber, water, wildlife, and fish resources and to manage each of them on a sustained-yield basis. This diversified approach to a more comprehensive set of objectives indicated that GFAs were beginning to change in response to public sentiment and political activity.

1970–2010: Modern GFAs

The reimbursement process for GFA forest harvest operations created a perverse incentive for forest managers to damage forests so that they could get greater reimbursement for rehabilitation costs (see O'Toole 2006). Resultantly, in 1970, the Forest Service was cutting four times as much timber as it had in 1952. It largely did so using the environmentally unfriendly practice of clear-cutting, which is removing trees regardless of maturity. The effects on recreation, wildlife, and watersheds were profoundly negative. In 1976, Congress instituted a comprehensive forest planning process, which was largely unsuccessful. Environmental groups grew and garnered public support for political outcry in response to the poor environmental practices. By the 1980s, GFAs were losing billions of dollars a year on their operations. The Forest Service and similar agencies were in crisis.

In response to criticism and pressure, the GFAs—and particularly the Forest Service—shifted their core competency from timber harvest to fire suppression (O'Toole 2006). In 1987, the Forest Service harvested more than 12 billion board feet of timber nationally (Gorte 2000). A decade later, in 1997, the federal government harvested over 4 billion board feet, and this had decreased to 2 billion in 2007. At the same time, fire spending increased from 13 percent of the Forest Service budget in 1990 to 45 percent in 2008 (Berry 2009). These figures underestimate total fire suppression expenditures, which regularly exceeded budgeted figures by up to $900 million. The 2012 Forest Service budget indicates that it will receive $5.3 billion, $1.7 billion of which is allocated to wildland fire management (USFS 2011).

Among wildfire critics, there is a widespread belief that GFAs are engaging in agency aggrandizement, attempting to increase their funding and importance. Randal O'Toole is a particularly outspoken critic of the cost structure of GFAs:

> "The Forest Service tries to put out fires by dumping money on them," firefighters commonly say. One Forest Service employee confided to me that his district had enough funds to pay its staff only 11 to 11.5 months of the year—and relied on fires to fill in the two- to four-week gap. Firefighters don't mind spending money on fires, since that is the source of their pay; [one firefighter] notes that [they] call smoke clouds "money bubbles" because they are ensuring more paychecks for somebody.
>
> (O'Toole 2006, 220)

O'Toole is not alone in this belief. A 2008 exposé in the *Los Angeles Times* reported that the government often pursued costly publicity stunts to garner media attention for firefighting efforts, although the stunts produced no fire suppression (Cart and Boxall 2008). Members of the forestry industry harbor similar views. One registered professional forester said, "CAL FIRE's strong union leadership is really attempting to create the world's largest fire protection entity, and they're doing this through use of enormously expensive and very PR savvy tools like the DC-10 [airplane], photo shoots with the Governor wearing CAL FIRE nomex, and the morally bankrupt promotion of firefighter fatalities."

GFAs' approach to suppression is currently under attack from a variety of stakeholders. On the one hand, conservationists believe GFAs fight too many fires and should more carefully weigh the costs and benefits of suppression. In 2003, the nonprofit organization Forest Service Employees for Environmental Ethics filed suit against the Forest Service, demanding the agency publicly and formally evaluate the environmental and social effects of wildland firefighting. The group's goals include "ending the war on fire" because "too many firefighters die each year in a fruitless and self-defeating war against fire." According to the group's executive director, "Everyone knows the system is broken and that bureaucratic inertia favors the status quo" (Devlin 2003).

On the other hand, landowners are dissatisfied with GFA practices for very different reasons. They believe agencies should suppress fires more rapidly, employ the use of backfire less frequently, and place a higher value on protecting timber. Landowners believe GFAs respond to situations with high likelihood of media coverage and allow suppressible fires to build to "campaign fire" size before attempting suppression to gain attention, revenue, and the experience fighting fires necessary for firefighters to advance within their agencies. Predictably, landowners continue to believe that wildfire suppression is essential to their long-term profitability, and they proactively seek to prevent and suppress wildfires at considerable cost.

During this period, private landowners have faced increased regulation, litigation, and public scrutiny of timber harvest practices. Despite increased regulation, annual timber harvest by the industry has remained relatively steady. In Oregon, for example, annual timber harvest decreased from an average of 3 billion board feet in 1989 to 2.7 billion board feet in 1995, while federal GFA timber harvest fell from 4.4 billion board feet to 0.6 billion board feet during that same time period (Associated Oregon Loggers 2007).

In sum, GFAs have recently shifted their core competency from timber harvest to fire suppression. Surprisingly, private landowners are very averse to this shift and believe their interests in fire suppression were better represented when the GFA acted as a land manager rather than a fire suppressor. Below, I trace how this shift has affected the norms surrounding fire suppression used by land managers and GFAs. This analysis explains the tensions by showing the divergent goals and practices of the groups.

Shared Norms among Land Managers and GFAs

This section examines how GFAs have ceased to share in the norms used for wildfire suppression by land managers. Deeply set norms among private land managers govern their actions regarding wildfire in cooperation with, and sometimes to the exclusion of, legal rules. Historically, during the period in which the goals of GFAs and landowners were aligned, GFAs also employed these norms. This resulted in an efficient, effective means of communication under exigent circumstances and means of sorting out the differences ex post. Today, land management goals of GFAs no longer include widespread timber harvest operations. Predictably, the strong norms between GFAs and landowners have eroded. Accordingly, GFAs are increasingly using legal rules and benefits of authority and immunity rather than local norms to deal with conflicts with local landowners.

Norms among Land Managers

Commercial activities on privately held institutional timberlands—including timber harvest operations, stream management, road development, and environmental compliance—are overseen by land managers. Ethnographic research indicates that foresters managing timberlands are a closely knit group given the fixed, adjacent proximity of their properties. Land managers have a rich, well-developed system of norms governing land management and wildfire suppression.

Land managers, for the purposes of this discussion, are registered professional foresters (RPFs) licensed by the California State Board of Forestry and Fire Protection. RPFs share a common knowledge base and education. They are expected to have an understanding of forest growth, development, and regeneration; soils, geology, and hydrology; wildlife and fisheries biology and other forest resources; fire management; road design; and the methods used to harvest timber (CAL FIRE 2002). To become an RPF, one must have seven years of experience in progressively difficult forestry work and pass an examination. The majority of RPF candidates graduate from college and then practice under the supervision of an RPF for three years prior to being eligible for the RPF designation. The minimum seven-year commitment to obtain licensure as an RPF limits the number of would-be candidates, as does the relatively low salary for newcomers to the field.

The close-knit relationship of foresters begins early: many know one another from college. The limited number of undergraduate institutions and small class sizes in forestry majors contributes to close bonds among graduates. The degree requires students to pick the major before coming to college and participate in summer programs and forestry-related work. Accordingly, forestry major students spend four continuous, consecutive years together, which produces strong bonds.[5]

As of May 2008, 1,200 RPFs were licensed to practice in California (BLS 2009a). The majority of foresters work for the federal, state, and local governments, leaving about 480 RPFs in private practice (BLS 2009b). Land managers, as foresters who have worked in private industry for the time necessary to reach executive positions, constitute a very small subset of foresters.

Land managers regularly interact with one another through transactions with adjacent land managers, in industry groups, and through socialization. Adjacent managers often work closely in managing their land. They operate under understood, oral, and written contracts governing subjects as disparate as snow removal, fire protection, and log selling. Conflicts sometimes arise, as in the case of timber conversion, when trees are accidentally cut by a nonowner. The relationships between adjacent managers are often decades-old. Land managers are also generally active participants in industry groups, such as the California Licensed Forester Association, and political organizations like the California Board of Forestry and Fire Protection. The frequent meetings of these organizations bring together land managers from disparate areas on a regular basis. Land managers feel compelled to become and stay involved, because the industry is perceived as being under constant attack by environmental groups, in public hearings and through litigation.

Also, the decisions made by the associations can have considerable consequences for the practices and profitability of the timber holdings land managers oversee. As a result, many of land managers sit, or have recently sat, on an industry-focused board or committee.

There is also a social component to associations: meetings often include activities for foresters' spouses, and social events accompany meetings. Friendships run deep among land managers. Many socialize together, belong to the same community organizations, and share political views. The conduct of land managers is governed by a set of deeply entrenched norms, reputational bonds, a system of social sanctions, and norm-based dispute resolution mechanisms. Agreements and dispute resolution systems are almost exclusively governed by internally developed norms and are developed and enforced without cognition of the legal rules that would otherwise govern such disputes. In discussing a contentious case of timber conversion, one RPF derided a party for seeking legal counsel, suggesting that the problem would have been better resolved using extralegal methods: "I don't know a problem in the world that can't be resolved by two guys and a pot of coffee." The landowners in far Northern California rely heavily on norms to govern their business transactions and social interactions. Norms and attendant reputation considerations and dispute resolution mechanisms are used to resolve problems; legal remedies are shunned.

Commercial institutional landowners have a well-developed system of practices and norms surrounding wildfire detection, suppression, regeneration, and recovery. These norms provide efficiencies over some legal default roles and have been the basis for creating other legal rules. But landowners have a limited role in wildfire suppression. Their efforts are limited by resource constraints. Instead, federal and state firefighting agencies bear the primary burden for coordinating suppression of wildfire. The question, then, is to what extent government fire suppression agencies adopt, employ, or influence the norms of commercial institutional landowners.

Landowner Norms vis-à-vis GFAs

From roughly 1920 to 1970, the core competency of GFAs was commercial timber operations. Just as private landowners cooperated to produce efficiencies in resource allocation and conflict resolution through the use of norms, so too did GFAs rely on local landowner norms. Essentially, they acted in large part as another landowner, interested in protecting the value of their timber and cognizant of a social obligation to take reasonable steps to protect other landowners' timber as well.[6] The use of norms was facilitated by the fact that GFA employees were members of the same closely knit group of foresters, with an expectation of mutual reliance for timber operations on an ongoing basis.

During this time, GFAs actively sought to cultivate relationships with local communities to better understand their norms and customs. To facilitate the adoption of norms, one GFA publication of the time encouraged appointment of a "contact man" to handle the primary interaction with locals: "One man should do all or most of the intensive prevention contact work on a given district. . . . It makes it possible for him to become thoroughly familiar with local customs and fairly well posted on local gossip, rivalries, etc." The ability of a ranger to interact with locals was specifically emphasized: "If possible, the [contact] man should possess some particular skill that local people value: in hunting, fishing, riding, stock-handling, etc." (Murphy and Weltner 1943, 2). Local men were hired for GFA jobs because their common background provided useful knowledge of local customs. Evidence of the success of GFA employees in adopting local norms can be seen in the diverse roles they played in the communities. The jobs of early GFA employees extended far beyond forestry or fire protection confined to their land; rangers also "settled disputes between cattle and sheep men, organized and led firefighting crews, build roads and trails, [and] negotiated grazing and timber sales contracts" (Murphy and Weltner 1943, 15).

When the primary aim of GFAs changed, so too did the composition of its workforce. One RPF explained that GFAs once were operated by foresters, but now "the Forest Service is staffed by a bunch of 'ists'—biologists, geologists, anthropologists." Accordingly, GFAs are no longer composed of members from the small, familiar world of forestry that share well-developed, accepted norms.

Another norm-detracting shift occurred when changes were made to the staffing of wildfire decision-making teams. Historically, wildfires were staffed by local wildfire officials. Now, incident command teams, which are made up of internal fire experts from around the United States, make the tactical decisions of how to fight a wildfire. The teams lack familiarity with local foresters and the norms that had previously governed fire suppression. From the perspective of landowners, cooperation and goodwill lessen when incidental command teams are used. Foresters allege that fires are being fought inefficiently, because their knowledge of the topography of the land is ignored by outsiders who blindly apply formulaic firefighting methods inappropriate to local conditions. Further, foresters now face another problem: incident commanders do not anticipate an ongoing relationship and so lack motivation to create goodwill for future reciprocation.

Norms in Fire Suppression

This section more specifically identifies chasms that have developed between the long-followed norms and modern GFA practices.

Ex Ante Precautions

Land Management

Land managers undertake continuous and extensive efforts to minimize wildfire risk. These efforts are fueled by a combination of self-interest in reduction of risk of wildfire spread on their land and also a shared understanding that one is obligated to reduce the risks to neighboring properties through appropriate maintenance. Risk mitigation techniques are standardized components of timber harvest practice. Precautions include tactical infrastructure building and maintenance, thinning, and monitoring.

Thinning—creating a greater distance between trees through selecting and removing trees from tightly condensed stands—is regularly done to reduce the spread of a potential fire. Should fire strike, the lessened fuel sources of a thinned timber stand will reduce its strength and speed of spread relative to an unthinned timber stand. Thinning produces economic benefits if merchantable trees that can be resold are removed. But other risk reduction practices are cost-justified only because they reduce the risk of wildfire. For example, logging crews are required to remove the slash, or woody vegetative debris, created by timber operations. Precautions such as these are reflective of the high costs wildfire imposes on landowners; even when risk is not imminent, such as during times of lower wildfire risk, landowners voluntarily undertake mitigation efforts.

Land managers build and maintain roads and landings to provide access to remote portions of their property. Managers coordinate the building of roads with adjacent land managers to avoid duplicative road systems; shared roads are governed by road-sharing agreements with provisions specifying contractual liability assignments for fire detection and damage on surrounding lands. Further, land managers sometimes create landings—cleared areas with the express intention of providing a headquarters from which GFAs will be able to coordinate firefighting efforts should fire strike in their area. The motivation for such preparation extends beyond self-interest: norms require collaboration and an eye to communal fire safety stemming from a common awareness that fire spreads quickly and without warning.

When GFAs engaged in widespread timber harvests, they also engaged in the thinning and road-building projects inherent in timber harvest operations. When harvest operations ceased, so too did many GFA fuel-reduction and thinning efforts. The result is that GFA lands, and those of surrounding landowners, are at risk of larger, more catastrophic fires.[7] Thus, GFAs no longer follow landowner norms concerning land management designed to mitigate wildfire risk. Land managers feel that a onetime member of their group is failing to uphold an important and widely recognized norm. An RPF employed by a state agency said, "The federal issue is the elephant in the room. By and large, our federal lands are not being managed in terms of wildfire resilience." He pointed out the example of the Moonlight Fire, which burned on public land and an adjacent parcel held by W. M. Beaty and Associates. After the fire, Beaty replanted trees, which grew 12 to 15 feet tall at the time of the conversation. The federal land was not replanted. "As a result, you have blackened snags and brush coming in. The risk of catastrophic fire is right at your doorstep after you've spent literally millions of dollars getting your ground back together. Once again the feds are posing a huge threat to private landowners."

This example illustrates the different objectives of the GFAs and landowners. Replanting is cost-justified only if it will be offset by future timber values. GFAs' policy of minimal harvesting means reforestation is not cost-justified based upon the future economic values of trees. But, by failing to reforest burned lots, GFAs create a wildfire risk that endangers the land of adjacent landowners and violates norms surrounding ex ante wildfire suppression.[8]

Detection and Reporting

Land managers or their employees seek to discover wildfires on their properties before they spread. One land manager explained that he assigns one employee to "fire duty" each weekend throughout the summer. The employee is tasked with staying near the property to provide an early response to any reports of fire and drive across the property to look for smoke or lightning strikes that might indicate a fire. The rural nature of many timberland holdings means fire may go undetected for some time, which is dangerous because fires are much easier to stop, and far less destructive, if suppressed early. This at first appears to fulfill only the self-interested motivation of detecting fires on one's own property. But, as with other activities, synergy is created through individual landowners fulfilling their socially prescribed duties. When surveying their lands, employees are indirectly also surveying the lands of others. Resultantly, each landowner has several employees viewing various portions of his or her property, which increases the likelihood of early wildfire detection.

Notably, the obligation among landowners to report wildfire they spot may not include reporting it to GFAs. If the fire is of manageable size, the landowner whose employee spotted it reports the wildfire to the landowner on whose property it is located, not to officials. This gives the affected landowner the opportunity to decide whether to fight the wildfire using his or her own private resources or to call authorities. If the fire is clearly too large to be managed by private resources, the fire spotter reports it first to government authorities and then to the landowner on whose property it is located. The bifurcated reporting techniques reflect that reporting is fueled by norms rather than legal obligation. Although there are some wildfire reporting laws in Western states, landowners have no duty in law to tell neighbors about damage occurring on their property. So in this scenario, the norm takes precedence over the law and governs the behavior of parties.

Early Suppression

There exists a strong norm—one landowner called it "absolute"—that any person spotting a fire must immediately engage in firefighting activities to try to stem the fire, regardless of whose property the fire is on. The norm of suppression on another property has no basis in law, but is instead entirely premised upon norms reflecting a common understanding that early suppression is vital to stemming a fire before it grows out of control. Some contracts among adjacent land managers and between land managers and logging contractors contain clauses requiring fire suppression attempts in sale areas or along road areas.

But the "good faith" expectations extend beyond these boundaries and impose a very broad extralegal duty. The early suppression norm extends beyond landowners immediately adjacent to one another. One forester described an incident in which he and his employees suppressed a small fire on someone else's land although they did not own land nearby and did not know the landowner. When driving to a remote worksite for a consulting position, the forester happened upon a small fire. He used rudimentary firefighting techniques and the equipment foresters carry in their trucks—including shovels and axes carried for this purpose—to suppress the fire and spent additional time monitoring the area to ensure that the fire did not reignite. The forester did not know the landowner or anticipate any reciprocation, but he still felt obligated to follow the norm of suppression.

Historically, GFAs also followed a norm of early suppression and sought to extinguish all wildfires within 24 hours; this goal was not always achieved, but rather marked the aspiration to suppress fires quickly with a strong initial attack. In contrast, GFAs no longer follow the landowner norm of early suppression. The delayed suppression may be consistent with modern GFA objectives, such as vegetative management or creating training opportunities for employees, but it goes against the interests of landowners seeking to protect the economic value of their timber and the norm of protecting a neighbor's land.

During a Fire

Coordination of Knowledge and Resources

Among landowners, coordinating efforts to fight wildfire—or, as is often the case during fire season, many fires burning at the same time—is seen as necessary collaboration. There is a strong sense that everyone is better off by following the norms outlined and, with them, sharing resources, information, and knowledge in light of a fire. This sentiment may be best expressed by one state fire agency, which described the need for cooperation among agencies: "None of the agencies in Alaska have all of the resources required to accomplish the fire protection job on their own. The Division of Forestry has cooperative agreements with the Departments of Agriculture and Interior, and numerous local government and volunteer fire departments to help get the job done. The state and federal agencies routinely utilize each other's personnel and resources to both manage and fight fires. This is efficient and cost effective" (Alaska DNR 2009). The same rationale applies to the shared resources of multiple private landowners. The coordination of these resources, unlike with state and federal agencies, is not formally delineated by legally prescribed suppression responsibility areas, but is instead predicated on an expectation that each landowner pull his or her own weight in helping suppress wildfires.

Traditionally, there has been a strong expectation that land managers provide manpower and equipment to GFAs suppressing wildfire on their property or adjacent properties. Landowners maintain small fleets of firefighting equipment, such as hoes and water trucks. Equipment used in timber operations, such as helicopters, backhoes, and bulldozers, is also used for firefighting. Land managers may employ their resources to extinguish small fires, avoid ceding tactical control to GFAs, or supplement the resources available to GFAs. Landowners offer private resources to the government even when doing so is not legally mandated. There is no expectation that the government reimburse landowners when their resources are used.

The tradition of sharing of resources among landowners was premised on a reciprocity norm that preservation of reputation and anticipation of future transactions would prevent parties from abusing advantages. Federal GFAs are immune from these considerations because of the transient, short-term structure of the Incident Management Teams. Accordingly, there is a final-period problem in which GFAs do not reciprocate for the loan of equipment, land, or resources by ensuring that what was used is replaced in as good or better condition. In *Dovenberg v. United States ex rel. United States Forest Service* (2009 WL 3756370 [D. Or. 2009]), a landowner brought suit against the Forest Service for extensive damage its employees caused to his property while using it as an incident command center. The case was dismissed on summary judgment after the court found that the Forest Service was protected by the Federal Tort Claim Act's discretionary function exception. The landowner was left without a remedy.

Landowners are quick to point out that such damage without recourse is exclusively a problem with federal GFAs. State GFAs, which are staffed by local officers who anticipate repeat transactions and often have preexisting relationships with landowners, are commended for returning equipment and land used in conducting firefighting operations in as good condition as it was in when lent, or better. This is reflective of the general sense that state GFAs are more responsive to landowner concerns and continue to share at least some landowner norms. A particularly poignant example of this is the story of a state GFA officer who refused to implement the tactics prescribed by the federal incident commander because he believed they would damage landowner property irreparably.

Private Firefighting

Increasingly, land managers choose to fight fire without the assistance of government firefighting agencies. For small wildfires that can be suppressed easily, there is a sense that it is better for land managers to extinguish the fire without alerting the government to the fire. This is a risky proposition: the fire can easily spread out of control and cause much greater damage if it is not controlled early. Liability for damage may attach to landowners if they do not report the fire to authorities. But this is a risk land managers are increasingly willing to undertake to protect their property values. Reporting fires requires ceding control for fighting them to GFAs. Once GFAs take control of a fire, they have exclusive authority to manage the strategy used to suppress it or to choose to let it burn. Historically, landowners gladly ceded authority to GFAs, confident that the firefighting officers would consult them for their institutional knowledge about the property.

They also had certainty that GFAs would act in landowners' interests: GFAs were subject to the same sanctions as other landowners if they harmed the interests of a landowner unfairly.

Recently, however, landowners have begun hiring private firefighters to protect their timber. In 2008, the Mendocino Redwood Company hired more than 100 firefighters and rented helicopters to battle 31 wildfires that threatened its 228,000 acres of timber. And this is a growing trend: "Across California . . . hundreds of private firefighters work alongside counterparts from government agencies, cutting fire breaks, setting backfires, and mopping up" (Cote 2008). More than 10,000 private firefighters are represented by the private firefighting industry group known as the National Wildfire Suppression Association, which estimates that 40 percent of the personnel and equipment used in wildfire suppression across the United States comes from private contractors (this includes contractors hired by GFAs). Landowners hire private firefighters for two reasons: (1) GFAs are unable or unwilling to fight fire on the landowner's property, or (2) the landowner wants to retain control of firefighting operations to avoid damaging tactics, such as backfire.

Land managers recognize the superiority of firefighters in fighting fires and respect the risks they take. An RPF acknowledged this contribution, saying, "They're experts. There is a reason they are paid the hazard pay that they get and retire at 50 with 90 percent pay." Landowners would prefer to have GFAs fight their fires, but they recognize that the government may simply not protect their land or may choose to fight the fire in a way that will cause a degree of harm perceived to be unacceptable.

Ex Post: Liability and Regeneration

Ex post, land managers do not pursue wildfire losses caused by other institutional land managers even in cases of negligence. Reciprocity norms—"it could happen to me next time"—preclude seeking recovery if, for example, a prescription burn grows out of control and burns an adjacent land. Even when a fire is set intentionally with good intent, there is an expectation that landowners will not seek recovery. One land manager recounted that his trees were burned by a backfire set by an adjacent landowner. The damaged landowner did not seek recovery.

In contrast, landowners perceive that GFAs are becoming increasingly aggressive in cost recovery efforts. In one case currently on appeal, a GFA had the opportunity to easily control a fire started by a landowner's employees, but chose not to. The fire burned for several days and spread across thousands of acres. Then the GFA chose to fight the fire at considerable expense. The landowner was assessed the entire cost of fighting the fire, rather than what the cost would have been had the GFA acted sooner. By attempting to assess high ex post costs on landowners that landowners would not impose on one another, GFAs again violate the norms of fire suppression. The once-shared norms of landowners and GFAs are now almost exclusively the domain of landowners and not followed by GFAs. (For a more complete discussion of the origin and status of liability rules, see Chapter 1.)

Are Shared Norms Desirable?

To assess the desirability of the norms once shared by landowners and GFAs, one must first take a large step back. What are the roles of the diverse group of stakeholders identified at the beginning of this chapter? The shared norms of GFAs and landowners ended when GFAs divested from timber harvesting in response to public pressure exerted by other stakeholders. Certainly, those opposed to timber harvesting did not foresee that ending forestry practices would lead GFAs to abandon norms aiding in fire suppression. In other words, the loss of norms is an unintended collateral effect, not the direct result of an expression of public will.

When the GFAs shifted roles from a commercial timber operator to a firefighter, it no longer needed the norms that once governed its interactions with private landowners. These norms once created desirable synergies that produced efficiencies in cost, safety, and resource preservation. Further, the breakdown in communication and trust between GFAs and landowners has produced the socially undesirable effect of landowners choosing to assume the risk of legal liability for not reporting a fire on their property to avoid ceding control to GFAs, which they believe pursue strategies that undermine the interests of timber operators. This is a serious concern that could result in the loss of not only resources, but also human life.

Regardless of the policies GFAs adopt regarding fire suppression, on-the-ground action will always involve a local topography managed by individuals intimately familiar with it. Ignoring the institutional knowledge of land managers results in unnecessarily ill-suited practices, which produce undesirable results. So, while GFAs should unquestionably retain the authority to unilaterally make decisions in conditions of wildfire, they should do so in consultation with the readily available knowledge of professional land managers.

On a broader level, studying the interaction between norms and law in fire suppression satisfies a need to understand how the two interact. This case study has presented examples in which norms govern behavior over law. Therefore, actively engaging the norms—as GFAs did in the 1940s—provides an inexpensive, feasible means of communicating desirable public-safety and fire suppression outcomes. GFAs should consider how to engage local stakeholder groups through actively seeking an outward-looking approach focused on understanding the content of norms and, where appropriate, seeking to adjust them to create better fire safety conditions. The efficacy of this approach could be expanded through further study of the existence and operation of norms within other stakeholder groups.

Conclusions

Current wildfire suppression efforts are universally acknowledged as troubled. This chapter focuses upon the relationship between institutional landowners and government agencies vis-à-vis wildfire suppression. Today, landowners bemoan the exit of GFAs from timber operator functions, because the shift has been accompanied by a break in the norms that once governed the interactions of the organizations. Historically, the decisions of government firefighters were made in cooperation with institutional landowners. The parties would combine resources, knowledge, and information to collaboratively develop and deploy firefighting tactics. Cooperation under such circumstances was possible because of a shared system of norms between the government agents and landowners, who regularly interacted in landowning capacities in an ongoing relationship spanning from before the beginning of a fire to well after its end.

Over time, federal land management agencies dramatically reduced their landowning functions. Reciprocity between institutional landowners and federal agencies eroded. The norms once governing their interactions further disintegrated with changes to the federal firefighting system that eliminated purely localized interactions. Today, institutional landowners are critical of federal firefighters for not following norms that the groups once shared. To examine these criticisms, this chapter engaged the study of norms to analyze shifts among GFAs. In doing so, it illustrated that norms scholarship plays the valuable role of explaining present behavior and serves as a basis for analyzing normative suggestions for improvement in wildfire suppression.

Notes

1. To avoid the unnecessary complexity of delineating the many agencies that serve similar land management and fire suppression functions, this chapter artificially conflates state and government firefighting agencies. This is at best inexact. Unlike federal agencies, some state agencies continue to operate in a landowner capacity and thus share in the norms of private landowners. Moreover, state firefighting efforts necessarily remain localized, which further strengthens the likelihood of anticipated future interactions between state agencies and private landowners. Accordingly, the relationship between such state agencies and landowners generally remains far more collaborative; landowners often use state agencies as an example of how federal agencies should operate.

2. See Sunstein (1996); Ellickson (1991), describing norms among ranches in Shasta County, California; Bernstein (1992), describing norms among New York diamond merchants; Feldman (2006); Meares and Kahan (1998), arguing that government policy-makers should attempt to enforce positive norms among inner-city groups to achieve policy objectives; and McAdams (1997).

3. Over the years, various stakeholders wanted the reserves to be used for a variety of reasons: foresters wanted appropriate land management to protect forests from fire, insects, disease, and unsustainable-yield forestry practices, conservationists sought big-game habitat, preservationists wanted parks, and western farmers and urban dwellers sought watershed protection.

4. In contrast, the clear-cutting approach adopted by timber barons is not dependent upon the future value of younger trees. Instead, all trees—regardless of age—are cut simultaneously, eliminating the need for buy-and-sell timber operators to encourage fire suppression.

5. One retired forester I interviewed was 87 years of age and continued to keep in touch with virtually all surviving members of his graduating class from forestry school. His class had held reunions every five to ten years over a 60-year time span.

6.   This is not to ignore the policing function of GFAs. In fact, there is some evidence that
     GFA used its policing function to reinforce norms among landowners. See *Oregon v.
     Gourley* (306 P.2d 1117 [Or. 1956]), noting that the state of Oregon sought to recover
     the cost of fighting a forest fire from a landowner's failure to use every effort to extinguish
     a fire, which violated Oregon law codifying norms among private landowners.
7.   Senator Diane Feinstein, a Democrat representing California, expressed concern that
     environmental efforts precluded GFAs from spending funds on hazardous fuel reduction
     projects in parts of the state. She noted that "increasing federal appropriations to reduce
     hazardous fuels at Lake Tahoe has been a top priority of mine since I have been in the
     Senate" and also wrote, "I believe we need to take immediate action to reduce hazardous
     fuels in the Tahoe Basin" (2007a, 2007b).
8.   Notably, there is a divide between the policies and perceptions of state and national
     GFAs. State and federal agencies take differing stances toward suppression, with state
     agencies favoring rapid response (such as the "10 a.m. rule," requiring efforts to have
     all new fires under control by the next morning) and federal agencies taking a more
     nuanced stance that allows for allowing fire to burn ("let-burn" policies). In a July 8,
     2010, memorandum, the National Wildfire Coordinating Group wrote, "With rare
     exceptions, state and local agencies support and carry out wildfire suppression programs
     that provide for rapid and aggressive initial response to wildfires with the intent of
     minimizing its [*sic*] spread. Federal agencies manage wildfires on federal lands considerate
     of protecting communities and other state or private resources" (NWCG 2010). State
     agencies often have oversight boards partially composed of industry representatives.
     Further, because they are committed to operating in a single local area, state agents are
     more likely to anticipate repeated ongoing interactions with landowners. Resultantly,
     they are generally more responsive to landowners' interests and view firefighting as a
     cooperative effort.

References

Alaska DNR (Department of Natural Resources). 2009. Division of Forestry Fire and Aviation
   Program: Interagency Effort. http://forestry.alaska.gov/fire/ (accessed April 24, 2011).
Associated Oregon Loggers. 2007. Timber and Forest Facts of Oregon. www.oregon
   loggers.org/harvestdata.html (accessed April 24, 2011).
Bernstein, Lisa. 1992. Opting Out of the Legal System: Extralegal Contractual Relations in
   the Diamond Industry. *Journal of Legal Studies* 21:115–157.
Berry, Alison. 2009. Two Forests under the Big Sky: Tribal v. Federal Management. Property
   and Environment Research Center Policy Series No. 45. http://westinstenv.org/wp-
   content/Alison_Berry_PERC_essay.pdf (accessed April 24, 2011).
BLS (Bureau of Labor Statistics). 2009a. Occupational Employment Statistics: Occupational
   Employment and Wages, May 2008: 19-1032 Foresters. www.bls.gov/oes/current/oes
   191032.htm (accessed October 1, 2010).
———. 2009b. Occupational Outlook Handbook, 2010–11 Edition: Conservation Scientists
   and Foresters. www.bls.gov/oco/ocos048.htm (accessed April 24, 2011).
CAL FIRE (California Department of Forestry and Fire Protection). 2002. California Forest
   Stewardship Program: What Is a Registered Professional Forester (RPF)? http://
   ceres.ca.gov/forststeward/html/rpf.html (accessed April 24, 2011).
Cart, Julie, and Bettina Boxall. 2008. Air Tanker Drops in Wildfires Are Often Just for Show.
   Los Angeles Times, July 29. www.latimes.com/news/local/politics/cal/la-me-wildfires29-
   2008jul29,0,6778040,full.story (accessed April 24, 2011).
CDF/USFS (California State Division of Forestry and USDA Forest Service). 1900. Forest
   Fire Fighting Fundamentals for Use by Fire Protection Agencies and Cooperators

Engaged in Fire Fighting on Forest and Other Wild Land. Sacramento, CA: CDF and USFS.

Cote, John. 2008. Private Firefighters' Role Growing in State. *San Francisco Chronicle*, July 27.

Devlin, Sherry. 2003. Group to Sue over Firefighting. www.headwatersnews.org/miss. firesuit.html (accessed April 23, 2011).

Ellickson, Robert C. 1991. *Order without Law: How Neighbors Settle Disputes.* Cambridge, MA: Harvard University Press.

Feinstein, Diane. 2007a. Letter from Diane Feinstein, U.S. senator from California, to Gale Kimbell, chief of the Forest Service, and John Singlaub, executive director of the Tahoe Regional Planning Agency. July 12.

——— . 2007b. Letter from Diane Feinstein to California governor Arnold Schwarzenegger. August 20.

Feldman, Eric A. 2006. The Tuna Court: Law and Norms in the World's Premier Fish Market. *California Law Review* 94:313–369.

Folweiler, A. D., and A. A. Brown. 1946. *Fire in the Forests of the United States.* St. Louis: John S. Swift.

Gorte, Ross W. 2000. Timber Harvesting and Forest Fires. CRS Report for Congress. http://ncseonline.org/nle/crsreports/forests/for-30.cfm (accessed April 24, 2011).

McAdams, Richard H. 1997. The Origin, Development, and Regulation of Norms. *Michigan Law Review* 96:338–433.

Meares, Tracey L., and Dan M. Kahan. 1998. Law and (Norms of) Order in the Inner City. *Law & Society Review* 32:805–838.

Murphy, Tom, and George Weltner. 1943. *Man-to-Man Fire Prevention: Personal Contacts.* USDA Forest Service, Southern Region.

Newsweek. 1952. Fabulous Bear, Famous Service Fight Annual Billion-Dollar Fire. June 2, 50–54.

NWCG (National Wildfire Coordinating Group). 2010. Memorandum, July 8. www. nwcg.gov/general/memos/nwcg-030-2010.pdf (accessed April 23, 2011).

O'Toole, Randal. 2006. Money to Burn: Wildfire and the Budget. In *Wildfire: A Century of Failed Forest Policy,* edited by George Wuerthner. Washington, DC: Island Press/ Foundation for Deep Ecology, 250–261.

Sunstein, Cass R. 1996. On the Expressive Function of Law. *University of Pennsylvania Law Review* 144:2021–2053.

USDA (U.S. Department of Agriculture). 1992. *Centennial Mini-Histories of the Forest Service.* Report FS-518. Washington, DC: USDA.

USFS (USDA Forest Service). 2011. USDA Forest Service Fiscal Year 2010 Budget Justification. http://www.fs.fed.us/aboutus/budget/2012/justification/FY2012-USDA-Forest-Service-overview.pdf (accessed July 10, 2011).

6

THE POLITICAL ECONOMY OF WILDFIRE MANAGEMENT

Saving Forests, Saving Houses, or Burning Money

Sarah E. Anderson and Terry L. Anderson

More and more people are moving into the wildland–urban interface, areas in or close to forests where their homes are at risk from wildfires. Theobald and Romme (2007) estimate that from 1970 to 2000, the wildland–urban interface expanded more than 52 percent to 179,775 square miles and is expected to increase to 198,333 square miles by 2030, with the greatest expansion occurring in the states of the intermountain West. The Forest Service, which manages 192 million acres of land, thus increasingly faces a trade-off between the ecological benefits of fire and the political economy consequences. Faced with different mandates and different pressures from interest groups, the Forest Service has the difficult task of balancing the role of fire in natural systems with safety considerations and the costs of property damage, particularly on private lands adjacent to public lands. Hence, in recent years, wildfire suppression has become more controversial.

One hundred years ago, the fledgling U.S. Forest Service, trying to find its niche in the federal bureaucracy, literally experienced "trial by fire" when thousands of forested acres burned in the fire of 1910. Timothy Egan (2009, 248) notes that "barely ten months after the fire, Congress doubled the money in the Forest Service budget for roads and trails, giving the rangers what they had begged for in the previous years." Fire became the tool for Forest Service founder Gifford Pinchot to wrest control from the Secretary of Interior and firmly ensconce a place for the service in the federal budget.

Following the 1910 fire, the Forest Service set a course of fighting forest fires at virtually any cost. Then in 1963, the Leopold Report suggested that the Forest Service take a more lenient approach to fire suppression, recognizing fire's role in forests (Leopold et al. 1963). The result was a "let burn" policy, which meant some natural fires would be allowed to take their course. In 1988, that course was partly responsible for the massive fires in Yellowstone National Park that burned over 1 million acres. Those fires brought political pressure to rethink fire policy again.

In 1995, the Interagency Ecosystem Management Task Force concluded that "the federal government should provide leadership in and cooperate with activities that foster the ecosystem approach to natural resources management, regulation, and assistance" (IEMTF 1995, 8). If the ambiguity of what is meant by an "ecosystem approach" was not enough to make fire management difficult, agencies found themselves subject to increasing political pressures. Because of the century-long buildup of fuels in western forests, Douglas MacCleery (Forest Service) and Dennis Le Master (Purdue University) conclude that there is "(1) increasing risk to federal and non-federal ecosystems . . . , (2) a rising toll of loss and degradation of watershed values and wildlife habitats . . . , (3) increasing risks to the human communities . . . , and (4) significant and increasing losses to taxpayers in fire suppression costs and resource values" (quoted in Nelson 2000, 50).

Losses from wildfires have left agencies and Congress with little choice but to spend huge sums fighting fires. During the last three decades of the 20th century, fire suppression expenditures ranged between $200 million and $600 million. Since 2000, expenditures have exceeded $1 billion (WFLC 2004). Once a fire is burning, the Forest Service must generally suppress the fire if it is near the wildland-urban interface.

Mainly because more and more people have moved into forested areas (see Kennedy 2006), the Forest Service has added fuels management to its tool kit for protecting communities near national forests. In 2000, the Forest Service set forth the National Fire Plan in an attempt to standardize fire preparedness and hazardous fuels reduction. In 2001, Congress appropriated $205 million for hazardous fuels reduction projects, including mechanical thinning and prescribed burns. Then in 2002, in an effort to provide some logging opportunities for the forest industry and reduce fuel loads, President George W. Bush proposed the "Healthy Forests Initiative," and Congress followed up by passing the Healthy Forest Restoration Act of 2003.

In most cases, Congress appropriates a lump sum for wildfire prevention or hazardous fuels management, and the Forest Service must allocate the funds to regions, districts, and projects. Despite reasonably clear congressional mandates, local incentives and expenditures may not always align with congressional intent.[1] Just as the literature on fire suppression suggests that expenditures may not be efficient due to bureaucratic incentives (Donovan and Brown 2005), wildfire prevention and hazardous fuels management funds may be influenced by political and economic pressures.

This chapter attempts to answer several questions about the factors that might influence fire management expenditures. Are the funds allocated based on the likelihood that forests are more susceptible to fire? Are they allocated based on political pressure from Congress? Or are they allocated to prevent damage to property, especially houses, on lands adjacent to national forests?

To answer these questions, we examine the political economy of forest fire expenditures on fire prevention (not suppression) and hazardous fuels reduction. Our purpose is to explain the significant variations in these expenditures across

Forest Service districts and across states. For example, in FY2001, spending on hazardous fuels reduction ranged from zero in some forests to $16 million in Six Rivers National Forest in California. Similarly, fire preparedness spending ranged from zero to $11 million. We attempt to quantify the factors that drive U.S. Forest Service expenditures and programs for wildfire prevention and fuels management at two different levels of aggregation. First, at the state level, we measure the agency's management effort by the amount of spending on both prevention and hazardous fuels reduction. At a more disaggregated level, we measure the agency's management effort by number of projects and by dollars spent on projects by ranger district in California. We hypothesize that these dependent variables will be a function of economic, environmental, and political considerations measured by such things as number of housing units, fire hazard, and congressional committee representation.

We test our hypotheses with two datasets. We use preparedness and hazardous fuels reduction spending for FY2001 and FY2002, and hazardous fuels reduction for FY2003 at the state level. These data were collected from the National Fire Plan Performance Reports and cover the entire United States, but they have the disadvantage of being aggregated to the state level when funding is, in actuality, spread among the smaller units of the ranger district. The second dataset disaggregates fuels management activities in California to the ranger district for 2004 to 2008.

Our analysis of these data suggests that politics is not important in spending decisions and that protection of housing assets is a major driving force. Especially for California, the agency's focus seems to be almost entirely on protecting property.

The Political Economy of Fuels Management and Fire Preparedness Policy

There are several stages at which management can occur: fire prevention—encouraging people to follow Smokey the Bear's adage that "Only you can prevent wildfires"; fire suppression—putting the fire out; fire preparedness—being ready to fight fire when it occurs; and fuels management—decreasing vegetation to reduce the likelihood and severity of fire. Fire suppression spending has been increasing substantially over time. Other agencies, such as the Federal Emergency Management Agency (FEMA), also tend to overinvest in disaster relief and underinvest in preparedness and mitigation (Healy and Malhotra 2009). When they do invest in fuels management and fire preparedness, the question we address is what factors determine the amount invested in the pre-fire management stage.

Donovan and Rideout (2003) posit that the efficient level of fire management expenditures minimizes the costs related to fire and net damages, where the latter includes positive effects that can result from wildfires. Building on this, Donovan and Brown (2005, 388–390) construct a model that subtracts the present value of wildfire-related benefits (e.g., reduced fuel loads) from the present value of wildfire-related damages (e.g., timber and housing lost) to get the "net value change." They then compare the optimal allocation of fire management expenditures with the incentive structure in the Forest Service and conclude that "the benefits of wildfire are ignored" and "the costs of wildfire suppression are not fully considered."

Somewhat offsetting the bias toward suppression is the budget for fuels management. Following the lead of Donovan and Brown, we can think in terms of maximizing the difference between the increased value of assets (e.g., trees and structures saved) minus the costs of fire management. In this context, investment in fire management is an input into the production process. The investment might protect or improve the capital stock of buildings and roads. It could protect the future flow of resources—timber, forage, or wildlife—from the land. Or fire management could reduce the liability for damage to other property owners (see Chapter 1 of this volume; Yoder et al. 2003). At the district level, fire managers may be very risk averse in not wanting their district to be the one in which "the big burn" occurs. For this reason, we might expect any discretionary budget to be shifted toward fuel management. Just as Donovan and Brown examine whether the Forest Service and Congress have the incentive to maximize "net change value," we consider what factors—environmental, economic, and political—affect the allocation of fire management budgets.

Related to risk aversion by agency personnel, we can expect the Forest Service to reduce fuels where housing stocks are more valuable, for several reasons. First, following Donovan and Brown (2005), the optimal allocation of the fire management budget would maximize the net present value of benefits from fire management (assets saved) minus the net present value of fire management costs. Second, the agency may be responding to direct pressure from influential homeowners. For example, when a fire was burning south of Big Sky, Montana, local Forest Service officials received a call from a wealthy landowner asking what would be done to protect his property. Thus, the capital stock of housing and other structures surrounding the forest is likely to weigh in maximizing the return on fire management expenditures. By its own description of priorities, the Forest Service should be expected to spend more money on preparedness and particularly hazardous fuels reduction, where more houses are at risk.

California exemplifies the importance of housing in the urban-wildland interface in fuels management decisions. Although only 7 percent of California's land is technically in the urban-wildlife interface, that area includes five million houses. Therefore, it is not surprising that property losses from fires in 2003 amounted to $2 billion (Kennedy 2006). The link between housing and fuels management is strengthened by insurance programs that subsidize building in fire-prone areas, thus creating a moral hazard problem. California has a program called the Fair Access to Insurance Requirements (FAIR) Plan, which Kennedy explains requires insurance companies operating in the state to join "a state-regulated association that acts as an insurer of last resort providing property insurance to homeowners who cannot obtain insurance in the private market, and offering it at generally subsidized rates" (2006, 243). The extension of the FAIR Plan in 2001 to encompass brush-fire losses in the entire state created a moral hazard problem because it "significantly underprices wildfire risk in California and encourages too much new development in the most hazardous areas" (Austin Troy, quoted in Kennedy 2006, 243). Such policies undoubtedly put pressure on land management agencies such as the Forest Service to reduce the risk of wildfire.

Investment in fuels management will also be a function of weather-dependent variables and susceptibility of land to fire damage—for example, ponderosa pine is a fire-tolerant species, whereas greater understory spreads fire rapidly—and of economic variables. At the disaggregated level, the Forest Service uses fuels inventories and weather and moisture measures to predict the risk of fires in a given area. These are the primary indicators for whether fires are likely to occur in a given year. We thus expect to see more spending on prevention in the areas where the drought conditions are worse, and we explore various environmental variables to understand the timing of decision-making.

In addition to considering economic and fire risk variables, the public land managers are likely to take account of public choice variables. This raises the important question of what it is that the agency—the Forest Service, in this case— is maximizing and what influence politicians have on the decision-making process (see Hird 1991 for a similar examination of Corps of Engineers projects; Garrett and Sobel 2003 for FEMA spending). The Forest Service's National Fire Plan 10-year Comprehensive Strategy, for example, dictates that the Forest Service should "prioritize hazardous fuels reduction where the negative impacts of wildland fire are greatest" (USFS 2006). Rarely does a federal agency have such a clear statement to guide its budget priorities.[2] Based on this mandate, we expect the Forest Service to spend more where the risks of wildfire (e.g., loss of life and property) are greater.

Yet as with any budget decisions, politics may play a role in how many projects there are and how much is spent on them, though this will depend largely on how much micro-budget management can occur at the congressional level. Legislators may distribute the spending universally (Shepsle and Weingast 1981), use it to facilitate the passage of other legislation (Evans 1994), or simply utilize it for their own benefit as "single minded seekers of reelection" (Mayhew 1974). The congressional dominance model argues that the bureaucracy is very responsive to members of Congress because they have budgetary control and oversight over the agencies (Moe 1987, 1997; Weingast 1984; Weingast and Moran 1983). Members of Congress serving on committees overseeing the Forest Service may be able to channel more fire prevention expenditures to their own districts, resulting in increased spending in those districts (Adler 2002; Bonneau et al. 2004; Stein and Bickers 1997). Although most of the appropriations for fire prevention are lump sum appropriations, earmarks in appropriations bills are a regular occurrence and may result in more spending for particular districts. In the appropriations bills for 2001, 2002, and 2003, there were six earmarks: one for Minnesota, one for Arizona, one for New Mexico, and three for California. They ranged in size from $263,000 to $19,900,000. These direct earmarks are in addition to the indirect influence that members of Congress can exert. Therefore, we hypothesize that there will be more projects and more funding if a ranger district is represented by a senator or member of Congress who has a seat on a relevant natural resource or appropriations committee.

Because congressmen and senators are also concerned with reelection, we would expect that interest groups can indirectly affect fire management budgets. Measures of interest groups such as logging companies, homebuilders, and environmental groups would therefore be useful. Unfortunately, such data are not available for the analysis here.

It is also possible that the Forest Service allocates its budget depending on pressure from its own constituents, rather than via the reelection incentive faced by elected officials.[3] The Forest Service may target spending on hazardous fuels reduction to the areas represented by the wealthiest clients, logging companies, livestock grazers, or environmental groups. Forest Service decision makers will also consider the agency's mission on a regional basis; that is, in some cases, timber management may be more important, whereas in others it may be grazing, wildlife, or wilderness. In the case of logging, we expect the agency to spend more money on preventing fires in forests with more employment in the logging sector.

Data and Analysis

In general, our theory is that fire management expenditures will be a function of economic, political, and environmental variables. The analysis uses two different datasets, one for a cross-state analysis and one for a more disaggregated analysis of Forest Service districts in California. The cross-state analysis offers more geographic coverage and corresponds to the spatial scale at which senators can be expected to make decisions, but it is also limited by the aggregation of spending. The finer-grained data in the California analysis enables a more specific match between the geographic attributes of the area, such as the number of houses surrounding a forest, and spending. An ideal specification would include the disaggregated data for the entire United States as well as control variables such as the district fire regime, ecosystem health, expenditures by other agencies such as California Department of Forestry and Fire Protection, and expenditures by private landowners. As with all empirical studies, however, such detailed data are not readily available.

Cross-State Dataset

The cross-state dataset includes spending on both preparedness and hazardous fuels reduction for FY2001 and FY2002. It also has spending on hazardous fuels reduction for FY2003. This analysis uses cross-sectional time-series data by state. The data were collected from the National Fire Plan Performance Reports. For this analysis, the dependent variable is spending on either hazardous fuels reduction per acre or fire preparedness per acre of Forest Service land in the state. Because there is no particular reason to believe that hazardous fuels reduction is consistently more expensive in some states than others, this specification provides a better assessment of the effect of spending than total spending by state. For example, California received the most money for hazardous fuels reduction over the time period because it has extensive national forests, especially compared with some southern and eastern states, but it ranked only seventh highest in spending per acre. These two categories of spending are treated as separate dependent variables, explained by the same independent variables and serving as a robustness check on the specification.

The data take account of environmental factors that affect fire risk. For the cross-state dataset, we use the Dai Palmer Drought Severity Index (PDSI) to measure this risk. The index combines temperature and rainfall data to provide a summary measure of dryness compiled at the state level by the National Oceanic and Atmospheric Administration (NOAA). In particular, this measure is most effective at measuring medium-term drought (several months). The Forest Service can be expected to have this data on hand while making the spending allocation decisions. But the index is for current conditions and is not a measure of longer-term fire risk, due to factors such as a buildup of fuel loads. Fuel management decisions may also be based on historical data or the overall risk of fire in a given type of forest, which are not captured in this index. Because it is not clear what the time period is for making these decisions, the analysis reported here uses the PDSI's value in June of the year the money will be spent, but the analysis is robust to many various averages of previous time periods, including the longer-term average of the previous two fiscal years. A zero value indicates normal levels of temperature and precipitation, whereas negative levels of the PDSI indicate drought conditions. For FY2001–FY2003, the PDSI ranges in value from −7.47 (severe drought) in Colorado in 2002 to 5.13 in Virginia in 2003.

Population density and per capita income measures are derived from census data aggregated to the state level. The analysis includes a dummy variable indicating, as appropriate, whether the state has a senator serving on the authorizing or appropriating committee or subcommittee. By reading the House, Senate, and Conference Committee Reports on the Interior Appropriations legislation for FYI2001–FY2003, we were able to determine whether states received specifically earmarked spending on fire preparedness or hazardous fuels reduction. Arizona, California, and Minnesota received earmarks in FY2001, but only California received earmarks in FY2002. California and New Mexico both received earmarks in FY2003. These variables are included as a control variable. It should be noted that inclusion of earmarks may deflate the coefficient on committee membership, because state earmarks are often related to committee membership.

Cross-State Estimation

We now turn to testing the political economy explanations for variations in fire management expenditures across states. Table 6.4 in the Appendix at the end of this chapter provides the distribution of the dependent variable across states and shows that many southern states received more spending per acre than many of the western states with more national forest acres. We estimate the following baseline model:

$$\frac{Spending}{100\,Acres} = \alpha + \beta_1 PDSI_{it} + \beta_2 Inc_{it} + \beta_3 Popn_i + \beta_{4,5} SenOnCmtee_{it}^j +$$
$$\beta_6 Earmarks_{it} + \beta_{7,8} Year_{it}^k + \epsilon_{it}$$

where i and t index states and years, respectively. *PDSI* is the drought measure by year and state, *Inc* is per capita income by state and year, and *Popn* is population density by year. *SenOnCmtee* takes a value of one when the state has a senator serving on j = {Agriculture Appropriations}, as appropriate. In some models, this variable represents a subcommittee member rather than a full committee member. *Earmarks* represents the value of an earmark in a given year for a given state. Finally, *Year* is a dummy variable for k = 2002, 2003.[4]

Using these data creates potential problems of autocorrelation, heteroskedasticity, and omitted variable bias. To solve these problems, two possible models are available: fixed effects and random effects. A fixed effects model is appropriate when the omitted variables may be correlated with the included explanatory variable, whereas a random effects model assumes strict exogeneity between the explanatory variable and the error term (which includes a component from the possible omitted variables). Compared with the fixed effects model, which requires 37 dummy variables with 109 observations, the random effects model is more efficient, and the Hausman test suggests it is appropriate. In addition, the model uses fixed effects for each year to assess whether there are systematic differences between years. Table 6.1 presents the results of the random effects model using both hazardous fuels and fire preparedness dependent variables.

The random effects model results indicate, most importantly, that more money is not spent in the states with higher levels of drought. The coefficient on the PDSI cannot be distinguished from zero. That is, the Forest Service does not appear to prioritize states that are at risk of fire when making hazardous fuels reduction decisions. This alone is an interesting finding, because it is counter to what we would expect if the agency were trying to minimize fire potential. Moreover, this lack of correlation between spending and drought conditions holds through many specifications of the drought measure, corresponding to the different information the Forest Service might use to make the decision and the different time period in which it might make the allocation decision. For example, the results are substantively the same if the measure of drought is the reading on the PDSI in June of the current year or the average of the previous two fiscal years. These represent the two extremes of the specifications we tested.[5] The average in June corresponds to using short-term contemporary information to make an allocation decision at the very beginning of the summer in which the money will actually

TABLE 6.1 Hazardous fuels spending and fire preparedness spending per acre using random effects model

	Hazardous Fuels Spending per 100 Acres (FY2001–2003)	Fire Preparedness Spending per 100 Acres (FY2001, 2002)
PDSI in June	1.59	6.19
	(2.62)	(5.08)
Per capita income	−0.00730*	−0.00601
	(0.00435)	(0.00985)
Population density	0.175	0.120
	(0.185)	(0.321)
Senator on appropriations	−13.42	20.3
	(22.0)	(41.9)
Senator on agriculture	−16.9	6.16
	(19.6)	(35.3)
Earmarks (in $)	0.00000302	
	(0.00000260)	
Year (2002)	24.5**	21.5
	(11.6)	(17.3)
Year (2003)	16.6	
	(12.2)	
Constant	291**	359
	(116)	(254)
N	109	84
R-squared	0.13	0.001

Notes

Standard errors in parentheses.

** $p < 0.05$

* $p < 0.1$

be spent, while the two-year average represents making the decision at the beginning of the fiscal year when large amounts of previous information about the drought conditions are available. Though neither of these may be the true model of decision-making, the specifications representing intermediate possibilities also fail to change the substantive results. Even in a naïve pooled regression, drought is not positively correlated with spending on fire prevention. Thus, this null finding is robust to many specifications of the model and explanatory variables, increasing our confidence that spending on hazardous fuels reduction is not being targeted toward areas with higher risk of forest fires. In fact, during this time period, the western states were generally experiencing drought and the southern states were not, but the southern states received more spending per acre.

The only variable that is significantly related to fire spending is per capita income, for which we can reject the null hypothesis that its effect is zero with greater than 90 percent confidence. However, the correlation is negative meaning that states with higher per capita income actually receive lower levels of hazardous fuels prevention spending, which is contrary to our expectation that the Forest Service would spend more in areas with higher per capita income. Here the level of aggregation may be masking the effect. Ideally, the measure of per capita income would only include those areas in the wildland-urban interface or those counties bordering national forests.

Using the alternate dependent variable of fire preparedness spending, the results are substantively similar, although the model explains less of the variation in spending. We cannot reject the null hypotheses that each of the explanatory variables is zero. Here, too, the interesting finding is that spending on fire preparedness does not seem to be correlated with drought conditions.

California Ranger District Dataset

The cross-state analysis highlights the problem with modeling at the aggregate level when money is spent at the disaggregated level. In particular, the economic variables are unlikely to capture the demands on the Forest Service with any specificity. Thus, this second analysis at the forest level within California is used to test for forest-specific conditions such as fire risk as well as other economic and political variables. The Forest Service tracks all of its activities using the Forest Service ACtivity Tracking System (FACTS). This chapter uses the subset of activities related to hazardous fuels reduction in Region 5 (activity codes 1000–1282),[6] which encompasses the national forests in California.

We use two different dependent variables for the years 2004 through 2008. The first is the number of projects in each of the 65 ranger districts in each year. The number of projects ranges from none to almost 5,000 in a given district in a given year, with more than a quarter of the district-years having no projects. The second dependent variable is the cost of those projects, ranging from zero to $113 million in a given district-year. These two dependent variables have a high correlation of 0.88. Nonetheless, they may capture slightly different dynamics.

The economic variables are derived primarily from the census. In particular, this analysis captures the capital stock at risk using the number of housing units within 10 miles of the boundary of each ranger district taking advantage of the disaggregated data.[7] The other economic variable is the percentage of employment in forestry in the counties that encompass the forest.[8]

We use dummy variables coded 1 when that ranger district is represented by a member of Congress who serves on the Committee on Resources and the Committee on Appropriations and zero otherwise.[9]

We take account of the potential for fire risk in California using the Fire Hazard Severity Zoning (FHSZ) developed in January 2007 by the California Department of Forestry and Fire Protection. This assigns a value of Moderate, High, or Very High Hazard based on expected chance of burning and the potential fire behavior for that site. These data were then aggregated by ranger district. This measure of fire potential is a longer-term risk than that captured by the PDSI and is a function of the fuel type in addition to temperature and precipitation.

California Estimation

For California, we use pooled time-series and cross-sectional data. Table 6.2 shows results from a random effects model, because fixed effects by district would make it impossible to estimate the coefficients on housing units or percent employment in forestry (since they are derived from census data that does not change during this time period). The model also includes fixed effects for each year to assess whether there are systematic differences between years.[10]

Like the state-level analysis, very few of the independent variables of interest exhibit the expected relationship with the level of spending or the number of projects in each California ranger district. The one variable that consistently has the

TABLE 6.2 Project spending by ranger district, 2004–2008

Variables	(1) Log of Spending per Acre	(2) Number of Projects per Acre
Representative on Resources Committee	−1.49e-07 (3.84e-07)	−8.31e-05 (6.73e-05)
Representative on Appropriations Committee	1.18e-07 (3.06e-07)	−9.08e-05* (5.32e-05)
Housing units within 10 miles	3.94e-09* (2.02e-09)	−3.98e-08 (2.14e-07)
% of county employment in forest-related industries	−0.000468 (0.000348)	0.0187 (0.0377)
Fire hazard level	1.98e-06*** (7.02e-07)	7.75e-05 (7.52e-05)
2005	1.90e-07 (2.44e-07)	5.40e-05 (4.44e-05)
2006	1.45e-07 (2.45e-07)	4.34e-05 (4.44e-05)
2007	2.88e-08 (2.79e-07)	−5.20e-05 (4.85e-05)
2008	4.48e-07 (2.75e-07)	−2.28e-05 (4.85e-05)
Constant	5.19e-06*** (1.59e-06)	−9.78e-05 (0.000176)
Observations	290	325
R-squared	0.565	0.264

Notes

Standard errors in parentheses.

*** $p < 0.01$

** $p < 0.05$

* $p < 0.1$

TABLE 6.3 Yearly project spending, 2004–2008

Variables	(1) Cost per acre	(2) Num per acre
Representative on	−1.02e-06	−0.000223*
Resources Committee	(1.48e-06)	(0.000116)
Representative on	−2.94e-07	8.25e-05
Appropriations Committee	(1.34e-06)	(0.000106)
Housing units within	4.53e-09*	−3.16e-07*
10 miles	(2.39e-09)	(1.87e-07)
% of employment in	−0.000443	−0.0513
forest-related industries	(0.000463)	(0.0364)
Fire hazard level	2.27e-06***	0.000151**
	(8.28e-07)	(6.51e-05)
Constant	6.70e-06***	−3.34e-05
	(2.04e-06)	(0.000160)
Observations	65	63
R-squared	0.186	0.187

Notes

Standard errors in parentheses.

*** $p < 0.01$

** $p < 0.05$

* $p < 0.1$

expected effect and is significant is housing units near the national forest. As explained earlier, significant amounts of California housing are in high-risk areas, making it likely that protecting property is a major driver in Forest Service fuels management decisions. Therefore, it is not surprising and is perhaps reassuring that more money is spent where the risk to property is greater. The dominance of this variable may explain why none of the other independent variables are significantly related to spending. When fire hazard is higher, spending is also higher. Results from the number of projects per acre show that having a representative on the Appropriations Committee results in fewer projects, contrary to what we expected. In addition, in neither specification are economic factors such as the degree of employment in forest-related professions related to hazardous fuels reduction. Thus, these results suggest that spending, at least, is driven by proximity to a greater housing stock and by the level of fire hazard.

As a robustness check, Table 6.3 shows that the results are similar when the yearly activities are aggregated across the time period.

Conclusions

Controlling wildfires has become a major policy issue, especially in the West, where federal lands dominate much of the landscape. Because the U.S. Forest Service was so effective in controlling forest fires after 1910, fuels have built up, making massive devastation more likely. Not surprisingly, the Forest Service and Congress have increased budgets for both fire prevention and suppression.

As with any federal budget item that is as large as the fire management budget for the U.S. Forest Service, we would expect that politics might play an important role in determining the level of expenditure, perhaps even a more important role than economic or environmental considerations. We tested for the impact of these variables using data across states for 2001–2003 and pooled time-series and cross-section data for California ranger districts for 2004–2008.

Our analysis suggests that the Forest Service does consider the severity of fire conditions and the housing stock in its decision, but that political variables have little significance. The two levels of analysis offer insight into the types of environmental variables that play a role in decision-making. The shorter-term and more limited PDSI that focuses on drought conditions is not related to spending, but the longer-term fire severity codes in California are. This suggests a focus on longer-term fire potential. Of course, this comes at the expense of spending more per acre in southern states without a drought during this time period than in western states that were experiencing drought.

One plausible explanation for the lack of political significance is that the data do not adequately control for political influence. Across states, we would expect congressional representation to self-select in a way that makes every state with many national forests have some political influence over expenditures. Moreover, because many fire-related expenditures are mandated by Congress, individual congressional members may not have much additional influence on how much is spent in their states or districts, except to the extent that they can include earmarks in the appropriations legislation.

In the California dataset, there are two plausible reasons for the insignificance of political variables. First, congressional districts may encompass multiple ranger districts, and congressional members may be more interested in regional expenditures than in individual ranger district expenditures. Second, congressional representation on the relevant resource committees does not change much over the period under consideration, making it difficult to find a correlation between our political measures and fire expenditures. Thus, future research will expand the scope of this work to encompass the other Forest Service regions.

It is not surprising that the housing stock is consistently significant. Whether we are considering private or public fire management decisions, protecting assets is important. Indeed, the housing variable may capture the influence of public choice variables that we were trying to model. For example, homeowners may be an important political constituency that puts pressure on Congress and the Forest Service to protect property. To the extent that houses are clustered and vary in value, the number of homes may be more important than the income level of people living in them. Without more data to capture variation in political influence, it is impossible to separate the relative contribution of these variables to fuels management expenditures. In summary, our data suggest that the Forest Service is trying to following Roger Kennedy's (2006) admonition in the subtitle of his book, namely that we should be seeking "how to save lives, property, and your tax dollars."

Acknowledgments

This chapter is dedicated to Cole Stancavage Anderson, to whom Sarah Anderson gave birth on October 22, 2010, which explains why she could not attend the conference. We thank Dan Benjamin and Dominic Parker for their comments on the statistics and Exley McCormick, Hylton Edingfield, and Shawn Regan for their research assistance.

Notes

1. Although it might seem important that the sum of the states' spending must be what Congress appropriates, this constraint does not seem to be binding. For example, in 2002, the Forest Service used forest-thinning funding to fight fires. Some senators, in particular Senator Bingamen (D-NM), were upset by this transfer, but there were no immediate repercussions.
2. Nonetheless, there is always some discretion at the local level on how and when the budget should be spent, which makes it difficult to know whether budget data reflect how the funds are actually used.
3. By client, we refer to any agent the Forest Service seeks to please. As discussed, this may include members of Congress or individual citizens.
4. Note that the model is actually a random effects model, so this representation is a simplification.
5. Additional specifications included average PDSI in the previous fiscal year, average PDSI between January and October of the previous fiscal year, average PDSI between January and June of the current fiscal year, average PDSI between January and March of the current fiscal year, and average PDSI between October and March of the current fiscal year. None of these specifications changed the substantive results.
6. These codes were consolidated, so more recent data only use the codes through 1182.
7. These data are derived from Census Bureau data at the census block level. Using geographical information systems (GIS), a 10-mile buffer was drawn around each ranger district. This boundary was overlaid on the census block data. Maintaining the assumption that housing is uniformly distributed across the census block, the percentage of the block or blocks that is within 10 miles of the boundary of the district was multiplied by the total number of housing units in that block. This gives an estimate of the number of housing units within 10 miles of the district boundary. The assumption that housing is uniformly distributed is potentially problematic, although it is less problematic at the smaller scale of the census block. If anything, this variable is an overestimate of the number of housing units, since housing is more likely to be located farther from forest boundaries. For each of the variables derived from census data, this chapter uses the finest-grained data available (census block, where available). Also note that this can count housing units twice (within 10 miles of two different ranger districts). This double-counting is desirable, since houses that are within 10 miles of two ranger districts do indicate an economic need to engage in hazardous fuels reduction in both ranger districts.
8. The average of employment in counties encompassing the forest is weighted by the proportion of the forest in that county.

9. Note that a ranger district can be represented by multiple members of Congress. It is considered sufficient here for one of them to serve on the committee.
10. When forest-level fixed effects are included, the results are similar, but the coefficient on the wildfire hazard code is no longer distinguishable from zero. This is perhaps because the majority of each forest receives the same fire hazard level.

References

Adler, E. Scott. 2002. *Why Congressional Reforms Fail: Reelection and the House Committee System.* Chicago: University of Chicago Press.

Bonneau, Emily, James Cottrill, and Jon Bond. 2004. The House Public Works Committee and the Distribution of Pork Barrel Projects. Paper presented at the annual meeting of the American Political Science Association. September 2004, Chicago.

Donovan, Geoffrey H., and Thomas C. Brown. 2005. An Alternative Incentive Structure for Wildfire Management on National Forest Land. *Forest Science* 51 (5): 387–395.

Donovan, Geoffrey H., and Douglas B. Rideout. 2003. A Reformulation of the Cost Plus Net Value Change (C + NVC) Model of Wildfire Economics. *Forest Science* 49 (2): 318–323.

Egan, Timothy. 2009. *The Big Burn: Teddy Roosevelt and the Fire That Saved America.* Boston: Houghton Mifflin Harcourt.

Evans, Diana. 1994. Policy and Pork: The Use of Pork Barrel Projects to Build Policy Coalitions in the House of Representatives. *American Journal of Political Science* 38 (4): 894–917.

Garrett, Thomas A., and Russell S. Sobel. 2003. The Political Economy of FEMA Disaster Payments. *Economic Inquiry* 41 (3):496–509.

Healy, Andrew, and Neil Malhotra. 2009. Myopic Voters and Natural Disaster Policy. *American Political Science Review* 103(3):387–406.

Hird, John A. 1991. The Political Economy of Pork: Project Selection at the U.S. Army Corps of Engineers. *American Political Science Review* 85 (2):429–456.

IEMTF (Interagency Ecosystem Management Task Force). 1995. *Ecosystem Approach: Healthy Ecosystems and Sustainable Economies.* Washington, DC: White House Office of Environmental Policy.

Kennedy, Roger G. 2006. *Wildfire and Americans: How to Save Lives, Property, and Your Tax Dollars.* New York: Hill and Wang.

Leopold, A. S., S. A. Cain, C. M. Cottam, I. N. Gabrielson, and T. L. Kimball. 1963. Wildlife Management in the National Parks: The Leopold Report. www.craterlakeinstitute.com/online-library/leopold-report/index-leopold-report.htm (accessed February 11, 2011).

Mayhew, David. 1974. *Congress: The Electoral Connection.* New Haven, CT: Yale University Press.

Moe, Terry M. 1987. Congressional Controls of the Bureaucracy: An Assessment of the Positive Theory of Congressional Dominance. *Legislative Studies Quarterly* 12:475–520.

——— . 1997. The Positive Theory of Public Bureaucracy. In *Perspectives on Public Choice: A Handbook,* edited by Dennis Mueller. Cambridge, UK: Cambridge University Press, 455–480.

Nelson, Robert H. 2000. *A Burning Issue: A Case for Abolishing the U.S. Forest Service.* Lanham, MD: Rowman and Littlefield Publishers.

Shepsle, Kenneth A., and Barry R. Weingast. 1981. Political Preferences for the Pork Barrel: A Generalization. *American Journal of Political Science* 25 (1):96–111.

Stein, Robert M., and Kenneth N. Bickers. 1997. *Perpetuating the Pork Barrel: Policy Subsystems and American Democracy.* Cambridge, UK: Cambridge University Press.

Theobald, David M., and William H. Romme. 2007. Expansion of the US Wildland-Urban Interface. *Landscape and Urban Planning* 83 (4): 340–354. www.sciencedirect.com/science?_ob=ArticleURL&_udi=B6V91-4P89900-1&_user=10&_coverDate=12/07/2007&_rdoc=1&_fmt=high&_orig=search&_origin=search&_sort=d&_docanchor=&view=c&_acct=C000050221&_version=1&_urlVersion=0&_userid=10&md5=a73ae41f03c573a1e722be00a1428e97&searchtype=a (accessed February 11, 2011).

USFS (USDA Forest Service). 2006. *A Collaborative Approach for Reducing Wildland Fire Risks to Communities and the Environment: 10-Year Comprehensive Strategy Implementation Plan.* www.westgov.org/wga/publicat/TYIP.pdf (accessed February 11, 2011).

Weingast, Barry R. 1984. The Congressional-Bureaucratic System: A Principal Agent Perspective (with Applications to the SEC). *Public Choice* 44:147–191.

Weingast, Barry R., and Mark J. Moran. 1983. Bureaucratic Discretion or Congressional Control? Regulatory Policymaking by the Federal Trade Commission. *Journal of Political Economy* 91 (October):765–800.

WFLC (Wildland Fire Leadership Council, Independent Panel). 2004. Large Fire Suppression Costs: Strategies for Cost Management. www.fs.fed.us/fire/ibp/cost_accounting/cost management_aug_04.pdf (accessed February 11, 2011).

Yoder, Jonathan, Marcia Tilley, David Engel, and Samuel Fuhlendorf. 2003. Economics and Prescribed Fire Law in the United States. *Review of Agricultural Economics* 25:218–233.

Appendix

TABLE 6.4 Hazardous fuels reduction spending by state

State	Average Hazardous Fuels Spending	Forest Service Acreage	Average Spending per 100 Acres	PDSI in June (– indicates drought)
Georgia	2,899,029	865,392	$335	0.757
Louisiana	1,539,667	604,256	$255	0.557
Florida	2,852,255	1,152,872	$247	1.50
Mississippi	2,707,185	1,169,219	$232	2.02
South Carolina	1,382,583	616,725	$224	−0.973
Alabama	1,405,788	665,981	$211	1.44
California	42,213,485	20,708,710	$204	−1.28
New Mexico	17,694,615	9,416,827	$188	−1.36
Nebraska	591,172	352,252	$168	−1.24
Minnesota	4,323,666	2,838,580	$152	1.99
Texas	1,094,802	755,104	$145	−1.28
South Dakota	2,762,555	2,012,805	$137	−0.22
Arkansas	2,977,339	2,586,621	$115	−0.16
Ohio	252,446	233,073	$108	0.463
Washington	9,669,535	9,251,930	$105	−0.393
Missouri	1,551,207	1,494,042	$104	0.243
Colorado	13,065,587	14,481,429	$90	−4.70
Oregon	13,955,301	15,662,276	$89	−2.73

TABLE 6.4 continued

State	Average Hazardous Fuels Spending	Forest Service Acreage	Average Spending per 100 Acres	PDSI in June (− indicates drought)
North Carolina	1,035,880	1,246,559	$83	−0.45
Arizona	8,051,901	11,261,846	$71	−3.13
Tennessee	473,386	699,814	$68	1.09
Vermont	258,838	385,820	$67	0.637
Utah	4,577,029	8,189,206	$56	−3.94
Kentucky	431,452	804,540	$54	0.857
Pennsylvania	266,001	513,359	$52	−0.21
Montana	8,552,334	16,903,238	$51	−3.88
Wisconsin	564,071	1,523,256	$37	1.75
Indiana	65,847	198,716	$33	0.167
Idaho	6,244,332	20,463,083	$31	−3.75
Michigan	692,748	2,863,953	$24	−0.323
Wyoming	1,988,980	9,237,566	$22	−5.31
North Dakota	218,591	1,105,977	$20	1.04
Virginia	315,814	1,661,100	$19	0.997
Illinois	42,203	292,966	$14	0.193
Alaska	2,608,258	21,987,024	$12	
Nevada	567,295	5,835,100	$10	−4.38
New Hampshire[b]	36,352	728,225	$5	−0.19
West Virginia	40,934	1,033,631	$4	2.02
Kansas	0	108,175	$0	−0.0333
Connecticut[a]		24		1.187
Delaware		0		0.78
Hawaii[a]	259,000	0		
Iowa		0		−0.103
Maine[b]		53,040		−1.82
Maryland		0		0.453
Massachusetts		0		1.00
New Jersey		0		0.5
New York		16,175		0.6
Oklahoma		397,610		0.000
Rhode Island		0		1.17

Notes

a   Connecticut and Hawaii have only research stations.

b   Maine and New Hampshire share the only national forest in Maine, but in this analysis, the spending is assigned to New Hampshire since the headquarters for the forest are there.

7

WHEN "SMOKE ISN'T SMOKE"

Missteps in Air Quality Regulation of Wildfire Smoke

Kirsten Engel and Andrew Reeves

Decades of fire suppression have taken their toll on America's forests. One legacy is severe wildfires. The last decade witnessed many severe fire seasons. In the last fifty years, there have been fifteen fire seasons in which the total acreage subject to wildland fires exceeded 5,000 acres. Eight of these occurred in the last decade alone. Five of the largest-acre fires have occurred since 2004 (NIFC 2011). Another legacy is degraded and altered ecosystems. In the absence of regular burns, the species that make up native habitats have given way to altered ecosystems.

Prescribed burning, or the intentional ignition of wildfires to reduce the buildup of fuels and otherwise manage natural resources, has long been understood as an effective tool to reduce the incidence of naturally ignited wildfires and maintain ecosystem health. Recent studies confirm that decreased fuel loads can lessen the impact of fires by limiting the number and severity of large wildfires, rendering it more difficult for crown fires to spread, and providing a space in which firefighters can safely work to contain large wildfires (see Finney 2001; Omi and Martinson 2004; Pollet and Omi 2002).

Despite their ability to decrease the incidence of wildfires, experts estimate that the amount of prescribed burning being done in the United States is currently far below levels that would be considered optimal from the vantage point of reducing damages from wildfires.[1] Variables contributing to the past and future underprovision of prescribed fires subject to prior study include liability risk for burners (see, e.g., Yoder 2008) and the lack of sufficient resources being devoted to prescribed burning. This chapter is devoted to one arguably underappreciated variable that we anticipate will grow in significance in the future: our current structure of air quality regulation.[2]

The air quality, or smoke, impacts of wildfires are subject to the framework of regulation established by (and derived from) the federal Clean Air Act. Federal regulation, however, makes a fundamental distinction between smoke from unplanned wildfires and that emanating from prescribed burns. To perhaps overly simplify the complex intersection of federal and state statutes, regulations, and policies on this topic, the law provides for the exemption of wildfire smoke from regulatory concern altogether at the same time that it stringently regulates smoke from prescribed fire. This differential treatment ignores the fact that smoke is smoke: wildfire smoke is just as harmful as the smoke from prescribed fires. Just as important and perhaps even more critically, it overlooks the fact that prescribed fire smoke may, in many situations, be necessary to reducing wildfire smoke; prescribed fires have proven instrumental in reducing the incidence and severity of wildfires.

We present three options for changes to the current air quality control regulatory regime to enable resource managers to reduce the total smoke load from planned and unplanned wildfires. Under the first, air quality regulators would build "room" for prescribed burning emissions within the emissions budgets of state air quality implementation plans so that prescribed burning would no longer be subservient to the emissions of nearby industrial or mobile sources. Under the second, or pure "smoke is not smoke" policy, regulators would provide for the exclusion, for air quality compliance purposes, of smoke from prescribed burning in the same manner and to the same degree as smoke from unplanned wildfires. Under the third, or "smoke is smoke" policy, all smoke from any type of wildfire activity would "count" for air quality compliance purposes, and regulators would be encouraged, so far as feasible, to meet air quality targets in view of the actual load of smoke from all wildfires.

We recommend the third option, the elimination of all regulatory exemptions for smoke from wildfires for air quality compliance purposes. We do so in order to ensure better protection of human welfare today by making sure that the adverse health effects of all types of wildfire, and not just prescribed fire, are taken into consideration in air quality planning.

Air Quality Regulation and Wildfire

Why Air Quality Is Relevant

Wildland fires, whether intentionally set or not, contribute large quantities of pollution to the country's air every year. Nationally, the size of the emissions of the pollutant of concern from wildfires, particulate matter less than 2.5 micrometers in diameter ($PM_{2.5}$), is comparable to that from industrial facilities. Thus, the Environmental Protection Agency (EPA 2009a) reports that in 2005, all fires combined emitted 411,470 metric tons of $PM_{2.5}$, while electricity generation and other industrial processes, long considered the primary culprits in particulate emissions, were responsible for 515,455 and 541,284 tons, respectively. Higher estimates are available (see, e.g., Wiedinmyer et al. 2006, who estimated that fires in the United States during 2004 were responsible for 2.4 million metric tons of $PM_{2.5}$). Nevertheless, wildfire is subject only partially to the U.S. comprehensive air pollution regulatory framework. This section gives some background on the rules and regulations governing air quality throughout the United States. These rules are complex—to a great extent on account of the Clean Air Act (CAA) itself, the most important and comprehensive legislation related to air quality. The 1970 Clean Air Act has been amended twice and now stands as the comprehensive framework for the control of all air pollutants contributing to a wide variety of air pollution conditions. These include ozone precursors found in urban smog, fine particulates that create regional haze, and, since the 2007 Supreme Court decision applying the Act to greenhouse gases, air pollutants contributing to global climate change (*Massachusetts v. EPA*, 549 U.S. 497 [2007]).

The core of the Act concerns EPA's authority to establish, and the states' obligation to attain, health- and welfare-based standards for specific pollutants. To this end, EPA has singled out for regulation six "criteria" pollutants: lead, sulfur dioxide, carbon monoxide, nitrogen oxides, ozone, and particulate matter.[3] For these six common pollutants, EPA has developed primary National Ambient Air Quality Standards (NAAQS) at levels designed to protect the health of sensitive populations.[4] For ozone, for instance, the NAAQS is set so that, in an 8-hour averaging period, the level of ozone recorded should not exceed .075 parts per million by volume. (This was the primary standard as of 2008. For a frequently updated table summarizing current requirements, see EPA 2011c.)

Under the Act, each state is responsible for developing plans, known as State Implementation Plans (SIPs), in order to ensure the attainment of the NAAQS within each air quality control region in the state. To develop SIPs, states create an emissions "budget" for each criteria pollutant. The budget is the maximum allocation of emissions of the pollutant that will still ensure that ambient levels of the pollutant are in compliance with national standards. Through the SIP planning process, states inventory current and planned sources of a given pollutant and impose a control strategy to ensure that emissions from such sources do not exceed air quality standards. States use computer models, incorporating data on emissions, dispersion, and meteorological conditions, to determine the levels of controls needed for compliance. Thus, for a typical industrial facility, the state will have estimated the emissions from such a facility and will incorporate in the SIP any controls upon the emissions from such a facility that, when viewed together with other sources of the same pollutant, the state deems necessary to attain the NAAQS. Finally, areas where the air quality is worse than the NAAQS level are designated by EPA as "nonattainment" for that pollutant. Sources of that pollutant within a non-attainment area must comply with more stringent requirements than similar sources located within an area that is in attainment with the NAAQS.

This particular structure—national standards enforced regionally through SIPs— has worked exceedingly well for four of the six criteria pollutants: by 2008, the number of nonattainment areas for sulfur dioxide, carbon monoxide, and nitrogen oxides had fallen to zero; of the thirteen nonattainment areas first established for lead in 1978, only two remained in 2008. For particulate matter and ozone, however, the results have been promising but much less dramatic. In the eleven years following the establishment of the ozone NAAQS in 1997, the number of nonattainment areas fell from 113 to 31. For the less stringent NAAQS dealing with particulate matter of 10 micrometers or less (PM_{10}), from 1987 to 2008 the number of nonattainment areas fell from 87 to 18 (EPA 2011c).

In relation to wildfires, these two particular NAAQS (and the fact that achieving 100 percent attainment has yet to become a reality) are especially important for two reasons: (1) EPA has begun planning further reductions in acceptable pollutant levels for both ozone and particulate matter, which will inevitably lead to greater incidence of nonattainment (see, e.g., EPA 2011b); and (2) the direct product of wildfires—smoke—is a major nonpoint-source contributor to both ozone and particulate matter pollution. (Point-source polluters are those, like factories, that emit pollutants from a stationary location.) As will be discussed later in this chapter, smoke from wildfires has generally been treated as an exceptional event, excludable in many instances from EPA monitoring data, that happens only erratically and on occasion. The reality, though, is that wildfires—especially in the West—contribute large quantities of both pollutants, and as far as human health is concerned, whether this harmful pollution results from forest fires or tailpipe emissions is irrelevant.

In addition to such concerns over human health, the Clean Air Act also addresses the problem of "regional haze" or the visibility of regional air sheds. Ozone and particulate matter are the primary culprits of regional haze, as ground-level ozone is the nation's primary constituent of smog and $PM_{2.5}$ serves as the primary cause of reduced visibility in much of the United States, especially in national parks and wilderness areas (see, e.g., EPA 2011b, 2009c).

The 156 areas affected by regional haze legislation consist of certain national parks, wilderness areas, national memorial parks, and international parks in existence as of August 7, 1977, in which visibility was found to be an important value (EPA 2001). These areas are, for the most part, located in the West. As with the NAAQS, the responsibility for improving visibility within these important air sheds has been delegated to the states. But whereas point-source emissions within any given state can readily be monitored and controlled, visibility presents additional difficulties, as large swaths of fire-prone land in the West fall under the control of federal agencies—not state governments.

The Air Quality Regulatory Structure Governing Wildfires and Prescribed Burning

Any explanation of the air quality regulatory structure governing fires is incomplete without also explaining the general practice—employed by EPA and many states—of distinguishing among (1) wildfires, (2) wildland fire use fires, and (3) prescribed burning.

According to EPA (2007), wildfires are considered "unplanned, unwanted wildland fire[s] (such as a fire caused by lightning) . . . where the appropriate management response includes the objective to suppress the fire." More simply, a wildfire is an unplanned fire that is not considered beneficial by regulators. Though originating in the same manner as wildfires, wildland fire use fires are those that are naturally ignited, such as by lightning, and are managed for the benefit of resources in accordance with a fire or land management plan. Finally, a prescribed burn is a fire intentionally lighted by managers to meet specific resource management objectives. Although the smoke from each of these three types of fires is substantively identical, this tripartite structure has led to differing regulatory policies for each type of fire. For the purposes of this chapter, the differing treatment of wildland fire use fire and prescribed burns is especially important.

In general terms, the Federal Wildland Fire Management Policy mandates that every acre of land under the control of the Departments of Agriculture and Interior —which includes all Forest Service lands, as well as lands managed by the Bureau of Indian Affairs, Bureau of Land Management, Fish and Wildlife Service, and National Park Service, 700 million acres in all—be subject to a Fire Management Plan (FMP) (GAO 2009). The purpose of these plans is to dictate how fire will be managed on the lands subject to them, whether wildfires will be suppressed or managed in whole or in part for resource benefits, and whether managers intend to treat the vegetation with prescribed fire. As explained in the EPA Interim Air Quality Policy on Wildland and Prescribed Fires:

> The [FMPs] are strategic plans that define how wildland and prescribed fires will be managed to meet land use objectives. The [FMPs] must contain prescriptive criteria which are measurable and will guide selection of appropriate management actions in response to fires. The criteria can relate to suppression actions or describe when fire can be managed to gain resource benefits. This allows the use of a full range of appropriate management responses to fire, which may include: full suppression of a wildland fire; suppression on part of a wildland fire while allowing another portion of the fire to continue playing a natural ecological role and achieve resource benefits; or the use of prescribed fire.
>
> (EPA 1998)

EPA also requires that FMPs be in place before either a prescribed burn or a naturally ignited fire can be managed for resource benefits. Importantly, the protection of health or welfare from wildfire smoke is neither the overriding objective of these plans nor much of their focus. FMPs are designed primarily with the possible harm to property and life potentially encountered with wildfires in mind. The Bureau of Land Management's FMP for its Amarillo Field Office, for instance, explains that "protect[ing] human life, both the public and firefighters," is the "single, overriding priority in fire management." The Amarillo FMP lists "meet[ing] federal and state air quality standards through proper management of emissions" from fires as one of its objectives, but as air quality in the region is already satisfactory, it does not address the impact of fire on air pollution in concrete terms (BLM 2010). This inattention to detail in relation to air quality impacts of FMPs is generally the norm. Thus, for purposes of smoke management, the importance of FMPs stands in relation to their prospective proposals for the treatment of useful wildland fires and prescribed burns on land use—not the management of air quality issues specifically.

Nevertheless, it is EPA's policy to allow states the flexibility to determine their own approach to governing wildfire—assuming such approaches "adequately protect air quality" (EPA 1998). EPA has identified important incentives for states to adopt Smoke Management Programs (SMPs), which are designed to mitigate the smoke byproduct of wildland fire use fires and prescribed fires.

Smoke Management Programs

SMPs generally establish a procedural framework for the management of smoke from fires being actively manipulated or employed for the sake of resource benefits. Thus, SMPs apply to prescribed fires, requiring land managers to follow certain requirements designed to reduce the incidence of smoke. As EPA has explained: "The purposes of [SMPs] are to mitigate the nuisance and public safety hazards ... posed by smoke intrusions into populated areas; *to prevent deterioration of air quality and NAAQS violations*; and *to address visibility impacts in mandatory Class I Federal areas*" (EPA 1998; emphasis added).

SMPs are not mandated by EPA. Nevertheless, EPA has identified certain situations when a state's adoption of an SMP would be appropriate: (1) there are increasing citizen complaints related to smoke intrusion; (2) managed fires are leading to a higher presence of criteria pollutants under the NAAQS; (3) $PM_{2.5}$ and PM_{10} NAAQS numbers are already dangerously close to acceptable levels; and (4) local and regional fires are already significantly contributing to haze/visibility impairment in protected Class I federal areas (EPA 1998).

EPA has also adopted important incentives to encourage states to adopt SMPs. In short, where prescribed or wildland fire use fires cause or significantly contribute to a violation of the particulate matter ambient air quality standard, EPA pledges to use its discretion *not* to designate the local geographic area as an area failing to comply with the NAAQS (a "nonattainment area") so long as the state has in place and is implementing either a smoke management plan or its equivalent. According to the agency:

> EPA [will] use its discretion *not to redesignate an area as nonattainment when fires cause or significantly contribute ... to PM NAAQS violations, if the State ... required those fires to be conducted within a basic SMP.* Rather, if fires cause or significantly contribute violations, States/tribes will be required to review the adequacy of the SMP, in cooperation with wildland owners/managers, and make appropriate improvements.
>
> [However, if] States/tribes do not certify that a basic SMP is being implemented, *no special consideration will be given to PM violations attributed to fires managed for resource benefits.* Rather, EPA will call for a SIP revision to incorporate a basic SMP and/or will notify the governor of the State ...

that the area should be redesignated as nonattainment. The SMP adopted in response to the [SIP] call must require mandatory participation for greater than de minimis fires, and must be adopted into the [SIP] so that it is Federally enforceable. Also, the [SIP] must meet all other CAA requirements applicable to nonattainment areas.

(EPA 1998; emphasis added)

Thus, Smoke Management Programs play a considerable role in the regulation of smoke and, importantly, in possibly excluding NAAQS violations resulting from natural fires in states that have adopted SMPs. In the West, every state has implemented such a plan, meaning that in California, Arizona, Nevada, Utah, and Montana—where nonattainment for PM_{10} and $PM_{2.5}$ is most prevalent—data from many wildland fires are potentially excludable (EPA 2011a).

In relation to prescribed burns, EPA has advised that SMPs include a permitting and approval process and that, ultimately, burn plans are utilized for any fire that is not de minimis.[5] Approval process for any given prescribed burn varies by state. In general, though, each burn must be preapproved by air quality regulators upfront, and burns must be consistent with state smoke management programs or policies. As EPA (1998) advised, "State/local wildland managers should notify air quality managers of long-range plans to use fire for resource management" and "should consider alternative management tools and evaluate the potential air quality impacts of fires." Additionally, "State requirements include any specific SIP requirements applicable to private land owners which are designed to ensure that the State complies with CAA requirements." In California, for instance, prescribed burning is governed by Title 17 of the California Administrative Code. This reads, in part: "No person shall knowingly set or allow agricultural or prescribed burning unless he or she has a valid permit from a district or designated agency. No burning shall be conducted pursuant to such permit without specific district approval." Further, California has codified procedures for determining whether any given day will be an allowable burn day, a no-burn day, or a "marginal burn day" reliant upon present meteorological conditions (17 CCR § 80120, 80110). Thus, a number of factors, from the bureaucratic (getting permits approved) to the natural (appropriate weather being present), must come together for any prescribed burn to occur, ensuring that prescribed burns are heavily regulated.

Many land managers, having recognized the difficulties associated with prescribed burn approval, have determined that, as an alternative, wildland fires should be used, usefully, to achieve regulatory goals. In Oregon, for instance, the Department of Environmental Quality has determined that "natural fires that are ignited by lightning and then managed like a prescribed burn are one way Federal Land Managers can achieve certain resource management objectives" (OAR 340-200-0040, § 5.8). By employing this technique, land managers may avoid possible NAAQS violations and, for that matter, the sometimes arduous permitting process associated with prescribed burns.

The Exceptional Events Rule

Regardless of whether land managers utilize preapproved prescribed burns or wild-land fire use fires to meet resource-planning objectives, EPA has put in place rules—such as the previously mentioned rule for determining attainment or nonattainment status relative to implementation of an SMP—for the exclusion of monitoring data related to wildland fires. Most importantly, in 2007, EPA updated its "exceptional event" rule.

The rule defines an exceptional event as an event that "affects air quality; is an event that is not reasonably controllable or preventable; is an event caused by human activity that is unlikely to recur at a particular location or a natural event; and is determined by EPA to be an exceptional event." In explaining the rule, EPA stated, "We believe that both wildfires and wildland fire use fires [useful wildland fires] fall within the meaning of 'natural events.' . . . Therefore, ambient particulate matter and ozone concentrations due to smoke from a wildland fire will be considered for treatment as an exceptional event if the fire is determined to be either a wildfire or wildland fire use fire" (EPA 2007).

Under this rule, then, two major nonpoint sources of PM and ozone pollution—wildfires and wildland fire use fires—are generally excludable from NAAQS determinations. Although prescribed burns are not as easily written off, EPA has also determined that, in many instances, they may fall within the exceptional event rule as well. According to EPA (2007), "A prescribed fire cannot be classified as 'natural,' given the extent of the direct human causal connection," but may still qualify as an event "affect[ing] air quality," being "unlikely to recur at a particular location," and "not reasonably controllable or preventable." Although the determination that a prescribed fire will affect air quality is straightforward, EPA provided guidance for the last two criteria. In relation to the "recurrence factor," the agency advised looking at natural fire return intervals for particular landscapes and ecosystems. If the "likelihood of recurrence is sufficiently small enough," data from such fires may be excludable if the other conditions of the rule are met. As for the "not reasonably controllable or preventable" factor, EPA (2007) advised "examining whether there are reasonable alternatives to the use of fire in light of the needs and objectives to be served by it." Specifically, if a significant "build-up of forest fuels [occurred] in a particular area that if left unaddressed would pose an unacceptable risk of catastrophic wildfire," this requirement may be met. Additionally, pest or disease outbreaks and issues of access problems and severe topography may also help meet this requirement. Thus, though less straightforward than the exclusion of wildfires and wildland fire use fires, under the exceptional event rule, it is possible for states to have data from prescribed burns excluded from NAAQS attainment data.

Potential Impact of EPA Smoke Policies on Wildfire Smoke

As discussed above, federal fire managers distinguish among three types of fires: wildfire, which consists primarily of naturally ignited fires (e.g., by lightning) or accidentally or intentionally ignited wildfires that are unwanted; wildland fire use fires, unplanned or unwanted fires that are used to accomplish resource management objectives; and prescribed fires, those intentionally ignited to meet specific resource objectives, usually a reduction in the buildup of forest fuels (NFAEB 2005). By providing for the total exclusion of air quality data related to unplanned wildfires as "natural events," regulators have codified the assumption that the air pollution impacts of such fires are not controllable. The result of this assumption is a failure to encourage states, working with federal land managers, to use available mechanisms—prescribed fire as well as mechanical fuel removal treatments—to their fullest extent to reduce the air quality impacts of unplanned wildfires.

As described earlier in this chapter, EPA has determined that wildfires and wildland fire use fires meet the definition of a "natural event" pursuant to Section 319 of the Clean Air Act. As a result, EPA authorizes states to exclude data related to particulate and ozone emissions from such fires for NAAQS compliance purposes. In essence, provided states are able to demonstrate that "but for" these emissions, the locality would not trigger a NAAQS exceedance, it is as if, for air quality purposes, the fires never occurred (EPA 2007). California has successfully petitioned for the exclusion of data from an unplanned wildfire for air compliance purposes and has at least one other petition pending before EPA at this time (Lakin 2010; see CARB 2010, 2011). In excluding such data, a state, together with emission sources of the same pollutants within the locality, avoids the onerous regulatory requirements that are triggered when an area shifts into nonattainment with the NAAQS or is considered in violation of a SIP. These requirements can consist of the required application of stringent technology standards on existing industrial sources and the withdrawal of highway funds from the locality (Clean Air Act § 171, 179).

Not only are the pollution impacts of wildfires and wildland fire use totally excludable for air quality compliance purposes, but the impacts are not required to be considered, at least to any great degree, in forestry planning procedures. Thus, for instance, federal Fire Management Plans generally do not regulate the air quality aspects of wildland fire use in much detail.

Also, as discussed earlier in this chapter, under the Clean Air Act, states are accountable for achieving and maintaining the national ambient air quality standards in each air quality control region. Unless specifically exempted by EPA, all air quality monitoring data gathered within a particular region "count" in determining whether a state has met its NAAQS attainment goal. Although states have considerable discretion in determining what sources of a NAAQS pollutant they will control in order to meet or maintain the NAAQS, and at what level of stringency (*Union Electric v. EPA*, 427 U.S. 246, 256 [1976]), they generally subject most major sources of permanent emissions to controls. As a default level, the Clean Air Act considers any source of 100 tons or greater to be a major source of pollution. In addition, federal law directly requires that new or modified stationary sources of criteria pollutants meet federal technology-based standards and in many situations requires that states impose controls upon certain stationary sources in SIPs (e.g., Clean Air Act, § 171, 173).

Air pollutant emissions from wildfires are dealt with in a completely different way. Of the three types of wildfire, only the regulation of prescribed fire is relevant, since, as discussed above, only the air quality impacts of prescribed fires are subject to regulatory controls before the event. With respect to prescribed burning, states do not explicitly reserve a portion of the total amount of emissions authorized under a SIP to prescribed burning. Instead, prescribed burning is authorized on a case-by-case basis when air quality regulators determine that the federal or state land manager's prescribed burn plan is consistent with the state's smoke management plan or, where a state lacks such a plan, "best management practices." Currently, 19 states have smoke management plans (Breininger 2009). Critically, the smoke management plan need not be incorporated into the state SIP (see, e.g., MNICS 2002). In fact, EPA offers the lack of a required connection between the smoke management plan and the SIP as an incentive to states to develop smoke management plans (EPA 1998). Hence, there is no mechanism by which state air quality regulators currently reserve "space" within their SIPs for emissions from prescribed burning.

This lack of connection between the SIP and the smoke management plan potentially restricts the times when air quality regulators will authorize prescribed burning. Prescribed burning is authorized only when air quality regulators can be assured that the emissions from the burning will not cause an exceedance of the NAAQS when added to preexisting emissions of the same NAAQS pollutant that are authorized by the SIP. Prescribed burning emissions are thus subservient to the emissions of more permanent sources of the same pollutant. This objective is accomplished through the mechanism of the state smoke management plans, which limit authorization of prescribed burning to those conditions where the burning would not cause an exceedance of a NAAQS or the impairment of visibility in certain areas protected by regional haze rules (EPA 1998). Many states make this policy operational by limiting "burn days"—days on which prescribed burning is permitted—to days on which such burning would not violate a NAAQS or impair visibility.

Suggested Air Quality Regulatory Options for Wildfire Smoke

The following are three alternative regulatory options for enhancing the use of prescribed fire and reducing the incidence of smoke from unplanned wildfires.

Make "Room" for Prescribed Burning Emissions within the State SIPs

The most easily implementable option for enhancing the use of prescribed fire would be to require or promote states—whether by EPA mandate or through incentive structures similar to those used to encourage the adoption of SMPs—to include "room" under their SIPs for liberal use of prescribed fires. As previously discussed, prescribed fires are currently dealt with on a "burn-by-burn" basis, and further, these burns stand in a subservient position in relation to other pollution sources under any given state's SIP. As a result, it is often difficult for land managers to successfully implement planned burns. If, however, ample room was made under SIPs for particulate matter and ozone emissions from such burns, land managers' plans for prescribed burning would not be subservient to the existing emissions from point sources such as cars and factories.

If, under this scenario, actual allowances for ozone and particulate matter under a state's SIP are not increased—a likelihood given the strict nature of NAAQS standards—fire managers will find themselves completely at odds with point-source polluters and, for better or worse, no longer standing in a subservient role. The likelihood of significant conflict (and potential backlash from the public) is high: to allocate pollution to prescribed burns, pollution from point sources would necessarily need to be reduced. This process would increase costs for many factory owners and perhaps would require factory closings (hence the public backlash) in some instances.

If successful, this option would enhance human welfare by increasing the amount of prescribed burning being done today. It would do nothing, however, to protect current generations from the smoke from unplanned wildfires, which would continue to be eligible for exemption for regulatory purposes under EPA's exceptional events rule.

Adopt a Pure "Smoke Is Not Smoke" Policy

Another alternative would be for air regulators to allow for the exclusion, for air quality compliance purposes, of air quality monitoring data related to prescribed burning in the same manner and to the same extent as EPA's natural and exceptional events policy currently allows for the exclusion of air pollution from unplanned wildfires. This might be considered the adoption of a pure "smoke is *not* smoke" policy.

The objective behind such a policy would be to liberate state and federal land managers who wish to perform prescribed burning from the necessity of demonstrating compliance with either the criteria for exceptional events or the requirements of the state smoke management plan. In fact, such a policy would likely eliminate any incentive for a state to adopt a smoke management plan in the first place, since EPA's promise to exempt prescribed burning data for compliance purposes has been the major incentive behind the adoption of such plans. The hope is that resource managers would step up prescribed burning in response to the alleviation of these various restrictions. However, to the extent current levels of prescribed burning are being limited by other factors—perhaps lack of resources or staff to carry out the prescribed burns—this policy would not seem to have much of an effect in increasing prescribed burning.

If successful, like the first option, this option could also enhance human welfare by increasing the amount of prescribed burning being done, which should reduce the incidence of future catastrophic wildfires. The total exemption of wildfire smoke for regulatory purposes today could, however, increase the possibility of harm, as health would be threatened by the smoke not only from unplanned wildfires but also from prescribed burning.

Adopt a Pure "Smoke Is Smoke" Policy

A third and, we will argue, much more effective strategy would be for air quality regulators to adopt a pure "smoke is smoke" policy. In other words, none of the data related to the air quality impacts from unplanned wildfires, wildland fire use fires, or prescribed burning would be eligible for exclusion for air quality compliance purposes. Under this policy scenario, wildfires could, and no doubt would, trigger nonattainment status for many air quality control regions.

Although prescribed burning would be similarly alleviated from restrictions under this scenario, there is a much greater likelihood that prescribed burning would increase. This is because the threat of throwing an area into nonattainment would act as a powerful incentive for an increase in prescribed burning so as to reduce the likelihood of an unplanned, exponentially more destructive, wildfire. This plan would likely be more effective in encouraging prescribed burning than the current regime. At present, federal and state land managers are the primary advocates for prescribed burning. But where the consequences of the failure to do prescribed burning is the triggering of nonattainment or a violation of the SIP, other pollution sources within the region, as well as the state itself, would likely become effective advocates of prescribed burning.

This policy does not play "smoke and mirrors" with the severe health impacts of wildfire smoke. Smoke *is* smoke, regardless of its source. Fine particulate matter and ozone have the same deleterious effects upon health and visibility, whether they derive from a raging wildfire (which is currently excludable), a prescribed fire (which is not easily excludable), or a coal-fired utility (which is not excludable). Hence, a "smoke is smoke" regulatory policy will force regulators to confront the total load of each pollutant of national concern and determine which sources can continue to pollute, which must cut back and to what level, and which cannot, in order to meet air quality regulatory objectives. Only by having this complete inventory of the sources contributing to harmful air quality can policymakers make rational decisions about which sources of particulate matter or ozone should have to reduce their emissions. One solution may be to increase prescribed burning, but in other situations it may be to reduce vehicular pollution.

This third option also protects human health and welfare most fully, as all wildfire smoke, of whatever origin, is considered for air compliance purposes. Although this may result in hardship to permanent stationary sources, it meets the objective of protecting health from air quality that exceeds the national health standards.

Conclusions

In setting primary National Ambient Air Quality Standards for criteria pollutants such as ozone and particulate matter, the Clean Air Act mandated that EPA set limits to protect public health, including the health of "sensitive" populations such as asthmatics, children, and the elderly (see, e.g., EPA 2011c). In addressing wildfire, however, EPA has refused to acknowledge that smoke from such sources is essentially the same (in relation to criteria pollutants such as ozone and $PM_{2.5}$) as smoke from point-source polluters like factories. By doing this—namely, by omitting large quantities of emissions data from wildfires and useful wildland fires—EPA has disincentivized the use of prescribed fire. And although prescribed fires do produce emissions, we are here presented with the case where, as Philadelphia's first volunteer firefighter, Benjamin Franklin, has said, "an ounce of prevention is worth a pound of cure." By reducing flammable substances—especially underbrush and dead organic matter—in our nation's forests through prescribed burns, the likelihood of catastrophic fires can be significantly reduced. Currently, our regulatory structure as laid out by the Clean Air Act and enforced by EPA has not recognized this, and as a result, fire is not well controlled through enforcement of national air quality standards. Nevertheless, especially if a "smoke is smoke" policy were to be adopted, our clean air regulatory structure does have the potential to help control catastrophic wildfires should we ever decide to more fully utilize it.

Acknowledgments

The authors thank the many state and federal officials who offered their time and perspectives on this topic, including Peter Lahm, National Wildfire Coordinating Group, Washington, DC; Trent Proctor, Regional Air Program Manager, Sequoia National Forest, Porterville, CA; Scott Nester, San Joaquin Air Quality Control District, San Joaquin, CA; Mark Lakin, EPA Region 9, San Francisco; Lisa Hanf, EPA Region 9, San Francisco; Jim Brenner, Fire Management Administrator, Florida Division of Forestry; Mark Fitch, National Park Service, National Interagency Fire Center; Karen Magliano, California Air Resources Board; and David Lighthall, Health Science Advisor, San Joaquin Valley Air Pollution Control District.

Notes

1. For example, one study finds the optimal rate of prescribed burning in Volusia County, Florida, to be 214 percent higher than current rates, which is already much higher than rates observed nationally (Mercer et al. 2007). Further, for the past decade, federal land managers have been seeking to implement a several-fold increase in the use of fire to sustain ecosystems (Sandberg et al. 1999). The estimates of the amount of acreage and associated emissions from the ecosystem management burning that local land managers believe is needed far surpass current levels (see Peterson et al. 1998).
2. We already perceive that air quality regulation is restricting the desired level of prescribed burning, but this effect is likely to be accentuated in the future. At the same time that federal, state, and tribal land managers are planning increases in the level of

prescribed burning occurring on federal lands (see WRAP 2008), air quality regulators are planning to make more stringent the national standards applicable to the air pollutants generated by prescribed burning.

3. These "criteria" pollutants are, per EPA, the principal pollutants affecting the nation's air quality and are called such because human health-based and/or environmentally based criteria are set for addressing acceptable levels of such pollutants.

4. EPA is required to establish primary and secondary standards under the NAAQS. Primary standards are set to protect the public health (including especially sensitive members of the population like asthmatics and the elderly), whereas secondary standards more generally protect the public welfare (visibility, damage to livestock and crops, and so on). Currently, though, only sulfur dioxide has a differing secondary standard. The secondary standards for ozone and both types of particulate matter—the primary concerns of this chapter—mirror the primary standards.

5. The following elements are recommended for inclusion in any given burn plan: (1) the location and description of the area to be burned; (2) personnel responsible for managing the fire; (3) type of vegetation to be burned; (4) area (acres) to be burned; (5) amount of fuel to be consumed (tons/acre); (6) fire prescription, including smoke management components; (7) criteria the fire manager will use for making burn/no-burn decisions; and (8) safety and contingency plans addressing smoke intrusions (see EPA 1998, 19).

References

BLM (Bureau of Land Management). 2010. Amarillo Field Office 2010 Fire Management Plan. www.blm.gov/pgdata/etc/medialib/blm/nm/programs/fire/fire_management_plans/amarillo_fmp.Par.93015.File.dat/AMFO_FMP_2010_final.pdf (accessed April 25, 2011).

Breininger, Todd. 2009. Smoke Management Program. DCNR Bureau of Forestry, Division of Forest Fire Protection. www.paprescribedfire.org/smoke%20management.pdf (accessed April 25, 2011).

CARB (California Air Resources Board). 2010. 2007 Southern California Wildfires and High Winds. www.arb.ca.gov/desig/excevents/2007wildfires.htm (accessed April 25, 2011).

———. 2011. 2008 Northern California Wildfires. www.arb.ca.gov/desig/excevents/2008 wildfires.htm (accessed April 25, 2011).

EPA (U.S. Environmental Protection Agency). 1998. Interim Air Quality Policy on Wild-land and Prescribed Fires. www.epa.gov/ttncaaa1/t1/memoranda/firefnl.pdf (accessed April 25, 2011).

———. 2001. Visibility in Mandatory Federal Class I Areas (1994–1998): A Report to Congress. nepis.epa.gov/Exe/ZyPURL.cgi?Dockey=00002RY5.txt (accessed April 25, 2011).

———. 2007. Treatment of Data Influenced by Exceptional Events. Federal Register 72, no. 55 (March 22): 13560–13581.

———. 2009a. Air Emission Sources: Particulate Matter. www.epa.gov/air/emissions/pm.htm (accessed February 7, 2010).

———. 2009b. Visibility: Basic Information. www.epa.gov/visibility/what.html (accessed April 25, 2011).

———. 2011a. Counties Designated Nonattainment for PM-10. www.epa.gov/airquality/greenbk/mappm10.html (accessed April 25, 2011).

———. 2011b. Ground-Level Ozone. www.epa.gov/groundlevelozone/ (accessed April 25, 2011).

———. 2011c. National Ambient Air Quality Standards (NAAQS). www.epa.gov/air/criteria.html (accessed April 25, 2011).

Finney, Mark A. 2001. Design of Regular Landscape Treatment Patterns for Modifying Fire Growth and Behavior. *Forest Science* 47 (2):219–228.

GAO (General Accounting Office). 2009. Wildland Fire Management. GAO-09-906T. www.gao.gov/new.items/d09906t.pdf (accessed April 25, 2011).

Lakin, Mark. 2010. Personal communication between Mark Lakin, U.S. EPA, Region 9, and Kirsten Engel, November 1.

Mercer, D. Evan, Jeffrey P. Prestemon, David T. Butry, and John M. Pye. 2007. Evaluating Alternative Prescribed Burning Policies to Reduce Net Economic Damages from Wildfire. *American Journal of Agricultural Economics* 89 (1):63–77.

MNICS (Minnesota Incident Command System Prescribed Fire Working Team). 2002. Minnesota Smoke Management Plan. http://files.dnr.state.mn.us/forestry/wildfire/rxfire/mnsmokemgmtplan.pdf (accessed April 25, 2011).

NFAEB (National Fire and Aviation Executive Board). 2005. Three Kinds of Wildland Fire. Directives Task Group Briefing Paper #03. www.nwcg.gov/branches/ppm/fpc/archives/fire_policy/general/3_kinds_of_wildland_fire_BP3_1_19_05.pdf (accessed April 25, 2011).

NIFC (National Interagency Fire Center). 2011. Fire Information: Wildland Fire Statistics. www.nifc.gov/fire_info/fire_stats.htm (accessed April 25, 2011).

Omi, Philip N., and Erik J. Martinson. 2004. Effectiveness of Thinning and Prescribed Fire in Reducing Wildfire Severity. In *Proceedings of the Sierra Nevada Science Symposium*, edited by Dennis D. Murphy and Peter A. Stine. Gen. Tech. Rep. PSW-GTR-193. Albany, CA: USDA Forest Service, Pacific Southwest Research Station, 87–92.

Peterson, Janice, David Sandberg, and William Leenhouts. 1998. Estimating Natural Emissions from Wildland and Prescribed Fire. www.epa.gov/ttn/faca/pbdirs/natur7.pdf (accessed April 25, 2011).

Pollet, Jolie, and Philip N. Omi. 2002. Effect of Thinning and Prescribed Burning on Crown Fire Severity in Ponderosa Pine Forests. *International Journal of Wildland Fire* 11:1–10.

Sandberg, David V., Colin C. Hardy, Roger D. Ottmar, J. A. Kendall Snell, Ann Acheson, Janice L. Peterson, Paula Seamon, Peter Lahm, and Dale Wade. 1999. *National Strategic Plan: Modeling and Data Systems for Wildland Fire and Air Quality*. Gen. Tech. Rep. PNW-GTR-450. Portland, OR: USDA Forest Service, Pacific Northwest Research Station.

Wiedinmyer, Christine, B. Quayle, C. Geron, A. Belote, D. McKenzie, X. Zhang, S. O'Neill, and K. K. Wynne. 2006. Estimating Emissions from Fires in North America for Air Quality Modeling. *Atmospheric Environment* 40:3419–3432.

WRAP (Western Regional Air Partnership). 2008. Western Regional Air Partnership 2008-12 Strategic Plan. www.wrapair.org/WRAP/documents/WRAP_2008-12_Strategic_Plan3_08final.pdf (accessed April 25, 2011).

Yoder, Jonathan. 2008. Liability, Regulation, and Endogenous Risk: The Incidence and Severity of Escaped Prescribed Fires in the United States. *Journal of Law and Economics* 51 (2):297–325.

8

PRIVATE AND PUBLIC PROVISION OF FIREFIGHTING SERVICES IN RURAL AUSTRALIA

Jeff Bennett

Southern Australia experiences a Mediterranean-type climate, with cool, wet winters and hot, dry summers. Pastures and the natural bushland grow strongly in spring and subsequently dry out as the summer progresses, leaving high fuel loads that are particularly susceptible to fire. This situation is made more volatile by the dominance of eucalyptus trees in the vegetation mix. The high oil content of eucalyptus leaves makes them highly flammable in conditions of low humidity, high temperatures, and strong winds (Cary et al. 2003).

With these conditions in place each summer, people living in rural areas and the peri-urban fringes of the cities face the prospect of wildfire causing losses of property and life. The history of the damage caused by fires, summarized in Table 8.1 for the States of Victoria and New South Wales (NSW), demonstrates the magnitude and frequency of these losses.

Most recently, wildfires in the State of Victoria in February 2009 resulted in the deaths of 173 people. Insurance claims for property and motor vehicle damage amounted to A\$1.2 billion, and animal deaths were estimated to be over one million.[1] In the aftermath, the Victorian Bushfire Reconstruction and Recovery Authority, established by the State government, spent over A\$1 billion, and the Commonwealth government provided almost A\$0.5 billion to the recovery effort (VBRC 2010).

Though such catastrophic fires capture international headlines, the provision of day-to-day firefighting services in southern Australia is part of the fabric of life in rural areas. Primary responsibility for the control of the numerous fires that break out on privately owned land in summer falls to the large number of men and women who are members of local area volunteer rural fire brigades. However, the public sector also plays a key role. First, government agencies that are responsible for land held by the Crown are also responsible for the control of fires on that land. Second,

TABLE 8.1 Fire history: New South Wales and Victoria

Date	Name	Location	Deaths	Homes and Farms Destroyed	Area Burned (000 ha)[a]	Stock Losses (000s)
Feb 1851	Black Thursday	Victoria	12		5,000	
Feb 1898	Red Tuesday	Victoria	12	2,030	260	
Feb 1926	Black Sunday	Victoria	60			
Jan 1939	Black Friday	Victoria & NSW	71	650	1,500	
Dec 1943– Jan 1944		Victoria	15–20	885	1,000	
Jan 1962		Victoria	32	450	—	
Feb 1965		Victoria		60	315	4
Mar 1965		NSW	3		330	
Feb 1968		Victoria		63	2	
Jan 1969		NSW	23	241	250	12
Dec 1969– Jan 1970	Roto fire	NSW			280	
Dec 1972		Victoria			12	
Dec 1972– Jan 1973		NSW			216	
Dec 1974		NSW			3,755	50
Feb 1977		Victoria		456	103	198
Dec 1979– Jan 1980		NSW	1	14	1,000	
Feb 1983	Ash Wednesday	Victoria		2,253	210	27
Jan 1985		Victoria	3	680	102	46
Dec 1985		NSW	4		3,500	40
Dec 1993		NSW	4		800	
Jan 1997	Dandenong fire	Victoria	3	41	1	
Feb 1998		NSW	4	10	500	
Dec 2002		Victoria			181	
Jan 2003		Victoria		41	1,300	9
Feb 2003		NSW (ACT[b])	4	530	—	
Jan 2006	Grampians fire	Victoria	3	416	160	64
Feb 2007		Victoria	1	51	1,081	1741
Feb 2009		Victoria	173	4,029	430	

Sources: DSE (2009); RFS (2011).

Notes

a ha = hectares.

b Australian Capital Territory.

the State has structured numerous institutional arrangements that provide the "rules" by which private-sector entities engage in firefighting activities.

This has resulted in a complex interplay between private- and public-sector interests. Fires that start on private land are the responsibilities of the volunteer rural fire brigades. Yet if such fires are predicted to spread to public lands, the effort of government agencies will be enlisted. Similarly, volunteer brigades may be called upon to assist fighting fires on public lands.[2] The coordination of efforts between the volunteer brigades and the government agencies has been the subject of much dispute and a focal point of the findings of the Royal Commission into the Victorian Bushfires (VBRC 2010).

But perhaps more important for the efficient provision of firefighting services are the institutions established by the State that drive both public- and private-sector actions. These institutions (or rules) are primarily established by legislation in each State, given that under the Australian constitution, the State governments have responsibility for emergency situations, including bushfires. Although each State has a different act, they have sufficient commonalities to establish some basic features.

First, the legislation sets up a statutory authority that is responsible for prevention, control, and suppression of rural area fires as well as the protection of life, property, and environmental assets from fire damage. In NSW, this is the Rural Fire Service (RFS); in Victoria, the Country Fire Authority (CFA); and in South Australia, the Country Fire Service (CFS). The individual local area volunteer brigades are con-stituted under these authorities, with various structures to organize brigades into groups and then regions. These structures also establish the chain of command. Hence, the head of a State-wide fire authority, who is an employee of the State, is ultimately responsible for the actions of the individual local area volunteer brigades. That person delegates to regional and group officers, who are also employees of the State. It is only at the local brigade level that private volunteers are involved.

Second, the legislation sets out the financial structure of the authority. The State fire services have two main sources of funds: payments from the government and payments from insurance companies. In South Australia, the Country Fires Act (1989) established the Country Fire Service Fund. This fund receives an appropriation from the State parliament and a sum prescribed by the government to be paid by insurers. The amount paid by insurers is specified in Sections 18 and 19 of the Act to be at least one-quarter but not more than half of the State Treasury's estimate of the CFS's expenditure for the coming year. The amount paid by individual insurers is dependent on their overall market share, defined in terms of premium income collected. However, Section 19A withdrew Sections 18 and 19 as of 1999–2000. The CFS reports from that date onward indicate only revenues from the State government (with some Commonwealth government supplementation).

In NSW, the Rural Fires Act (1997) follows a similar approach, but a contribution from local government is also required. The proportions of expected expenditure to be met by the various parties are set out in Section 107: (a) the

State government, 14.6 percent; (b) relevant councils, 11.7 percent; and (c) insurance companies, 73.7 percent. In Victoria, the Country Fire Authority Act (1958) requires that the projected expenditures of the CFA are funded in advance, with 22.5 percent coming from the State's consolidated revenue and 77.5 percent sourced from insurance companies insuring against fire on rural property (Section 76).

Third, the Acts specify the responsibilities of individual landholders in the prevention, control, and suppression of fires. All make reference to landowners taking practical or reasonable steps regarding fire prevention and control, thus reflecting the position established in civil law relating to negligence, whereby individuals have an obligation to take "reasonable care." This position has evolved over time (Eburn 2010a, 2010b). English common law originally established a doctrine of strict liability for the release of an inherently dangerous substance such as fire (*Rylands v. Fletcher* UKHL 1 [1868]). However, subsequent case law in Australia weakened that liability, initially by excluding fire caused by lightning (*Hargrave v. Goldman* HCA 56 [1963]; (1963) 110 CLR 40), and then in a High Court decision (*Burnie Port Authority v. General Jones Pty Ltd* HCA 13 [1996]; (1994) 179 CLR 529) where ordinary negligence was made specific.

However, the Acts go further by creating a range of obligations to prevent fire. These are epitomized by the establishment of the right to declare fire danger seasons and total fire bans. Breaches such as lighting a fire on a day of total fire ban are punishable under the criminal code and can involve fines and imprisonment.

An Economic Framework

The Australian Emergency Management Institute states that "Australians expect their governments at all levels to do their best to ensure that their communities are as well protected from emergencies as is reasonably possible . . . [and to] . . . bring together the efforts of all governments and private and volunteer agencies" (AEMI 2009, 4).

Beyond this statement of expectation, little by way of economic justification for government involvement in the provision of firefighting services can be found in government policy documents. A valid first step in understanding the public policy issues surrounding firefighting provision is to consider aspects of "market failure" that may be at work.

Property rights are key to this consideration. Where property rights to assets and the flows of goods and services resulting from their use are well defined, robustly defended, and traded competitively, markets are generally agreed to deliver resource allocations that are comparatively efficient. The occurrence of fire can be the result of either a landowner's own actions or the actions of others. Insofar as a landowner decides to release a fire that impacts on his or her own property, it would seem that no breach of rights occurs and no failure of decentralized decision-making is evident. Complexities arise when the right to use of property is infringed by neighbors who allow fire to escape across a property boundary. This breach of rights is clearly defined and defended through the law of ordinary negligence.

However, it is not defended when the initiation of the fire cannot be attributed to the actions of any individual. For instance, when a fire starts as a result of a lightning strike or when the cause of a fire is unidentified, there is no defined liability. The situation then becomes one of managing the risk of loss.[3]

The situation is further confounded when the focus is shifted from the initiation of a fire to the control of a fire that has already spread beyond the property of the initiator. The actions of those seeking to control the blaze on their own land are motivated by the prevention of loss to their property. So long as the marginal costs of effort are lower than the expected marginal benefits they receive from attempts to control the fire, they will fight it. However, their efforts also determine the probability that the fire will move onto others' properties. The rights involved in this circumstance are not well defined. There is no clear indication that the person fighting the fire will be rewarded (or penalized) for their effort (or lack of it) by their neighbors. Furthermore, the transaction costs of negotiating an agreement among individual neighbors are unlikely to be sufficiently low to enable timely outcomes, especially as the spread of the fire may involve an exponentially growing number of affected parties.

The case of fire control therefore indicates a role for collective rather than individual action (Libecap 1989). The question then becomes whether such collective action is best arranged endogenously, within the group of people involved, or exogenously, imposed on the group by an outside authority. Endogenous action would be typified by the voluntary formation of neighboring landholder groups who agree to assist in the fighting of fires on each other's properties. Exogenous action would involve governments setting up professional firefighting brigades.

The alternative models of collective action will have different operating characteristics and organizational costs. Voluntary groups may have good local knowledge and be able to respond quickly because of their local residency in relatively sparsely settled areas. However, the formation of such groups may be inhibited by freeriding behavior, and the complexities of local interpersonal relationships may cause friction among members and even exclusion from the group. Professionals may be better trained and unaffected by local disputes but also may be more expensive, more widely spread across the community, and hence slower to react.

The transaction costs involved in limiting free riding within local volunteer groups and collecting and managing the funds needed to form a professional brigade are an important consideration in comparing the alternatives. As Ostrom (1990) has demonstrated, the existence of the potential for free riding resulting from the nonexcludability characteristic of a good does not necessarily preclude the formation and operation of successful voluntary groups. With sufficiently repeated experiences among groups with small numbers of relatively homogeneous members, endogenous institutions can form at lower cost than exogenously imposed institutions. Yet as numbers in the group grow and interests become more heterogeneous, exogenous collective action becomes more efficient.

The bigger the group, the larger-scale the fire is likely to be, and a further complication arises. This involves the appropriate scale at which to fight a fire. Small-scale fires can be controlled using locally deployed small-scale capital equipment. Large-scale regional fires are likely to be more appropriately tackled using larger-scale, more specialized capital equipment (Chapter 4). Local voluntary groups may enable the collective application of individual farm-scale firefighting equipment. This may be an inefficient scale for attacking larger fires. Establishing the endogenous institutions to facilitate group purchase and then utilization of larger-scale equipment may be costly, and the utilization of the larger-scale capital equipment may be inefficient. Such equipment may suffer shorter periods of downtime if shared across local groups. Again, the transaction costs of such broader cast endogenous agreements are higher, with free riding becoming an increasingly difficult obstacle.

The choice between endogenous and exogenous institutional structures—voluntary or professional firefighting operations—across different scales of operation is, however, not an absolute one. A mixture of the two forms is prospective, and current operations of firefighting services in rural Australia demonstrate how private, voluntary effort is mixed with exogenously directed public effort. The conceptual analysis presented in this section provides some justification for the presence of both voluntary and government-instituted firefighting effort. The next question to be addressed is whether the current mix could be changed to improve provision efficiency.

The Public-Private Interface

The split between private and public effort in firefighting has changed, and continues to evolve, over time. In general, the extent of private involvement as a proportion of the total effort has been falling. Tables 8.2, 8.3, and 8.4 set out the key data for the last ten years for NSW, Victoria, and South Australia to illustrate that trend. An indicator of the extent of voluntary, private effort is the number of volunteers who are members of local brigades. Number of volunteers is a very broad indicator only, as it does not take into account any possible substitution of capital for labor (for example, more on-farm firefighting equipment using less labor), nor does it account for changing population distributions, both between rural and urban areas and among different rural areas (despite overall population growth in rural areas, some regional populations have declined while others have expanded). Nevertheless, an overall trend is clear: volunteer effort is relatively steady and even declining in terms of the number of volunteers per head of rural population. In NSW, volunteer numbers have risen slightly, whereas in Victoria and South Australia, decreases have been recorded. The number of brigades registered in each State has also fallen over the ten-year period.

In contrast, the public-sector-driven effort has increased in terms of both labor input and overall spending. The professional staff employed by the fire services (and funded by the exogenously generated funds) has increased markedly in all

TABLE 8.2 NSW Rural Fire Service

Year	1999–2000	2000–2001	2001–2002	2002–2003	2003–2004	2004–2005	2005–2006	2006–2007	2007–2008	2008–2009
Brigades	2,301	2,164	2,259	2,099	2,094	2,069	2,100	2,077	2,058	2,065
Volunteers	68,983	68,350	65,395	67,058	69,375	70,964	70,745	71,441	70,159	70,701
Rural population	2,417,120	2,446,945	2,465,952	2,481,703	2,492,941	2,511,412	2,534,099	2,560,267	2,595,812	2,629,952
Professional staff	144	161	490	570	601	649	680	685	710	752
Expenditure[a]	67,195	70,233	131,199	17,0551	9,7900	105,173	11,6865	162,785	123,416	148,756
State govt. contribution[a]	10,481	10,978	12,584	11,446	13,351	17,210	20,189	20,660	22,696	24,561
Local govt. contribution[a]	7,907	8,440	11,009	11,370	11,541	12,098	12,285	14,346	16,287	17,978
Insurance contribution[a]	47,364	50,489	61,008	63,679	63,952	67,042	68,075	79,642	90,257	101,702

Source: RFS (2009).

Note:

a Thousands of A$, adjusted by the Consumer Price Index (CPI).

TABLE 8.3 Victorian Country Fire Authority

Year	1999–2000	2000–2001	2001–2002	2002–2003	2003–2004	2004–2005	2005–2006	2006–2007	2007–2008	2008–2009
Brigades	1,229	1,228	1,228	1,240	1,213	1,193	1,213	1,209	1,211	1,211
Volunteers	64,340	61,657	57,985	59,136	58,583	58,662	58,849	59,509	58,362	58,943
Rural population	1,318,617	1,333,101	1,339,138	1,346,074	1,355,464	1,367,993	1,383,525	1,403,504	1,424,919	1,447,691
Professional staff	838	1,055	1,129	1,175	1,212	1,244	1,301	1,331	1,398	1,481
Expenditure[a]	97,522	107,370	109,370	100,788	129,437	134,773	153,025	185,693	173,723	240,840
State govt. contribution[a]	20,315	20,037	25,710	24,861	28,652	28,242	31,433	48,647	35,456	35,516
Insurance contribution[a]	72,134	70,523	91,581	92,313	102,564	106,673	110,125	118,283	129,849	143,941

Source: CFA (2009).

Note

a Thousands of A$, adjusted by the CPI.

TABLE 8.4 South Australian Country Fire Service

Year	2001–2002	2002–2003	2003–2004	2004–2005	2005–2006	2006–2007	2007–2008	2008–2009
Brigades	434	431	434	434	428	428	422	422
Volunteers	16,412	16,280	15,695	15,590	15,134	15,550	15,711	15,711
Rural population	406,137	409,536	413,236	418,001	422,076	426,663	431,426	436,124
Professional staff	71	NA	67	73	105	105	102	108
Expenditure[a]	29,464	31,162	33,087	35,880	35,302	35,293	36,386	36,217
State govt. contribution[a]	30,123	30,715	31,354	34,539	33,479	34,597	36,497	37,012

Source: CFS (2009).

Note

a   Thousands of A$, adjusted by the CPI.

three jurisdictions. Similarly, overall (real) expenditure has risen significantly, more than doubling in NSW and Victoria, with smaller rises in South Australia. The increase in NSW expenditure has been sourced from similar-magnitude increases in all three major sources of funds (State government, local government, and insurers), and the Victorian increase similarly has been spread across State government and insurers.

The data suggest a negative correlation between the number of volunteers per head of rural and regional population in each State and the number of professional staff employed. The results of simple regressions relating these two variables in their logarithmic transformation form support this relationship for Victoria and South Australia (SA), but not for New South Wales:[4]

$$\text{Victoria: } \ln(\text{volunteers}/\text{rural population}) = -2.81 - 0.0003 \ln(\text{staff})$$
$$R^2 = 0.69$$
$$(-39.11) \, (-0.298)$$

$$\text{NSW: } \ln(\text{volunteers}/\text{rural population}) = -3.56 - 0.00004 \ln(\text{staff})$$
$$R^2 = 0.16$$
$$(-170.9) \, (-1.24)$$

$$\text{SA: } \ln(\text{volunteers}/\text{rural population}) = -3.13 - 0.0018 \ln(\text{staff})$$
$$R^2 = 0.65$$
$$(-57.34) \, (-3.04)$$

In these equations, the constants are all significant at the 5 percent level, and the coefficient on the log of staff variable is significant at the 5 percent level for Victoria and SA. However, correlation does not necessarily imply causation. Increases in the number of professional staff may have induced a negative response in volunteering, or staff numbers may have been boosted because of falling volunteer numbers. These relationships deserve more complete exploration, but this will be possible only with more extensive data.

The extent of public-sector involvement is understated by these data. Not included are the expenditures by the Commonwealth government, particularly through the operation of the National Aerial Firefighting Centre (NAFC). In 2007–2008, total expenditures for NAFC amounted to A$1.5 billion, and the organization had assets valued at more than A$9 billion. Over that year, the 37 rotary-wing and fixed-wing aircraft that the national fleet comprises were activated on 502 occasions and made more than 7,000 drops of suppressant, amounting to about 12.5 million liters. The aircraft are stationed strategically across southern Australia.

Furthermore, the Commonwealth government has periodically injected funds into the firefighting activities of the State organizations, usually in response to major fire outbreaks. Though these funds are usually directed at recovery activities (for instance, the national partnership on the Victorian bushfire reconstruction and recovery plan has been endowed with A$31.1 million over two years), they are also used to supplement the State firefighting organizations' finances.

In overview, the current situation is as follows. Landowners in rural areas may hold firefighting equipment on farms. They may be (voluntary) members of a local rural fire brigade. That brigade will be equipped with capital items, ranging from tankers to overalls, that are largely financed from the State firefighting organization (RFS, CFA, CFS). Some local brigade finance (often generated by local fund-raising activities) will also be available to finance expenditure. Beyond fires with only limited localized impacts, the local brigade effort will generally be coordinated by a staff of professionals employed at the regional level. State-wide efforts are coordinated by professional staff at the organizations' headquarters. Major fires will involve resources (including volunteers) being drawn from the rest of the State and interstate. Landowners in Victoria and NSW who insure their properties pay premiums, a portion of which is returned to their State's firefighting organization. Separate from this are the firefighting operations of the government land management agencies, whose responsibilities are for fires that start on public lands.

The increasing relative prevalence of exogenously determined institutions governing firefighting reflects a society-wide trend in the provision of collective goods. Goldsmith et al. (2010) point to four stages of this trend. Private efforts prevail in the first stage. In the second, public-sector engagement emerges and begins to "crowd out" the voluntary effort.[5] A reemergence of the private sector through the State's deliberately fostering public-private partnerships embodies the third stage. The fourth stage involves a less prescriptive role for the private sector in delivering "disruptive transformative innovation." The current state of Australian firefighting provision would appear to be set in the second stage, with increasing public-sector involvement. Emergence of the third and fourth stages in other contexts has been driven by a combination of public-sector budgetary limitations and recognition of the merits of private-sector involvement—specifically, the lowering of transaction costs that can be achieved through using endogenous rather than exogenous institutions. Ironically, in order to take advantage of the opportunities afforded by private volunteer effort, government policy reform is required. The next section identifies a number of opportunities for public policy reform that provide for an expansion of the role of the voluntary component of the rural firefighting services.

Opportunities for Reform

A first step would involve the removal of the legislative requirement for insurers to fund fire services. In NSW and Victoria, the levying of a firefighting surcharge on rural property insurance has resulted in higher insurance premiums and hence lower levels of insurance demand.[6] Removal of the levy would reduce the cost of insurance, and a consequential increase in the demand for insurance could be expected. An increase in the proportion of the community covered by insurance would reduce the calls for public-sector disaster relief. Frequently in the post-fire media coverage, the public is exposed to cases where property damage has not been insured. The response to such press coverage is normally a call from the public for government-funded assistance to those adversely affected by the fire. The perverse consequence of this is even lower levels of insurance coverage, as people who were insured see themselves as having wasted the money spent on their insurance premiums when they were no better off than those who had not paid. If the public "safety net" were removed given an increased level of insurance coverage, there would be a further increase in the incentive to take out insurance.

The removal of the insurance levy may also encourage growth in the flexibility of insurance products offered. For example, premium discounts may be given where fire protection measures, including investments in firefighting equipment and fire preparation strategies, are in place. This in turn would provide incentives for individual property owners to lower the probability of fire damage exposure. (Chapter 3 of this volume outlines the strategy of the State Farm Insurance Company in the United States to require compliance to wildfire risk mitigation standards prior to policy renewal.) For such flexibility to become a feature of property insurance (just as car insurance and life insurance premiums are tailored to specific cases), actuarial information relating actions to the probability of damage and then monitoring information would be required. The costs of the collection of this information may be a significant barrier to the development of flexible insurance products. These transaction costs for insurers may be lowered with collaboration with local brigades that could act as information collection agents.

These insurance reforms would shift incentives toward greater self-reliance on the part of individual landowners. However, with any insurance product, there is also the risk of moral hazard. Insurance providers guard against this occurrence through the practice of coinsurance, whereby the insured party bears some of the risk of the insured event. For instance, insurance "excesses" mean that the insured party must pay some of the damage costs. No-claim bonuses also work to protect against moral hazard.

Without payments made through insurance policies, other arrangements would be required to secure funding for the collective elements of the firefighting services. One option would be to fund local brigades by a rural area council rates surcharge. This strategy would help avoid the free-riding problem in securing collective action by keeping the funding local and clearly linked. Payments from councils to brigades could also be designed on a dollar-for-dollar basis to encourage local fund-raising activities and further strengthen the anti-free-riding incentives of close community engagement. This would require that council payments not be made to the headquarters of the State fire service. Rather, the financial arrangements would be kept local to ensure the link (both perceived and real) between payment and provision. A danger of the South Australian system of funding, whereby an "emergency services levy" applies to a wide variety of State charges, is that the public perceives that it has paid for the provision of these services and as such does not see any further need to be involved through volunteering.

Beyond these local funding sources, State government contributions raised from general revenue sources should be used to fund the control and coordination functions of the State fire services. This would include the operational expenses of the State-wide and regional command centers. To ensure that all local brigades are able to work together, consistency in training would also be advisable. This suggests that the training for local brigade members should be carried out at a regional level using State-sourced funds.

A potential difficulty with a funding regime that is more focused on links with the local community is that brigades in areas with a low ratable land base will be less well resourced than those in more wealthy regions. Where the poorer areas are also more prone to fire because of their environmental characteristics and act as fire "source" areas, an argument can be made for state funding to be used to support the brigades here.

In terms of organizational reform possibilities, it is important for the State government to resist the temptation to increase its role in the production of fire control services. This includes the appointment of salaried staff at regional coordination centers. Such pivotal positions can have important "signaling" roles as to the importance of the volunteering effort relative to state provision. If volunteers hold these positions, not only does this result in State budgetary savings, but also the importance of volunteering and self-reliance is stressed throughout the community.

A further organizational point is to avoid the amalgamation of local brigades. Because of the importance of organizational structure in the process of avoiding the free-rider problem, brigades need to be relatively small in number of members with homogeneous characteristics. This maximizes peer group pressure against free riding.

A potential negative consequence of having many small brigades is the under-utilization of capital equipment. Alternatively, brigades may not be large enough to afford capital appropriate to the task of firefighting at the scale required. This calls for organizational reform that permits the better utilization of equipment by regional groupings of brigades. Pooling of individual brigade funds for larger-scale equipment purchases and the sharing of that equipment makes some economic sense. Optimal location of the equipment would need investigation for rapid response. But given that the scale of a fire normally builds only over time, this would not appear to be an insurmountable logistical exercise.

An example of the capital scale issue comes in the form of the aerial firefighting capacity. This is currently managed at the Commonwealth level to allow operational flexibility and capacity utilization. Duplication is thus avoided, and rapid deployment across large distances is comparatively straightforward.

The regulatory environment in which volunteer brigades operate is also worth noting as an area for potential reform. On top of training requirements for volunteers, operations are limited by occupational health and safety regulations. Clearly, bushfire fighting is a dangerous activity, and volunteers need to be aware of the risks they are taking and be equipped to make decisions that are appropriate to the circumstances. However, the imposition of regulations regarding behavior that is aimed at preventing "lowest common denominator" behavior is likely to be counterproductive. Anecdotally, an example of such regulatory "overkill" was the insistence on safety certification for food being prepared by volunteer brigade members for those fighting a blaze. Such measures reduce both the incentives for volunteering and the effectiveness of the volunteer effort.

Conclusions

Collective action in the control of bushfires can be justified with reference to the lack of well-defined and defended property rights when damage results from fires that have poorly defined origins and cross multiple land holdings. Exogenous institutions have become relatively more important in the coordination of bushfire fighting in such cases in southern Australia. This is despite a long history of voluntary activity through local bushfire brigades. The implication is higher transaction costs.[7] Elements of government policy can be identified as playing a role in the relative importance of exogenous institutions and of professional State-funded firefighting efforts. The use of insurance premiums as a source of funds and the growth of occupational health and safety regulations are primary suspects.

Reform options that will encourage the reemergence of private-sector, voluntary activity are available. The free-riding incentive, which is key in restricting voluntary effort, can be reduced by more closely linking the source of funds with the firefighting effort. Local council rates are an option that is likely to be superior to the insurance premium mechanism used in Victoria and NSW, particularly in light of the perverse incentives the insurance premium route gives in the insurance market. More direct funding provides incentives for creative innovation in both fund-raising and efficient provision of effort.

Ensuring that poorer but more fire-prone areas are adequately resourced to fight fires that may escape across areas would require some redistribution of funds sourced from centralized funding sources. Such centralized funds would also be required to ensure coordination across brigades.

Although it is clear that a mixture of endogenous and exogenous institutions is required to achieve an optimal balance between private- and public-sector activity, the danger of moving toward a situation of public-sector dominance is one of higher cost structures, less efficient delivery of services, and provision of services that satisfy political interests rather than social well-being. The "crowding out" of voluntary activity by state-provided services would thus be deleterious to society on a number of levels, including the destruction of social capital within small rural communities.

Notes

1. A$1.00 = US$1.09 as of May 3, 2011.
2. The significance of the volunteer firefighter in the Australian context is in marked contrast to the approach taken to wildfire suppression in the United States. Chapter 4 describes the U.S. approach as a "centralized, military-style hierarchy of highly specialized crews, managers, and equipment operators" that evolved from an original structure composed of volunteers and conscripts, including prisoners.

3. With property rights defined and defended, there would appear to be no efficiency failure inherent in the decentralized market-based resource allocation process in such cases of "natural disaster." The equity implications are another matter and are considered later in this chapter.
4. Other independent variables relating to the occurrence of major fires either within the State or across the nation, lagged for up to two years, proved to be insignificant in explaining the number of volunteers per head of rural population.
5. The history of the Rural Fire Service in NSW is illustrative. Before 1900, individuals fought fires on a fragmented basis, and it was not until the widespread and serious fires of 1896 that local volunteer brigades began to form. Government became involved in 1906 when the Local Government Act authorized local councils to form brigades. The proliferation of brigades and statutory authorities was "rationalized" in 1970 under amendments to the Bush Fires Act that saw the formation of the Bush Fire Committee. It was only in 1997 that the RFS was formed under the Rural Fires Act after a coronial enquiry into the severe fires of 1993–1994.
6. A recommendation of the 2009 Victorian Bushfires Royal Commission was the removal of insurance funding of the CFA. This recommendation has now been accepted by the Victorian government.
7. The move from volunteer-based to professional wildfire fighting in the United States can be seen as a progression from the situation currently observed in Australia. As suggested in Chapter 4, this came about largely because of "blank check budgeting," which allowed for the payment of professionals but has resulted in considerable inefficiencies, including those brought about by some perverse incentives that see firefighters wanting fires to burn longer. Chapter 5 also points to the emergence of private firefighting businesses as a reaction to these inefficiencies.

References

AEMI (Australian Emergency Management Institute). 2009. *Australian Emergency Management Arrangement.* Canberra: Attorney General's Department.

Cary, G., D. Lindenmayer, and S. Dovers. 2003. *Australia Burning: Fire Ecology, Policy and Management Issues.* Melbourne: CSIRO Publishing.

CFA (Victorian Country Fire Authority). 2009. Annual Report 2008/2009. www.cfa.vic.gov.au/publications/aboutcfa.htm (accessed September 7, 2010).

CFS (South Australian Country Fire Service). 2009. 2008/2009 Annual Report. www.cfs.sa.gov.au/site/about_us/publications/annual_reports.jsp (accessed September 2, 2010).

DSE (Victoria Department of Sustainability and Environment). 2009. Bushfire History: Major Bushfires in Victoria. www.dpi.vic.gov.au/dse/nrenfoe.nsf/childdocs/-D79E4FB0C437E1B6CA256DA60008B9EF?open (accessed April 28, 2011).

Eburn, M. 2010a. *Emergency Law: Rights, Liabilities and Duties of Emergency Workers and Volunteers.* 3rd ed. Sydney: Federation Press.

——. 2010b. Personal communication with the author, August 27.

Goldsmith, S., G. Georges, and T. Burke. 2010. *The Power of Social Innovation: How Civic Entrepreneurs Ignite Community Networks for Good.* San Francisco: Jossey-Bass.

Libecap, G. 1989. *Contracting for Property Rights.* New York: Cambridge University Press.

Ostrom, E. 1990. *Governing the Commons: The Evolution of Institutions for Collective Action.* New York: Cambridge University Press.

RFS (New South Wales Rural Fire Service). 2009. Annual Report 2008/2009. www.rfs.nsw.gov.au/file_system/attachments/State08/Attachment_20091223_B96345FF.pdf (accessed September 7, 2010).

RFS (New South Wales Rural Fire Service). 2011. Brief History of Bush Fires in NSW. www.rfs.nsw.gov.au/dsp_content.cfm?cat_id=1180 (accessed April 28, 2011).

VBRC (2009 Victorian Bushfires Royal Commission). 2010. 2009 Victorian Bushfires Royal Commission Final Report. www.royalcommission.vic.gov.au/Commission-Reports/Final-Report (accessed August 1, 2010).

9

FIRE SUPPRESSION POLICY, WEATHER, AND WESTERN WILDLAND FIRE TRENDS

An Empirical Analysis

Jason Scott Johnston and Jonathan Klick

Over the period 1970–2003, the United States witnessed an increase in wildfire activity, as shown in Figure 9.1. The increase in large wildfires (we define large, for reasons explained below, as those exceeding 400 hectares in extent) was particularly striking, especially in the western part of the country.

During several of these years, wildfires were catastrophic, in terms of the sheer acreage destroyed, as with the Yellowstone fires of 1988; lives lost, as in 1994, when 34 firefighters died; or extensive property damage, as with the Cerro Grande Fire in 2000, a prescribed (intentionally set) fire in New Mexico that burned out of control and destroyed part of the Los Alamos National Laboratory. After yet another catastrophic fire season in the summer of 2002—with 21 firefighter deaths, over 7 million acres burned, and 3,000 structures destroyed (Hakanson 2006)— the president and Congress reacted in 2003 with the Healthy Forests Initiative (HFI) and Healthy Forests Restoration Act (HFRA), respectively. Both of these 2003 policy responses reflected a view stated in the 2001 Interagency Fire Plan that a decades-long policy of fire suppression by the Forest Service in particular had led to major ecological changes in many forest types, with a buildup of diseased and dying trees and forest floor litter that set the stage for major forest fires during periods of drought (see Glickman and Babbitt 2000).

Fire ecologists generally agree that decades of aggressive fire suppression policy could well have set the stage for more wildfires, but only in forest regimes that under natural conditions would have been subject to relatively frequent low-intensity fires, such as the open ponderosa pine forests found in the lower elevations of the Southern Rockies (see Turner et al. 2003). They have been skeptical, however, that even decades of aggressive fire suppression could have made much difference in forest regimes that under natural conditions were subject to very infrequent, albeit severe fires, such as the high-elevation ponderosa pine and spruce fir forests

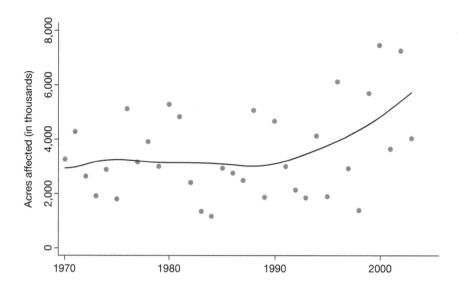

FIGURE 9.1 U.S. wildland fires, 1970–2003

Note: Fitted values generated by locally weighted regression technique.

Source: NIFC (2011).

found in the Northern Rockies (Stephens 2005; Turner et al. 2003). In such stand-replacing fire regimes, fire ecologists believe that it is climate, and not policy, that is the major determinant of whether large wildfires occur in a given summer.

A number of recent studies have provided empirical support for the hypothesis that summer weather—more specifically, severe regional drought—is a major determinate of fire season severity. A consistent finding, appearing in both studies of 20th-century wildfire trends and also longer-term studies, is that drought and wildfire are statistically correlated (Trouet et al. 2010; Westerling and Swetnam 2003). In stand-replacing fire regimes such as characterize the Northern Rockies, recent work has found a statistically significant correlation between the number of fires and periods of drought (Schoennagel et al. 2004, 2007), and an apparently robust positive statistical association between the area burned by wildfires and dry and warm conditions in the fire season and preceding seasons (Littell et al. 2009).[1]

None of this empirical literature attempts to control for changes in forest management policy or in other variables, such as changes in land use, which might be expected to influence the number of large wildfires. Fire suppression policy in fact underwent a virtual sea change early in the period 1970–2003—precisely the study period of so much research on climate and wildfire trends. During this period (beginning even earlier, in the 1960s, in some national parks), fire suppression policy moved from immediate suppression of fires toward what is now known as "wildland fire use" (and, on a more limited basis, prescribed fire). Wildland fire use means "managing lightning-caused fires as they burn naturally instead of putting them out," whereas prescribed fire is defined as a "manager ignited fire" (Wells 2009, 2).

To be sure, a radical change in fire suppression policy was not the only important change that occurred during the period 1970–2003 that might have been expected to contribute to the increase in large wildfires over the period. As discussed in Chapter 5, beginning around 1990, the Forest Service cut back greatly on timber harvest from national forests, managing national forests in a way that private forest managers at least perceived as greatly increasing the risk of catastrophic wildfire. In addition, housing density near many western national forests and parks dramatically increased during this period, and housing density is known to correlate positively with the number of fire ignitions. Gan (2006), the only study of which we are aware that actually attempts to statistically test for multiple causality in western wildfire time series, indeed finds that wildfire trends may be more sensitive to urban population density trends than to climate or timber harvest.

Below we provide extensive qualitative detail on the series of changes in Forest and Park Service wildland fire suppression policy that occurred over the period 1970–2003, and we also describe the vast expansion of settled areas near national forests and parks. We then take a closer statistical look at observable measures of potentially important policy change, the change in initial suppression policy as coded by on-the-ground Park and Forest Service personnel.

We do not attempt here to present a statistical analysis of all the factors—including inter alia development density and fire fuel loads—that might be expected to have contributed to the recent trend of an increasing number of large wildfires. Rather than attempt such a complete statistical analysis of all the variables that might be expected to have contributed to the recent multi-decadal increase in western wildfires, we instead focus our analysis on simple specifications that add measures of policy change to climate measures. The importance of our results is not in providing a full explanation for recent western wildfire trends, but rather in cautioning against drawing policy implications from the observed correlation between climate and wildfire trends. Our results indicate the value of letting the statistical analysis reveal potential causal relationships and their significance, rather than simply rejecting some potential causal variables on a priori grounds.

Additionally, our results show that in estimating the impact of climate variables on fire frequency and sizes, omitted variables bias must be taken into account. Specifically, omitted variables bias arises when the researcher fails to control for variables that affect the outcome (in this case, fire metrics) and are correlated with the explanatory variables of interest (climate metrics). Effectively, the estimated correlations represent both the true relationship and part of the effect of the omitted variable (see, e.g., Hamilton 1994; Wooldridge 2002). In the presence of such biases, it is not possible to confidently assess either the underlying direction of any relationship between fire outcomes and climate variables or the statistical significance of the estimated relationships. Even if the researcher has sufficient ancillary reasons and evidence to believe the direction of the estimated effect and its statistical significance, biased parameter estimates will make the estimates unsuitable for policy purposes. For example, though the estimated effect may suggest that a particular policy intervention is cost justified, if the true relationship were known, it could be the case that a benefit-cost analysis would lead to the opposite conclusion.

Nonclimatic Factors Influencing the Number of Large Wildland Fires

In this section, we describe qualitatively a number of changes that occurred in the western United States over the period 1970–2003, all of which could plausibly have contributed to an increase in the number of large wildland fires over this period. We focus on two such changes: in public wildland fire management policies and in land development in what is known as the wildland-urban interface, settled areas adjacent or close to wildlands. In the next section, we explain the consequences of omitting one potentially important explanatory variable—fire suppression policy change—from statistical analyses of wildland fire time trends.

Changes in Forest Service and National Park Service Wildland Fire Management Policies

In response to widespread fires after severe droughts during the 1930s, the USDA Forest Service (USFS) in 1934 adopted the "10 a.m. policy" (Pyne et al 1996). Under this policy, the USFS aimed to get wildland fires under control by 10 o'clock the morning following report of a fire, or if unsuccessful, by the next day, and so on ad infinitum. Under the 10 a.m. policy, the USFS attempted to put out all reported fires, even those in remote wilderness areas or low-value backcountry.

By the 1960s, this policy of immediate fire suppression had come under criticism. The creation of the National Wilderness System in 1964 heralded a new philosophy of natural fire use (Stephens and Ruth 2005). It was recognized that fires were part of the native ecology and that to preserve or restore ecosystems, natural, lightning-set fires had to be tolerated and "surrogate, prescribed fires" sometimes deliberately set (Pyne et al. 1996). According to some observers, the managers in the Selway-Bitterroot and Gila Wilderness Areas had begun to implement a program of prescribed natural fires as early as the late 1960s; others record the prescribed burn policies in these wilderness areas as beginning a bit later —in 1971 in the Big Sage Management Unit of the Modoc National Forest (Husari and McKelvey 1996), in 1972 in the White Cap Fire Management Area in the Selway-Bitterroot, and by 1975 in the Gila Wilderness (van Wagtendonk 2007). During this early period in the movement to natural fire use, the USFS operated under a planning objective of confining 90 percent of all such prescribed natural fires to 10 acres or less (Husari and McKelvey 1996). Yet as early as 1973, the Fritz Creek Fire, a prescribed natural fire, escaped the bounds of its management area and burned over 1,600 acres in the Whitecap Management Area of the Bitterroot National Forest (plus another 1,600 outside the remote Whitecap Creek drainage) (van Wagtendonk 2007; Wells 2009). By 1978, the USFS officially replaced the 10 a.m. rule with a trio of wildland fire suppression strategies: *control*, old-fashioned aggressive firefighting that continued until the fire was out; *confine*, limiting the fire within natural or preconstructed barriers, with little or no suppression effort; or *contain*, an intermediate strategy of keeping the fire within a control line (Husari and McKelvey 1996). Under the new policy, the strategy mix was to be chosen to accomplish a cost-effective approach to fires that escaped initial attack. In that very same year, a prescribed natural fire in the Gila Wilderness Area in New Mexico burned 1,295 hectares (van Wagtendonk 2007).

A similar transition occurred during the late 1960s and 1970s in the National Park Service (NPS). In 1968, the NPS edited the "Greenbook" and recognized fire as an ecological process (Rothman 2007).[2] Sequoia–Kings Canyon National Park immediately changed its policy by establishing a natural fire management zone (for areas above 3,000 meters) within the park and beginning to allow experimental prescribed fires (two during the initial year). By 1971, 52 fires had been allowed to burn in Sequoia–Kings Canyon, with the largest burning 183 hectares (van Wagtendonk 2007). Other national parks soon followed: in 1972, both Yellowstone and Yosemite began prescribed natural fire programs, with the natural fire zones in both parks gradually enlarged by 1975 to include elevations down to 1,220 meters in Yosemite and the entire park other than developed areas in Yellowstone (Rothman 2007; van Wagtendonk 2007). By 1974, all major national parks had prescribed fire programs, and lightning-caused fires could be allowed to burn within more than 3 million acres of designated natural fire zones within national parks (Kilgore 2007; Rothman 2007). That same year, the first prescribed fire in Yosemite, the Starr King Fire, burned over 1,500 hectares (van Wagtendonk 2007).

By 1978, both the USFS and the NPS had officially adopted prescribed natural fire policies. The NPS was first, in 1977 implementing NPS-18, which superseded all existing fire management policies for national parks by delineating guidelines for prescribed fire uses and distinguishing between prescribed fires that were to be suppressed and those that were to be allowed to burn (Rothman 2007). In 1978, the Forest Service officially scrapped the 10 a.m. policy, along with the related 1971 management objective that had set 10 acres as the wildfire containment goal, replacing it with a new policy favoring prescribed natural fire (Husari and McKelvey 1996; Pyne et al. 1996). That same year, a prescribed natural fire, the Lagstroth Fire, burned 1,295 hectares in the Gila Wilderness in New Mexico, and the Ouzel Lake Fire in Rocky Mountain National Park was allowed to burn for over a month in a high-altitude, low-risk zone of the park before it spread and burned over 1,000 acres, threatening the mountain town of Allenspark (Perry 2008; van Wagtendonk 2007).

During the 1980s, fire management planning, as it came to be called, moved to the forefront in both the national parks and national forests. In 1983, federal agencies were allowed to use "confine, contain, and control" as strategies during initial attack firefighting (Husari and McKelvey 1996). The number of national parks with prescribed natural fire policies steadily increased, reaching a total of 26 park units by 1988 (Kilgore 2007).

Just when the prescribed natural fire policy had become well established, it encountered the extremely hot and dry summer of 1988, when a series of large fires in Yellowstone burned out of control, including nine major fires that destroyed almost 1.4 million acres of parkland. Fifty fires started within the park, six were ignited outside the park, and four were human-caused (Wells 2009). Of the fires that started inside the park, 28 were allowed to burn naturally, but in what has since been generally perceived as a political decision, after July 21 all the 1988 Yellowstone fires were actively suppressed (Sanders 2000). That same summer, the Canyon Creek Fire escaped the Bob Marshall Wilderness in the Lewis and Clark National Forest, eventually burning over 100,000 hectares and threatening the town of Augusta, Montana (van Wagtendonk 2007).

After the Yellowstone and Canyon Creek Fires of 1988, the Secretaries of Agriculture and Interior temporarily suspended all prescribed natural fire programs in parks and wilderness areas until new plans could be prepared. By 1990, however, Yosemite, Sequoia, and Kings Canyon National Parks restarted their prescribed natural fire programs, with 20 such fires burning in Yosemite's prescribed natural fire zone that year, and in 1994, the Howling Fire in Glacier National Park was allowed to burn over 906 hectares despite public outcry and calls for suppression (van Wagtendonk 2007). In 1995, the Joint Federal Wildland Fire Management Policy and Program Review was released. Interestingly, prior to the mid-1990s, no Forest Service wilderness area in California had adopted a prescribed natural fire program, and even by 1996, wilderness areas with such programs were rare in the state (Stephens and Ruth 2005).

Thus the period 1970–2000 was a time of major change in federal wildland fire policy, with the beginning of this period corresponding almost perfectly to the onset of a move to allow at least some natural fires to burn. By the period 1983–2000, the general, system-wide official federal wildland fire policy had changed to allow the least aggressive policy of natural confinement even as an initial attack strategy. As described by the ecologist in charge of the Forest Service wildland fire use program in 2009, the goal of the wildland fire use policy was not simply to "let fires burn," but instead called for "actively managing fires—protecting values at risk while achieving resource benefits in those places where fire has a positive effect" (Wells 2009, 2). Still, it is inevitable that some managed wildland fires will escape the predesignated areas in which they are supposed to be confined. As one Forest Service manager put it, "It's chainsaw surgery. I can't draw a line and promise the fire will stay on this side. I'm dependent on weather: wind, tempera-ture, humidity . . . it's not scalpel surgery" (Wells 2009, 5). Many of the largest and most damaging fires that occurred in western national forests and parks during the 1970–2000 period—from the Fitz Creek Fire in Montana and the Ouzel Lake Fire in Colorado in the 1970s to several of the Yellowstone fires of 1988 and on to the Cerro Grande and Grand Canyon Fires of the last decade—were allowed to burn or were deliberately set under the new policy of natural wildland fire. Moreover, as discussed above, the change in wildland fire suppression policy implemented by the Forest and Park Services during the 1970s and 1980s was directed to higher-elevation fires—since lower-elevation fires almost invariably risk danger to settled areas if not immediately controlled. It seems at least plausible that a policy change intended to confine rather than immediately put out higher-elevation fires in remote areas of national parks and forests could have contributed to some extent to the observed increase in large higher-elevation fires occurring over the period during which such policy was implemented.

The existing literature recognizes that differences and changes in forest fire suppression policy can strongly influence the number of large fires and acres burned by fires. Stephens (2005), for example, observes that over the period 1940–2000, the relative number of fire ignitions in national forests in California significantly increased, but without any significant increase in the relative area burned. Stephens infers from this that "California's initial attack system has been effective in preventing the burned area from increasing; no other area in the USA had significant increases in ignitions without a corresponding increase in relative area burned" (2005, 218). Thus both anecdotal and more systematic evidence strongly suggests that policy changes, including the 1983 decision to allow federal agencies to adopt the least aggressive "confine" strategy as an initial control strategy, might well have contributed to an increase in the number of large fires over the study period 1970–2000.

Ignition Factors: The 1980s–1990s Expansion in the Wildland-Urban Interface

Federal firefighting policy is not the only important determinant of time trends in the frequency and severity of western U.S. forest fires on the federal lands. Another important factor identified in the literature is the tremendous growth in the so-called wildland-urban interface (WUI) that occurred in recent decades in the western United States. While there is no single standardized definition, the WUI is the area where "houses and wildlands meet or overlap" (Stewart et al. 2007, 202). From 1940 to 2000, there was a large expansion in the amount of housing located in and near forests (Radeloff et al. 2005), with a nationwide increase of 52 percent in the WUI from 1970 to 2000 (Theobold and Romme 2007). Higher housing density is known to contribute significantly to higher rates of human-caused wildfire ignitions (Cardille et al. 2001; Sapsis 1999). By one estimate, fire ignition rates increase by 0.17 fires per square mile per year with the addition of every 100 housing units (Spero 1997).

If these numbers on ignition rates and housing density are even roughly accurate, then they suggest that expansion in the WUI could explain some of the increase in large western wildland fires over the period 1970–2000. The reason, according to Theobold and Romme (2007), is that the states that had the greatest proportionate expansion in the WUI were mostly in the west, with approximately

90 percent of western WUI being found in high-severity forest fire regimes—those that are prone to large and catastrophic fires. In southern California alone, more than 6 million people live in the WUI, with over 800,000 living in the highest wildfire hazard zones (Xu and Wu 2009). California, Oregon, and Washington all experienced rapid housing growth in the WUI in the 1990s; during that decade, 61 percent of all new housing units built in these three states were located in the WUI, and the size of the WUI in these states increased by 11 percent (Hammer et al. 2007). By 2000, homes had been built on 14 percent of the forested wildland interface in the west, with some of the largest areas of WUI found in northwest Montana and northern Idaho (Gude et al. 2008). Lands within national forests (so-called inholdings) and near wilderness areas are especially prized for development: housing near 50 kilometers of wilderness areas grew at rates exceeding 400 percent over the 1940–2000 period over much of the west, and housing growth within national forests consistently exceeded the national average since 1970 (Radeloff et al. 2010).

Although the analysis of how changes in the WUI has influenced fire risk is still in its infancy, researchers in the lead of this effort have recently concluded that "current housing growth patterns are exacerbating wildland fire problems in the WUI" (Hammer et al. 2007, 263). There are, it seems, strong regional differences in how WUI expansion has impacted forest fires: there is a very strong positive correlation between population density and fire frequency in southern California, but no relationship between housing count and fire in, for example, northern Florida (Syphard et al. 2007). Still, any time-series analysis of trends in western wildfires that fails to attempt to control in some way for the rapid expansion in the WUI over the past several decades will be missing one of the pieces of the wildland fire trend puzzle: a monotonic increase in ignition sources over this period.

Climate, Policy Change, and Western Wildfire Trends: The Omitted Variables Bias Problem

As lucidly explained in Chapter 10 of this book, a number of problems confront a researcher attempting to statistically identify the various factors that may be causally related to recent wildfire trends. First, as a matter of model specification, it is not enough to consider only changes in public policy, for one has to properly account for how various policies affect the incentives of private landowners to manage their lands in a way that reduces fire risk and then take steps to suppress fires that do occur (see Chapter 3). Second, when one takes account of both private and public incentives, causal relationships may be much more complex than they would appear at first. Consider, for example, the relationship between federal fire suppression expenditures and the number of large wildfires. Over recent decades, as the number of large wildfires has been increasing, so too have been the fire suppression expenditures of the USDA Forest Service, the major federal fire agency (see Chapter 4). As an a priori matter, it may seem obvious that an increase in total acres burned by wildfires has caused an increase in federal fire suppression expenditures. But upon closer and more nuanced analysis, one sees that the causal relationship could run in the other direction—that an increase in the amount spent on fire suppression could have contributed to the increase in large wildfires. This is because as a matter of economic incentives, federal fire suppression acts to subsidize development of private lands in fire-prone areas. Kousky and Olmstead (2010) show that the move back to active fire suppression in the aftermath of the 1988 Yellowstone fires had a statistically significant impact in stimulating development of nearby private lands. Inasmuch as development of the wildland-urban interface is known to positively relate to the ignition rate, the possibility that active fire suppression could actually contribute to the increase in large wildfires is perhaps not so implausible as a priori reasoning might suggest.

The lesson from this recent work is that climate, policy, and land development incentives interact in complex ways to explain recent wildfire trends. A large fraction and the most highly publicized of the recent work by fire ecologists and climate researchers, however, singles out climate change as the potential cause of recent increases in the number of large wildfires. For example, Westerling et al. (2006) find that temperature and a melt variable (i.e., an indicator for whether the spring snowmelt occurred early in a given year) are statistically significant positive predictors of fire frequency and the duration of the fire season, with the relationship between climate and large-fire frequency found to be particularly pronounced at mid-elevation (2,130 meters) in the Northern Rocky Mountain Region. Without attempting to statistically control for either land use or policy changes during their study period, Westerling and colleagues assert that "increased wildfire activity over recent decades reflects sub-regional responses to changes in climate" and argue that the warmer springs and summers predicted for western forests by some climate models "will accentuate conditions favorable to the occurrence of large wildfires, amplifying the vulnerability the region has experienced since the mid-1980's" (2006, 942, 943).

Such an approach exhibits a fundamental problem with respect to statistical identification. By relying merely on time series variation, the researchers have no contemporaneous counterfactual. That is, in such analysis, all regions are exposed to the same temperature and melt measures. Implicitly, this kind of analysis relies on the hope that what happened in previous years is a good guide to what will happen in future years. However, such an assumption is often incorrect, given that many factors other than temperature influence forest fires and change over time. A failure to control for such factors will lead to a statistical bias if those factors are correlated with the temperature trend. This omitted variables bias can affect the magnitude and even the sign of an estimated relationship. Worse yet, the extent and the sign of the bias are generally not discernible, since they depend on the conditional correlation between the omitted variables and the temperature variable, as well as the conditional correlation between the omitted variables and the outcome (i.e., fire) variable.

An Illustration

For purposes of illustration, one plausible omitted variable bias story suggests that there could be either upward or downward bias in the relationship between fire outcomes and climate metrics. Assume that the volume of visitors to U.S. forests is positively related to temperature, since people like to hike when it is warm. Further, assume that hikers have a tendency to start fires. (For our purposes, it does not matter whether this tendency is the result of carelessness or intentional acts.) In this case, failure to account for the changing visitation patterns would lead to an upward bias in the relationship between temperature and fires. It is simple to come up with an example with an opposite bias by simply changing the assumption that hikers are encouraged by warmer weather to one where hikers prefer cooler weather. In that case, the relationship between temperature and fires would be biased downward. The omitted variable bias could be even more complicated. Perhaps hikers do not like weather that is too hot or too cold, in which case the effect of the bias is nonlinear, with the resulting bias being positive or negative depending on the domain of the temperature data in the sample. In some cases, the bias could average to zero by complete chance.

Even more complicated bias stories can be imagined. For example, perhaps lagged temperatures and expected future temperatures affect the price of timber. Current and expected prices of timber will affect cut practices, which will affect the potential fuel load available for fires, leading to fewer big fires when a larger area has been timbered. Because past, present, and future temperatures are correlated, these influences lead collectively to a bias.

Unfortunately, pure time series data do not generally provide much confidence in causal inferences. Even if a researcher were to include data on use by hikers in the analysis, dozens of other sources of bias may be lurking in the background. Further, as suggested by the timber price example, some of the relevant omitted variables may be inherently difficult to quantify, such as people's expectations about future temperatures and the effect of those expectations on timber prices. Other omitted variables, such as a metric capturing fuel load, are very likely to be measured with error, leading to attenuation bias with respect to the relationship between fires and fuel load, which will then generate bias in the other estimated relationships as well.[3]

The Impact of Considering Variables Omitted
from the Fire-Climate Model

In our view, it is likely that the factors considered earlier—a virtual revolution in federal fire management policy that allowed many natural fires to burn while being monitored and a dramatic increase in housing density near national forests and parks—contributed to the increase in large wildfires that occurred in the western national parks and forests over the period 1970–2000. We view it as also almost obviously true that summertime weather contributed, in that the western summers with a large number of big wildland fires in areas such as the Northern Rockies (stand-replacing fire regimes) were also anomalously hot and drought-prone. The point of statistical analysis is to try to get some more precise sense of the relative importance of the potential contributing factors. In this section, we provide some initial evidence that because of omitted variables bias, the importance of climate may be overstated in analyses such as that done by Westerling et al. (2006).

The Basic Relationship between Large-Fire Frequency and Summertime Weather

In order to draw comparisons with previous results in the literature, we focus on data from what Westerling et al. (2006) call the "Northern Rockies" region,[4] which is where they find the greatest weather-related increase in large wildfires. Again to provide some point of comparison with previous results in the literature, we define "large" wildfires as those exceeding 400 hectares in scope.

As do Westerling and colleagues, we find that the basic relationship between the number of large fires and mean summertime temperature is well specified using a second-degree polynomial of the temperature variable. This is confirmed in Figure 9.2, which uses the lowess regression technique (a variant of locally weighted regression) to allow for a nonlinear relationship between temperature and the fire frequency variable.[5] For simplicity of comparisons, we will instead use the natural log of the number of fires as our outcome variable, since, as is also shown in Figure 9.2, the relationship between this transformed measure and temperature is linear, except for the single outlier for which the mean temperature is 55 degrees Fahrenheit.

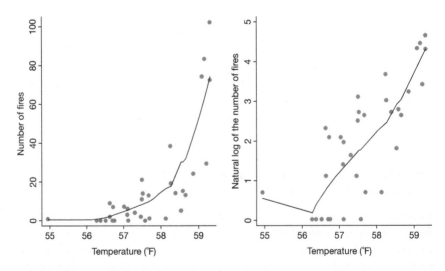

FIGURE 9.2 The relationship between fire frequency and mean temperature

Note: Fitted values generated by locally weighted regression technique.

TABLE 9.1 Relationship between ln(number of fires) and
temperature

	(i)	*(ii)*
Temperature	1.05***	
	(0.17)	—
Early melt	—	1.15**
		(0.49)

Source: Westerling et al. (2006).

Notes

Heteroskedasticity robust standard errors are in parentheses. Each regression
includes an unreported constant term.

*** p < 0.01 (against a two-sided test of a zero effect)
** p < 0.05 (against a two-sided test of a zero effect)
* p < 0.10 (against a two-sided test of a zero effect)

For purposes of a baseline comparison, we present the results of an ordinary
least squares regression of ln(number of fires) and temperature in column (i) of
Table 9.1. Column (ii) presents the relationship using the early melt indicator.

These results indicate a strong positive relationship between the summertime
weather metric and fire frequency. However, as suggested before, it is difficult to
rule out the possibility that part or all of this relationship is the result of an omitted
variables bias.

Fire Suppression Policy Change

Although, as mentioned above, a number of factors might have been expected to
contribute to the increase in large western wildfires over the 1970–2000 period,
one specific factor that seems a priori likely to have had a causal impact is changing
federal policy toward fire suppression. As discussed above, federal fire suppression
policy started to undergo some major changes at the very outset of the 1970–2000
study period, and by the mid to late 1970s, more and more natural wildland fires
were being allowed to burn in western national parks and forests. By 1983, federal
agencies were officially allowed to use the least aggressive "confine" strategy—
under which natural fires were allowed to burn within predetermined boundaries—
even as an initial attack firefighting strategy.

The data we rely upon for measures of fire suppression policy change clearly
depict these changes in policy. Our data come from the Forest Service's Kansas
City Fire Access SofTware (KCFAST) database (formerly National Interagency Fire
Management Integrated Database, or NIFMID) (see USFS 2011). This database
contains extensive data on fires for each national forest and every national park
with a fire management plan. For national parks, over the period 1972–2009, this
dataset allows us to identify fires that were coded as "wildland fires ignited by

lightning . . . or other natural ignition sources and managed as wildland fire use for resource benefit."[6] As the literature suggests that the wildland fire use policy has been implemented more cautiously in California national parks and wilderness areas, we compared changes over time in the fraction of fires managed for wildland fire use in major California national parks with those in the Northern Rockies region: Yellowstone, Grand Teton, and Glacier. As can be seen in Figure 9.3, the

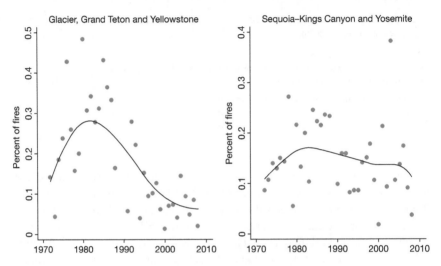

FIGURE 9.3 Fire suppression strategy in national parks: managed as wildland use fire

Note: Fitted values generated by locally weighted regression technique.

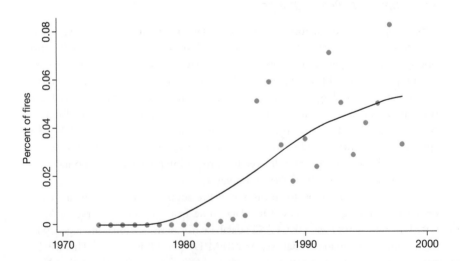

FIGURE 9.4 Use of confine strategy in national forests in the Northern Rockies region

Note: Fitted values generated by locally weighted regression technique.

fraction of fires managed for wildland fire use dramatically increased during the 1970s and 1980s in the Northern Rockies and then rapidly declined, whereas in California national parks, although there was an increase during the 1970s, wildland fire use remained an uncommon approach and eventually began a slow but continuing decline.

In the national forests, for the period 1983–1999, our dataset gives us a coding for the initial suppression strategy of confine, contain, or control, and during this period, official policy allowed forest managers to choose among these as an initial suppression strategy.[7] This possibility appears to be borne out in Figure 9.3, which shows the fraction of time that the least aggressive wildland fire use strategy of "confine" was used in the Northern Rockies region. As we can see from Figure 9.4, the use of the confine strategy increased substantially as of the mid-1980s in national forests in the Northern Rockies region.

Impacts of Fire Suppression Policy Change on the Number of Large Fires and Estimated Weather Effects

When we look solely at the time series of the number of large fires in the Northern Rockies, depicted by Figure 9.5, it does seem that the number of large fires began to increase most rapidly in the late 1970s, just as Forest and Park Service policy had strongly moved toward wildland fire use. Panel (b) in Figure 9.5 shows that this change in the rate of increase holds even when we partial out the summertime temperature effect. This suggests that the mid to late 1970s—the period when more and more national forests and parks were moving to a policy of allowing prescribed

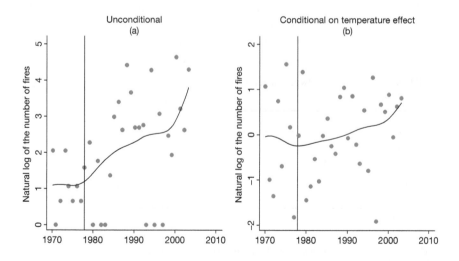

FIGURE 9.5 Effect of change in suppression strategy on fire frequency in the Northern Rockies region

Note: Fitted values generated by locally weighted regression technique.

natural fires—does mark a turning point in large-fire frequency. Even more significantly, it suggests that an important influence has not been accounted for in the statistical analysis of the relationship between fires and summertime weather.

To examine more closely the influence of fire suppression strategy on fires and the extent to which controlling for differential strategies affects the estimated relationship between temperature and fires, we looked at KCFAST data for the Northern Rockies national forests for the period 1983–1999. As noted above, during this period, national forest fire supervisors generated an informative report of initial suppression strategy (confine, contain, or control), and official policy allowed them to choose among these as an initial suppression strategy. We then collapsed the individual fire data into year X national forest region unit (national forest) cells, noting how many fires occurred in each cell, as well as the total number of acres involved. We also created a metric for the share of fires for which the service used aggressive suppression tactics.

We do not make claims of causality in the analysis that follows. It is almost surely the case that the estimated strategy effect suffers from a reverse causality problem (a form of omitted variables bias itself) in that the service is likely to use more intensive measures for larger fires. We merely present the analysis to illustrate how volatile estimated effects are when no strong statistical identification strategy is available.

For baseline comparison purposes, Table 9.2 examines the relationship between the climate metrics and the natural log of the number of acres involved in fire during the season. We use Huber–White standard errors to account for heteroskedasticity in the error term.

Using this dataset, we again find the basic result in the literature (as in Westerling et al. 2006) that the total acreage destroyed by fires is positively associated with the climate metrics, with both higher temperatures and an early snowmelt leading to more fires. The results are statistically significant.

TABLE 9.2 Relationship between ln(acres involved) and temperature

	(i)	(ii)
Temperature	0.62*** (0.05)	—
Early melt	—	1.44*** (0.12)

Source: USFS (2011).

Notes

Each regression includes an unreported constant term. Heteroskedasticity robust standard errors are in parentheses.

*** $p < 0.01$ (against a two-sided test of a zero effect)
** $p < 0.05$ (against a two-sided test of a zero effect)
* $p < 0.10$ (against a two-sided test of a zero effect)

If we allow the forest units to have differential baseline fire rates through the use of a so-called fixed effects model, as well as a unit specific trend, things change little, as seen in Table 9.3.

However, when we add the suppression strategy metric—the percentage of fires fought most aggressively (the "control" strategy)—we observe more of a change, as seen in Table 9.4.

Although the statistically significant positive result for summertime weather variables still shows up, the point estimate has moved substantially. If we compare the weather coefficients between Tables 9.3 and 9.4, we can reject the hypothesis that the two column (i) temperature coefficients are equal at better than the 1 percent

TABLE 9.3 Relationship between ln(acres involved) and temperature, including fixed effects

	(i)	(ii)
Temperature	0.61*** (0.04)	—
Early melt	—	1.39*** (0.10)

Source: USFS (2011).

Notes

Each regression includes a separate unreported constant term and linear trend for each forest unit. Heteroskedasticity robust standard errors are in parentheses.

*** $p < 0.01$ (against a two-sided test of a zero effect)
** $p < 0.05$ (against a two-sided test of a zero effect)
* $p < 0.10$ (against a two-sided test of a zero effect)

TABLE 9.4 Relationship between ln(acres involved) and temperature, conditional on fire suppression strategy

	(i)	(ii)
Temperature	0.52*** (0.05)	—
Early melt	—	1.23*** (0.10)
Percent of fires fought aggressively	1.11*** (0.20)	1.27*** (0.20)

Source: USFS (2011).

Notes

Each regression includes a separate unreported constant term and linear trend for each forest unit. Heteroskedasticity robust standard errors are in parentheses.

*** $p < 0.01$ (against a two-sided test of a zero effect)
** $p < 0.05$ (against a two-sided test of a zero effect)
* $p < 0.10$ (against a two-sided test of a zero effect)

level (F > 30) and the hypothesis that the two column (ii) early melt coefficients are equal at a comparable Type 1 error level (F > 37).[8]

We provide these examples for illustrative purposes only. The unfortunate reality of models lacking statistical identification is that it is not possible to tell which of various models generates estimates that lie closer to the truth. Including an additional variable that was formerly incorrectly omitted might move the estimate closer to the correct parameter, but if other variables were incorrectly omitted, it can just as easily move the estimate away from the true parameter. Lacking a strong identification strategy, the best we are left with is a search for model robustness. That is, in a well-identified model, inclusion of additional covariates should not move parameter estimates significantly. However, as is the case here, in poorly identified models, inclusion of additional control variables will generally lead to significant variation in estimates. Again, we have no confidence in the coefficients we estimate for the fire suppression effect, since the design does not rely on plausibly exogenous measures of this strategy. We do have confidence, on the other hand, that if the estimated climate effects are correct, they are so only by chance.

Conclusions

As suggested before, our results are not provided to suggest that the existing estimates in the literature regarding the association between temperature and wildfires are necessarily "wrong." In fact, our results suggest that even if conventionally estimated effects are too big, there does seem to be an association between temperature and fire frequency. However, we flag the identification problem and show how the addition of a plausibly important covariate substantially changes the parameter estimates. This suggests it is problematic to draw policy conclusions from findings generated by models where the only statistical identification comes from time series variation.

The upshot of our exercise, in addition to suggesting that policy and other land use variables are potentially important in analyzing the relationship between large fires in the Northern Rockies and mean annual temperatures, is to demonstrate the fragility of parameter estimates arising from statistical models that lack a strong identification strategy. In principle, a strong identification strategy could yield results that are even stronger support for the climate-driven wildfire hypothesis just as easily as it could undermine claims in the literature.

From the point of view of policy design, it is crucially important to get reliable estimates of the true causal impact of the various variables that contribute to wildfire trends. As described clearly in Chapters 4 and 10, the human and monetary cost of large western wildfires is large and increasing. But policy responses to the wildland fire problem themselves are costly. If one thinks that climate alone is responsible—a constraint imposed on statistical analysis found in recent noneconomic work—then one will overestimate the contribution of climate. Such an overestimation of the role of climate in causing recent wildland fire trends not only will lead to a systematic bias in climate policy design, with the potential benefits of, for example, greenhouse gas emission reductions overestimated, but also likely will affect wildland fire policy. If one believes incorrectly that climate alone is responsible, then one can easily miss changes in federal land use and fire suppression policies that could be much more cost-effective in altering the amount of land lost to and damage done by wildland fires. Fire ecologists severely criticized the Healthy Forests Restoration Act as ignoring scientific work on the natural role of fire in different types of forest ecosystems.[9] Such a commitment to science-based wildland fire policy requires that increased effort be devoted to work analyzing the role of economic incentives in influencing wildland fire trends, and to statistical analysis of the complex causes of wildland fire trends that properly controls for the omitted variables and identification bias problem that we have identified here.

Acknowledgments

The authors are grateful to Jon Ashley and Katie Watlington of the University of Viriginia School of Law for outstanding research and data management assistance on this project, and to Dean Lueck, Sheila Olmstead, and Roger Sedjo for very helpful comments and suggestions on previous drafts of this chapter.

Notes

1. Differently, in dry southwestern forests, Littell et al. (2009) find that one- and two-year lagged rainfall associates positively with fire frequency.
2. The "Greenbook" is the budget justification that accompanies every annual budget request by the Park Service and contains wildland fire suppression budget requests.
3. Note that attenuation bias occurs even if the error is random, as distinct from the case of measurement error in the outcome variable. If the outcome variable is measured with random error, the resulting model will be less precisely estimated but will not suffer from a systematic bias. Measurement error in a predictor, on the other hand, leads to bias even in the case of a completely random error.
4. As can be gleaned from Figure S2 in the supporting online material for Westerling et al. (2006), what they call the "Northern Rockies" region consists of Glacier, Yellowstone, and Grand Teton National Parks; Forest Service Region 1 (the USFS's Northern Region); plus the Malheur, Ochoco, Umatilla, Wallowa Whitman, and Colville Forests from USFS Region 6 (the USFS's Pacific Northwest region).
5. The lowess method is similar to the standard ordinary least squares regression technique while allowing for nonlinearities in the model. This is accomplished by fitting a low-order polynomial model to the data weighting local observations more heavily than more distant observations at each observation in the data.
6. This is the definition of fires coded as "49" in the KCFAST database. For this definition, see www.nifc.blm.gov/fire_reporting/annual_dataset_archive/index.html.
7. After 1999, the definitions for initial suppression strategy changed, with old coding numbers reused for different definitions, leading to numerous inconsistencies in reporting and, finally, completely uninformative reporting.
8. Models were estimated allowing for joint estimation of the variance-covariance matrix given the non-independence of the models using a seemingly unrelated regression technique.
9. Whitlock (2004, 28), for example, called the HFRA a "travesty that limits scientific analysis and public participation in decision-making and policy."

References

Cardille, J. A., S. J. Ventura, and M. G. Turner. 2001. Environmental and Social Factors Influencing Wildfires in the Upper Midwest, United States. *Ecological Applications* 11:111–127.

Gan, J. 2006. Causality among Wildfire, ENSO, Timber Harvest and Urban Sprawl: The Vector Autoregression Appoach. *Ecological Modelling* 191:304–314.

Glickman, D., and B. Babbitt. 2000. Managing the Impact of Wildfires on Communities and the Environment: A Report to the President in Response to the Wildfires of 2000. U.S. Departments of Agriculture and Interior. clinton4.nara.gov/CEQ/firereport.pdf (accessed May 2, 2011).

Gude, Patricia, Ray Rasker, and Jeff van den Noort. 2008. Potential for Future Development on Fire-Prone Lands. *Journal of Forestry* 106 (4):198–205.

Hakanson, Erik Kaj. 2006. Fuels Management Policy and Practice in the U.S. Forest Service. PhD diss., University of Montana.

Hamilton, J. D. 1994. *Time Series Analysis*. Princeton, NJ: Princeton University Press.

Hammer, Roger B., Volker C. Radeloff, Jeremy S. Fried, and Susan I. Stewart. 2007. Wildland-Urban Interface Housing Growth during the 1990's in California, Oregon and Washington. *International Journal of Wildland Fire* 16:255–265.

Husari, Susan J., and Kevin S. McKelvey. 1996. Fire-Management Policies and Programs. In *Sierra Nevada Ecosystem Project: Final Report to Congress*. Vol. 2, *Assessments and Scientific Basis for Management Options*. Davis: University of California, Centers for Water and Wildland Resources, 1101–1117.

Kilgore, Bruce. 2007. Origin and History of Wildland Fire Use in the U.S. National Park System. *George Wright Forum* 24:91.

Kousky, C., and S. M. Olmstead. 2010. Induced Development in Risky Locations: Fire Suppression and Land Use in the American West. Working paper. Washington, DC: Resources for the Future.

Littell, J. S., D. McKenzie, D. L. Peterson, and A. L. Westerling. 2009. Climate and Wildfire Area Burned in Western U.S. Ecoprovinces, 1916–2003. *Ecological Applications*: 19 (4): 1003–1021.

NIFC (National Interagency Fire Center). 2011. Fire Information: Wildland Fire Statistics: Total Wildland Fires and Acres (1960–2010). www.nifc.gov/fire_info/fires_acres.htm (accessed April 20, 2011).

Perry, Phyllis J. 2008. *It Happened in Rocky Mountain National Park*. Guilford, CT: Globe Pequot Press.

Pyne, Stephen J., Patricia L. Andrews, and Richard D. Laven. 1996. *Introduction to Wildland Fire*. 2nd ed. New York: John Wiley & Sons.

Radeloff, V. C., R. B. Hammer, and S. I. Stewart. 2005. Sprawl and forest fragmentation in the U.S. Midwest from 1940 to 2000. *Conservation Biology* 19:793–805.

Radeloff, V. C., S. I. Stewart, T. J. Hawbaker, U. Gimmi, A. M. Pidgeon, C. H. Flather, R. G. Hammer, and D. P. Helmers. 2010. Housing Growth in and near United States Protected Areas Limits Their Conservation Value. *Proceedings of the National Academy of Sciences* 107 (2):940–945.

Rothman, Hal K. 2007. *Blazing Heritage: A History of Wildland Fire Use in the National Parks*. New York: Oxford University Press.

Sanders, Kevin. 2000. Yellowstone Park's Year of Fire: The Great Fires of 1988. Bearman's Yellowstone Outdoor Adventures. www.yellowstone-bearman.com/yfire.html (accessed April 20, 2011).

Sapsis, D. 1999. *Development Patterns and Fire Suppression*. Sacramento: California Department of Forestry and Fire Protection's Fire and Resource Assessment Program.

Schoennagel, T., T. T. Veblen, D. Kulakowski, and A. Holz. 2004. The Interaction of Fire, Fuels and Climate across Rocky Mountain Forests. *BioScience* 54 (7):661–676.

———. 2007. Multidecadal Climate Variability and Climate Interactions Affect Subalpine Fire Occurrence, Western Colorado (USA). *Ecology* 88 (11):2891–2901.

Spero, J. 1997. How Will Increased Population Affect Wildland Fire Incidence: Is Ignition Frequency in the Sierra Nevada Related to Population Density? Sacramento: California Department of Forestry and Fire Protection's Fire and Resource Assessment Program.

Stephens, S. L. 2005. Forest Fire Causes and Extent on United States Forest Service Lands. *International Journal of Wildland Fire* 14:213–222.

Stephens, S. L., and L. W. Ruth. 2005. Federal Forest-Fire Policy in the United States. *Ecological Applications* 15:532–542.

Stewart, Susan I., Volker C. Radeloff, and Roger B. Hammer. 2007. Defining the Wildland-Urban Interface. *Journal of Forestry* 105:201–207.

Syphard, Alexandra D., Volker C. Radeloff, Jon E. Keeley, Todd J. Hawbaker, Murray K. Clayton, Susan I. Stewart, and Roger B. Hammer. 2007. Human Influence on California Fire Regimes. *Ecological Applications* 17 (5):1388–1402.

Theobold, D. M., and W. H. Romme. 2007. Expansion of the US Wildland-Urban Interface. *Landscape and Urban Planning* 83 (4):340–354.

Trouet, V., A. H. Taylor, E. R. Wahl, and C. N. Skinner. 2010. Fire-Climate Interactions in the American West since 1400 CE. *Geophysical Research Letters* 37: L04702, doi:10.1029/2009GL041695.

Turner, M. G., W. H. Romme, and D. B. Tinker. 2003. Surprises and Lessons from the 1988 Yellowstone Fires. *Frontiers in Ecology and the Environment* 1(7):351–358.

USFS (USDA Forest Service). 2011. KCFAST: Kansas City Fire Access Software. http://fam.nwcg.gov/fam-web/kcfast/mnmenu.htm (accessed April 20, 2011).

van Wagtendonk, J. W. 2007. The History and Evolution of Wildland Fire Use. *Fire Ecology* 3 (2):3–17.

Wells, Gail. 2009. Wildland Fire Use: Managing for a Fire-Smart Landscape. *Fire Science Digest* 4:1–11.

Westerling, A. L., H. Hidalgo, D. R. Cayan, and T. Swetnam. 2006. Warming and Earlier Spring Increase Western U.S. Forest Wildfire Activity. *Science* 313:940–943. Supporting online material at www.sciencemag.org/content/early/2006/07/06/science.1128834/suppl/DC1 (accessed April 20, 2011).

Westerling, A. L., and T. Swetnam. 2003. Interannual to Decadal Drought and Wildfire in the Western United States. *Eos, Transactions, American Geophysical Union* 84:545–560.

Whitlock, C. 2004. Forests, Fires and Climate. *Nature* 432:28–29.

Wooldridge, J. M. 2002. *Econometric Analysis of Cross Section and Panel Data*. Cambridge, MA: MIT Press.

Xu, Wenchao, and JunJie Wu. 2009. Wildland Fire and Urban Development Pattern: Why California Civil Code 1103 Fails to Protect Households from Wildfire. Paper presented at AAEA & ACCI Annual Meeting. July 2009, Milwaukee.

10

IN HARM'S WAY

Homeowner Behavior and Wildland Fire Policy

Carolyn Kousky, Sheila Olmstead, and Roger Sedjo

Wildfires in the United States generate annual emergency suppression expenditures at the federal and state levels reaching into the billions of dollars, as well as economic damages for insured and uninsured losses (and loss of life) on an even greater scale. The impacts of wildfires on human life (both homeowners and firefighters), built structures, and natural resources have drawn significant public attention to this issue in recent years. The Station Fire north of Los Angeles, which began in August 2009, required fire suppression expenditures of more than $100 million, killed two firefighters, burned many civilians, and destroyed about 90 homes. The 1991 Oakland/Berkeley Hills fire, the costliest in California's history, killed 25 people, injured 150, and did an estimated $1.5 billion in damage (Carle 2002). The subject is of international importance as well. In February 2009, more than 200 people were killed when brushfires in Australia burned out of control through residential areas. Forest fires in southern Greece in the summer of 2007 killed 84 people. In the summer of 2010, wildfires in Russia caused billions of dollars of damage, and later that same year, the worst wildfire in Israel's history burned thousands of acres and killed more than 40 people.

Despite these high-profile events, land development in the wildland–urban interface (WUI), where housing and fire-prone vegetation mix or exist in close proximity, has proceeded at a rapid pace. In 2000, 12.5 million U.S. homes were located within the WUI, a 52 percent increase over 1970, and a substantial majority of these (65 percent) were in high-severity fire regime classes (Theobald and Romme 2007). This trend is likely to continue; U.S. land in developed uses is expected to increase by 70 million acres between 2003 and 2030, with the largest fraction converted from forests (Alig and Plantinga 2004). California has the highest number of homes in the WUI (Radeloff et al. 2005), which, along with fire risk, often makes this state of particular concern, although the problem in the United States is not isolated to California or the West.

Although empirical economic analysis should have much to contribute to the challenging questions regarding the interaction of wildfire risk and household behavior, the existing literature on the topic is thin. Most chapters in this book enhance our understanding of the social and institutional problems of managing fire through theoretical modeling and qualitative descriptions of important economic and legal issues. This chapter focuses, instead, on the significant potential contributions of empirical microeconomic analysis to the understanding of the impacts of fire risk and fire policy on household behavior, and vice versa, which have important implications for social welfare.

We examine several key questions at the intersection of private homeowner behavior and wildfire that deserve greater attention from empirical economists. We introduce each of these topics in turn, discussing the nature of the empirical relationships predicted by economic theory and what is currently known from the literature. Then we turn to identifying the challenges for conducting new empirical research in these areas and suggesting how they can be overcome. We conclude by discussing how the empirical analyses we recommend can inform public policy decisions regarding wildfire management.

Homeowners and Wildfire: Four Research Topics

In this section, we consider four key economic issues regarding household behavior that, if examined empirically in greater depth by economists, have the potential to improve the efficiency of wildland fire policy: (1) the possible incentive for development provided by fire suppression; (2) the links between information disclosure about fire hazard and household location decisions; (3) the importance of private insurance markets in generating efficient fire policy outcomes; and (4) free riding in household private mitigation expenditures.

Land Development and Wildfire Suppression

Natural and social science research has focused on the increasing incidence of large wildland fires in the western United States (Allen et al. 2002; Westerling et al. 2006; Whitlock 2004).[1] Mirroring this trend, and the trend in damages discussed earlier in this chapter, annual federal fire suppression costs in the United States have increased significantly since 1970 (Calkin et al. 2005).

Figure 10.1 illustrates the increase in suppression expenditures over the past 35 years by the USDA Forest Service (USFS), which receives about 70 percent of the funds appropriated by Congress for wildfire preparedness and operations. During the decade ending in 1980, USFS spent $340 million per year, on average, fighting fires. For the decade ending in 2005, expenditures averaged $685 million per year, with annual expenditures in three of those years exceeding $1 billion

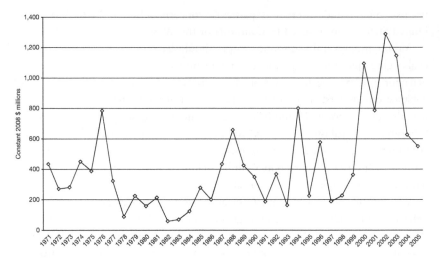

FIGURE 10.1 USFS annual fire suppression expenditures, 1971–2005

Source: Graphed from data made available by the U.S. Forest Service, Rocky Mountain Research Station, converted to constant dollars.

(Calkin et al. 2005). (All fire suppression expenditures have been converted to constant 2008$.)

These trends could be explained by more development in the WUI, which can contribute to increases in fire incidence (Cardille et al. 2001); by climate change (Westerling et al. 2006); as well as by the effects of decades of suppression, which increases the intensity of fires in some ecosystems through fuel buildup (Prestemon et al. 2002). Development also raises suppression costs, since firefighting is complicated by development (Gill and Stephens 2009).[2] Some have suggested that incentives within the Forest Service, which has by necessity shifted away from resource extraction since the 1990s (Thomas 2000) and now finds a significant portion of its budget devoted to suppression efforts, play an important role in the escalation of these costs (see Chapter 4).[3] It is also possible that federal fire suppression efforts contribute to increased development in fire hazard areas, further increasing costs.

Intuition from Economic Theory

Public suppression activity is an implicit subsidy, driving a wedge between private benefits and costs in household and firm location decisions (Kousky and Olmstead 2010). Since the benefits of development in forested and fire-prone regions are enjoyed by landowners, if the costs of fire suppression, when fires occur, are borne by taxpayers at large, excessive development may result. The implicit subsidy represented by public fire suppression may skew land use toward residential and other development, further increasing both the costs of the next fire (because additional structures and populations are now affected) and the costs of future suppression (because it is more difficult and dangerous to fight forest fires when structures and people must be protected). When combined with the known effects of climate change and fuel buildup, the effects of induced land development on suppression expenditures may be very important.

Conclusions from Related Literature

Economists have shown in other contexts that this disassociation of the benefits and costs of locating in a hazardous area can lead to an overinvestment in risky locations (Krutilla 1966), a phenomenon that has been called the "safe development paradox" (Burby 2006). For example, subsidies that reduce crop insurance premium rates below actuarially fair levels may increase the amount of land farmers cultivate, and agricultural disaster payments have a similar effect (Goodwin et al. 2004; Wu 1999). Such induced development has not been found in coastal areas behind shoreline protection, likely due to the high amenity values of locating on the coast (Cordes and Yezer 1998; Hillyer et al. 1997). Examination of coastal areas does, however, suggest that the availability of flood insurance through the National Flood Insurance Program may spur development and certainly does not hinder it (Cordes and Yezer 1998; Cross 1989).

Subsidized insurance is not the only means through which governments may induce land development in hazard-prone areas. Consider the fact that the construction of flood control and drainage infrastructure by the U.S. Army Corps of Engineers caused 30 percent of the observed conversion of land from forested wetlands to agricultural use in the Mississippi Delta between 1935 and 1984 (Stavins and Jaffe 1990). Through direct expenditure on risk reduction, the public sector provides an implicit subsidy for development. In the case of fire, the welfare costs of this activity include not only rapidly escalating suppression costs, but also the fire losses attributable to the subsidy (lives, structures, and natural resources) and other social costs of excessive land conversion.

Research by economists is beginning to investigate this potentially critical link between fire suppression and development, and suggests that suppression does induce some development (Kousky and Olmstead 2010).[4] As with all natural hazards, the degree to which the public sector subsidizes fire risk reduction may vary depending on the distribution of land ownership within a region. For example, large private landowners may internalize the costs of wildfire risk by engaging in their own suppression or mitigation activities (Chapter 4). Small-scale landowners likewise may contract to divide up responsibility for providing these public goods (see Chapters 3 and 8). Such contracts, like all Coasian solutions, are less likely to arise among a large number of small private landowners, or in any other case in which transaction costs are high. If fire suppression and mitigation activities are impure public goods (offering some private benefit, as well as pure public benefits), then, in theory, federal suppression activities could either crowd in or crowd out such spending (Kotchen 2005). As discussed in Chapter 8, it appears that in Australia, a greater state role in fire management may crowd out private provision.

Disclosure of Fire Hazard Information

Several states have enacted policies that disclose fire hazard information to homeowners. For example, following the 1991 Oakland Hills fire, California required its Department of Forestry and Fire Protection (CAL FIRE) to identify Very High Fire Hazard Severity Zones (VHFHSZs). Maps designating these zones were made in 1996 and updated in 2008. A disclosure law passed in 1998 addressing multiple natural hazards requires sellers of property in VHFHSZs to disclose to buyers the fire risk. As another example, under Oregon's Forestland-Urban Interface Fire Protection Act (ODF 2010), sellers must disclose if a property is located in a forestland-urban interface area. The Act also requires certain landowners to create fuel breaks along property lines and roadsides, the size of which varies by fire risk classification, which ranges from "low" to "extreme."[5] Several other states have developed fire hazard rating systems that can be applied by local land use and fire management officials to map fire risk within their communities (for a comprehensive list, see WUIWT 2008). The extent to which this information is easily available to landowners varies by state, an interesting source of variation that could be exploited for empirical analysis of the effectiveness of such policies.

Intuition from Economic Theory

The risks of natural disasters, such as wildfires, earthquakes, and floods, represent disamenities and should be reflected in home prices, and thus development patterns, to the extent that the buyers and sellers of property can accurately assess risk. However, if landowners are mistaken in their understanding of the risk they face, they will not fully internalize expected costs. Underestimation of wildfire risk by WUI homeowners is well documented (Beebe and Omni 1993; Cohn et al. 2008; Kumagi et al. 2004). In theory, this will lead to inefficiently high levels of development and inefficiently low levels of risk mitigation, such as the creation of defensible space in wildfire-prone regions. Property values will be too high, and development patterns may be skewed toward more "safe" uses (e.g., residential) than would occur if the true risk were known. If information disclosure induces an upward correction to landowners' risk perception, the effect should be empirically measurable as a drop in home values or land prices or a shift in development patterns.

Conclusions from Related Literature

As theory would predict, disclosure of risk information alters consumer behavior in many different settings. Mandatory food safety labeling, such as mercury advisories for fish consumption (Shimshack et al. 2007), nutrition labeling (Brown and Schrader 1990; Foster and Just 1989), and the surgeon general's tobacco warning label (Fenn et al. 2001; Sloan et al. 2002) provide several examples that have been examined empirically. The findings from the literature on these types of information disclosure programs indicate that consumers react rationally to quality or hazard labeling (reducing consumption of "bads" and increasing consumption of "goods") in many, but not all, cases.

The literature on land development patterns and risk information is much less substantial. One survey found that disclosure of earthquake information did little to alter home purchases (Palm 1981). Another suggests that after the provision of information about relative earthquake risk by California in the late 1970s, and the requirement that prospective buyers be notified of a property's location within a zone of heightened risk, individuals paid relatively less for homes in more earthquake-prone areas in Los Angeles County and the San Francisco Bay Area, suggesting that home prices do capitalize earthquake risk (Brookshire et al. 1985).[6] Flood risk has been found to be capitalized into property prices, and major flood events can lower home prices, suggesting an updating of risk assessments by home-owners (Bin and Polasky 2004; Carbone et al. 2006; Kousky 2010). Of course, homeowners may over- or underestimate risk, so the simple observation of capital-ization of risk into prices does not necessarily imply an efficient market. It does, however, indicate they are aware the risk is not zero.

Previous studies of wildfire risk and housing prices suggest that homeowners do recognize the risk of wildfire in the WUI in the aftermath of a fire event or when information about risk is readily available. For example, home prices in a community two miles from a major wildfire that burned 12,000 acres in Colorado experienced a 15 percent drop, which can be explained by a change in risk percep-tions and decreased amenities after the fire in the surrounding region (Loomis 2004). The Colorado Springs fire department rated the wildfire risk of 35,000 parcels of land in the WUI, using information on the construction material of structures as well as proximity to dangerous topography and flammable vegetation, and made risk information available on the Internet beginning in 2002 (Donovan et al. 2007).[7] The availability of risk ratings online in this case seems to have enabled the capitalization of wildfire risk into housing prices, at least in the short run. Evidence from California suggests that the combination of hazard disclosure and a recent fire are both necessary for a decrease in property prices due to wildfire risk (Troy and Romm 2006).

From these studies, it is clear that wildfire risk information can be capitalized into housing prices, but does it alter development patterns, and if so, how? Theoretical models and simulations suggest that development patterns should be impacted by hazard designations (Xu and Wu 2009). There is some suggestive evidence from California that a high fire hazard designation lowers development. In state responsibility areas (non-federal, non-incorporated land where primary responsibility for fire suppression lies with the state), the fire hazard determinations made by CAL FIRE represent the official public estimation of risk. In so-called Local Responsibility Areas (LRAs), CAL FIRE provided suggestions of what land should be designated as a VHFHSZ based on fuels, fire history, terrain influences, housing density, and occurrence of severe fire weather, and then local jurisdictions were allowed to alter or reject these maps. Many communities chose to alter or reject the maps, suggesting they believed the stigma of hazard designations would reduce development and lower property values (Troy 2007). For example, although the devastating 1991 Oakland Hills fire was the impetus for the legislation, Oakland Hills removed all designations of VHFHSZs in its jurisdiction and eliminated ordinances that required setbacks and other protective measures (Lefcoe 2004; Troy 2007).

Insurance for Wildfire

Many homeowners at risk of wildfires may choose to insure their property against damage. In most places, wildfire damage will be covered under a traditional homeowners policy. In very high-risk areas, homeowners may instead need to purchase a specific wildfire policy. Premiums will generally be higher in the highest-risk areas, and many insurers may make coverage conditional on certain mitigating actions or offer discounts to homeowners who reduce risks. Inspectors can be sent to homes to ensure compliance.

Intuition from Economic Theory

Economic theory predicts that a risk-averse homeowner, maximizing his or her expected utility (the sole function of which is wealth), will fully insure when the premium of the insurance equals the expected loss. In practice, private insurance costs more than the expected loss, but levels of risk aversion are often high enough to cover this difference. Further, homeowners' insurance is usually required by mortgage lenders. For these reasons, theory would predict that the cost of insurance is internalized by homeowners when making location decisions (assuming they are aware of the rates before purchase). In areas where the risk of damage from wildfire is greater, policies will cost more, reflecting that higher level of risk. This should lead to higher prices for insurance and different development patterns than in low-risk areas, all else equal.

In some cases, however, the rates homeowners face may not adequately reflect this risk, distorting decision-making in ways similar to the case of inadequate information or subsidized suppression, both described above. Insurance prices are regulated by the states, and some insurance commissioners may artificially compress rates—allowing less spatial differentiation than a company may desire—introducing some cross-subsidization into insurance markets. They may also suppress rates, capping the premiums insurance companies can charge. Some very high-risk areas for other perils, such as the Gulf Coast areas at risk of hurricanes, have seen problems in insurance markets when states restrict the ability of insurers to charge prices they think reflect the risk or when homeowners balk at high prices in risky locations. In many of these instances, the state has stepped in, offering insurance-of-last-resort to homeowners, often at artificially low prices.

California offers wildfire coverage to homeowners through its Fair Access to Insurance Requirements (FAIR) Plans. FAIR Plans were established following riots and civil disorder in the late 1960s. States that offered FAIR Plans were provided with federal riot insurance. Many of the programs have expanded to offer broader lines of coverage to homeowners that cannot find a private policy. In most areas of California, FAIR coverage is available only to those residents that have been turned down by private insurance companies, and the wildfire coverage is available only in certain high-risk areas. By offering coverage in locations that the private sector deems too risky to insure—indeed, in areas where some insurers dropped policies after large fires made them wary of underwriting the risk—this practice subsidizes development in risky locations (Troy 2007).

Some insurance companies offer reduced premiums to homeowners that adopt risk-mitigating activities. State programs may do this as well. For example, California's FAIR Plan provides lower rates for homeowners that clear brush or have an approved roofing material, to induce adoption of such practices by homeowners. Whether these spur additional investment in risk reduction depends on the magnitude of the expected savings compared with the cost of the investments. Further, many other variables may influence a homeowner's decision to adopt risk mitigation measures, as discussed further below.

Conclusions from Related Literature

American insurance markets, including pricing, are regulated by the states. Insurance companies have been moving to more detailed modeling of wildfire risk using GIS technologies. This allows them to combine information on vegetation, topography, climate, building codes, accessibility, and details of the home to generate property-specific rates (Miller 2007). However, in other settings, some state insurance commissioners appear to weight low prices and availability of policies more heavily than solvency considerations or management of catastrophe risk, limiting the ability of private companies to charge rates that fully reflect the risk (Klein and Wang 2007). As noted above, this may lead to rate compression and suppression, potentially leading to lower home prices and excess development.

Subsidized insurance for other natural hazards, such as floods and droughts, influences land development, particularly for agricultural and residential use (Galloway et al. 2006). As mentioned earlier, subsidies that reduce crop insurance premium rates below actuarially fair levels may increase the amount of land farmers cultivate; agricultural disaster payments have a similar effect (Goodwin et al. 2004; Wu 1999). There has been little empirical work, however, on the effects of subsidized insurance on development in fire-prone regions.

Insurance may, however, play a limited role in decision-making if homeowners are unaware of the difference in premiums between high- and low-risk areas until after they have closed on a property. For instance, one study found that in Boulder, Colorado, a majority of home buyers did not know of the flood risk or the cost of flood insurance until the time of closing or later (Chivers and Flores 2002). Without such information known ex ante, homeowners will not make substantively different decisions.

Private Fire Risk Mitigation and Free Riding

In addition to location decisions and the purchase of insurance, there are several actions that homeowners can take to reduce the risk of fire damage to their homes. These include clearing areas of defensible space around the homes and choosing fire-resistant building materials. At the community level, actions such as making roads easily accessible to firefighting crews can also reduce the risk of damage.

Intuition from Economic Theory

Risk-reducing activities like these generate both private goods (in the form of reduced risk of personal damage from fire) and public goods (in the form of reduced risk to one's neighbors). Public goods are non-excludable, meaning it is impossible to prevent others from consuming the good, and non-rival, meaning one person's consumption does not diminish another's. Economic theory predicts that individuals will underinvest in public goods, "free riding" on the investment of others. Just as in the case of suppression, private homeowners do have an incentive to create organizations that capture some of the potential benefits from increased public good provision through private contracts (see Chapter 4). However, private markets will generally provide less than the efficient quantity of public goods. With respect to reducing fuel loads, homeowners may free-ride not only on their neighbors' actions, but also on those taken by subdivision associations, city and county governments, state governments, and federal agencies.

Conclusions from Related Literature

Though none of the research topics we cover in this chapter has received significant attention from empirical economists, the question of private homeowner investment in fire risk mitigation has generated a great deal more research than the other three topics. Economists have noted the propensity for homeowners in fire-prone areas to underinvest in averting activities such as fuel treatment and the development of "defensible space," with a key explanation appearing to be the public good nature of these investments. For example, a household's defensible space decision in Boulder County, Colorado, appears to depend on defensible space outcomes at neighboring sites (Shafran 2008). Research on other hazards suggests several additional reasons why homeowners may underinvest in risk reduction measures, including an under-estimation of the probability of a loss, budget constraints, myopic behavior, and not wanting to be the only one in the neighborhood adopting such behavior (Kunreuther 2006).

Unlike private mitigation activities for other natural hazards (e.g., earthquakes), mitigation to reduce the risk of wildland fire may involve activities that reduce household utility by diminishing the amenity values of a property—for example, felling trees near the home may reduce the quality of a view (Winter and Fried 2000). This provides an additional disincentive to invest in mitigation. These issues have been explored using game theory, experimental economics, and mail surveys of homeowner preferences (Busby and Albers 2010; Holmes et al. 2009; McKee et al. 2004).

In theory, the landowner's decision about the desired level of private mitigation should be made jointly with his or her decision about investment in private insurance. As pointed out in Chapter 3, these choices are also made within the context of legal liability for mitigation, prevention, and suppression activities. Talberth et al. (2006) find that households do, in fact, make investment decisions about wildfire insurance, private averting activities, and public mitigation at the neighborhood level jointly.[8] Insurance companies have begun to recognize this fact—for example, as mentioned above, California's FAIR program, while subsidizing wildfire risk, has introduced economic incentives for the creation of defensible space, the use of fire-resistant building materials, and improved firefighter access (Monrovia Fire Safe Council 2004). Household investment in risk mitigation is also linked with the question of information disclosure addressed earlier. Providing households with information on their objective fire risk seems to reduce the number of households that overinvest in averting activities (those in low-risk classes), as well as the number in high-risk classes that are underinvesting (Talberth et al. 2006).

Challenges for Empirical Work on Homeowners and Fire Policy

Several challenges plague empirical investigation of the topics discussed above, the most notable of which we will review here: endogeneity, data availability, sample selection, and determining the optimal level of public good provision. Some are challenges for research on all of the topics we discussed, and others are specific to a subset of these topics. We address each of these challenges in turn in the paragraphs that follow.

The Challenge of Endogeneity

One key challenge for empirical work on household behavior and wildfire policy is endogeneity, a ubiquitous source of bias in statistical analysis. Trying to untangle the relationship between suppression policy and location decisions offers an intuitive example. Development may increase suppression efforts, because human-ignited fires are more common in developed areas, and fire agencies exert tremendous effort to protect structures, compared to areas with no development. But from a policy perspective, we may want to identify the opposite relationship—the causal impact of suppression on development. This problem of "reverse causality" can be overcome through the use of statistical natural experiments and quasi-experimental techniques. Exogenous variation in suppression efforts can be exploited to estimate the relationship between development and suppression.[9] Shifts in federal suppression policies over time have been used for this purpose, and preliminary analysis suggests that suppression does induce development on private land near federal land affected by federal fire suppression efforts (Kousky and Olmstead 2010). State-level variation in suppression efforts, or variation over time in the costs of suppression, could also be used for this purpose.

A related challenge is underlying heterogeneity across land parcels that may be correlated both with development (or another measure of land values, such as home prices) and with the wildfire policy of interest. In the case of wildfire policy, amenity values may play this role. Several of the characteristics that increase the risk of wild-fire damage (such as location on a ridge, or the density of trees on a property or in nearby forested land) also have an amenity value, such as improving views or increasing access to recreation. Thus, the underlying variables of a wildfire risk index are likely to be positively correlated with home prices or development. Researchers thus may need an instrument for risk ratings to statistically identify the negative impact of information disclosure of a property's risk rating on market value.[10] As another example, amenity values are a source of positive correlation between insurance prices and home prices, again requiring an instrument for insurance prices. Identifying valid instruments can be difficult in practice.

The Challenge of Data Availability

The sparse availability of data on land use change over time impacts the possibility of new empirical work on each of the topics we broached earlier. Comprehensive land cover and land use data are a satellite-era phenomenon; the publicly available land use data for the United States, for example, begin around 1970 and in most cases offer snapshots of land use over intervals of five years or more, with "current" observations lagging the present day by several years. The available time series on land cover have improved tremendously since 1970 in the fineness of spatial resolution (helpful in cases where policy shifts differ across small geographic units), but the temporal scale remains quite coarse. This is a real challenge for the natural experiments and quasi-experimental approaches needed to deal with the problem of endogeneity discussed above, in which we ideally would observe land use choices immediately before and after some important discontinuity over time.

Again, taking the case of research on the impacts of fire suppression is instructive. The relatively "late start" of land use observations in 1970, relative to the onset of large-scale federal fire suppression efforts (around 1910), makes questions about the impacts of early federal suppression policy on household location decisions statistically unanswerable. For post-1970 policy analysis, it must be true that the relatively large windows represented by the time-step of most land use data overlap sufficiently with the policy change of interest, but not too much with other confounding policy changes; otherwise, the data cannot be used to assess policy impacts. For example, if you observe land use in 1992 and 2000, but you want to assess the impact of a policy shift that took place in 1996, it is difficult to build a statistical case suggesting an effect of that policy change if the case cannot be made that no other important confounding events took place during that eight-year window.

On the positive side, current or relatively recent geographical information system (GIS) snapshots of land use are now available for most of the United States, opening up new opportunities for research. To examine trends in the WUI, such databases must also identify low-density development. A new database, Land Cover Trends, from the U.S. Geological Survey, begins to help overcome these difficulties.[11] Land cover types include "developed" land, which comprises both intense urbanization and low-density residential development. Land cover is available for five observation periods between 1973 and 2000, ranging from six to eight years in length. As a substitute for land use data based on satellite observations, some authors investigating wildfires have turned to census data (Gude et al. 2008), which is available for much earlier periods than land use data, though the 10-year temporal resolution is at least as coarse. At the level of the census tract (or higher levels of aggregation), maps of housing density can be developed based on census estimates. For the particular question of the impacts of fire suppression policies on development, land values or home values might prove to be a fruitful source of data, since they may be observed much more frequently than land cover (e.g., monthly). However, obtaining these data from private sources can be costly.

For many research questions, parcel-level data would be ideal. Even if such data are available on home prices, they may not contain information on mitigating actions the homeowner has adopted, and they certainly will not indicate whether the property has wildfire insurance. Both private insurance companies and public programs are concerned about privacy issues in releasing property-level data. Without such information, research on the effects of insurance on mitigation decisions is difficult. In research on hazards other than wildfire, some progress has been made using insurance data aggregated to the census tract or another geographic unit. This may be possible for wildfire research as well.

The Challenge of Selection Bias

A third challenge to empirical research is selection bias. Attempting to estimate the effects of risk disclosure on land development patterns provides an example. In California, communities could adopt, alter, or reject outright the maps that designated VHFHSZs. Any empirical assessment of the impact of disclosure on development would have to carefully control for this sample selection problem. Which communities chose to disclose the information to the buyers and sellers of land, which did not, and to what extent is the selection into disclosure itself correlated with development patterns? To the extent that this correlation exists, empirical estimates of the impact of disclosure on development that do not account for selection will be biased. Similar questions of voluntary disclosure have been examined in financial markets, environmental regulation, and other areas in which incentives to disclose clearly vary depending on costs. Selection is thus not an uncommon problem in empirical microeconomics, and although it is a valid concern, it can often be addressed econometrically.[12]

The Challenge of Determining the Optimal Level of Public Good Provision

A final challenge relates to research on all of the topics we have investigated in this chapter. Fundamentally, wildfire suppression, mitigation, and information provision are public goods. And determining the optimal level of public goods provision is a classic problem in microeconomics. The demand curve for a public good sums over the willingness to pay of all parties benefiting from the good, but consumers' true willingness to pay is difficult to estimate, for reasons related to free riding. If one conducts a survey, asking homeowners how much they are willing to pay for fire risk reduction through mitigation activities, and the survey respondents believe that they will realistically have to bear these costs in the future, and that the costs depend on their answer, their answer will lie below their true willingness to pay. If, on the other hand, they do not anticipate that their answer will affect their future costs, they will overstate their willingness to pay. This problem is a significant empirical challenge to establishing efficient public policies regarding public and private fire suppression and mitigation of fire risk—after all, if a state or local government cannot determine the optimal level of these activities, this is a difficult starting point for policy-making. Survey methods in economics, including contingent valuation, can be designed to reduce this bias.

Once efficient levels of suppression or mitigation have been determined, policies must be adopted to achieve these goals. It is in this process that the empirical research we recommend in this chapter may be most useful.

Potential Contributions to Public Policy from Empirical Research

U.S. western and southeastern states are plagued by annual fire seasons that put people (residents and firefighters) and structures at risk. The location of development, the mitigation and insurance choices adopted by homeowners, and the information available to homeowners about wildfire risk are undoubtedly behavioral determinants of the damages wildfires will cause. Applying empirical economic research to illuminate the impact of past, current, and potential future public policies affecting homeowner decisions through these levers is key to improving outcomes.

Current fire management policy does not account for the possibility that suppression itself may draw additional people and structures into harm's way, though the opposite problem, the increase in suppression expenditures due to development in the wildland-urban interface, is widely recognized (USDA 2006). Expanding our understanding of the potential of wildfire policy to affect development patterns is essential for informing suppression policies at the federal and state levels. Research on the impacts of suppression policy on location decisions is also tightly linked to the issue of disaster mitigation, more broadly, through the safe development paradox—an issue that is increasingly important as climate change is expected to increase the frequency and/or magnitude of many natural disasters (e.g., hurricanes, floods, and droughts) as well as wildland fires. Research in these areas can prove useful in both thinking about policy responses to the existing context, in which significant populations are already at risk, and policy strategies going forward (e.g., zoning), which may influence the direction of future land development so as to mitigate risk.

Over the past two decades, there has been significant growth in the use of information disclosure programs as a method of environmental and natural resource management. Relatively little is known, however, about behavioral responses to information disclosure policies.

Particularly when they do not mandate any particular behavioral change, disclosure policies may be more politically palatable than more prescriptive policies. If they do not provide new information or if the involved parties do not think the information is relevant, however, they may not be worth the cost. Essentially all of the public and private solutions to managing wildfire risk in the WUI rely on informed homeowners. Empirical research on the effectiveness of information disclosure policies with different characteristics can assist in the design of such disclosure policies for wildfire as well as other hazards, from flooding to earthquakes.

Following Hurricane Katrina, there has been increased discussion at the federal and state levels of the role of the government in catastrophe insurance markets. In high-risk areas, private insurance companies may choose not to offer policies if they cannot charge prices that will cover the risk. This has largely been a concern along the Gulf Coast with hurricane risk, but it has anecdotally been a difficulty in some high-fire-risk areas as well. State insurance programs, such as the California FAIR program discussed above, often fill the gap. To date, in most of the country, availability of wildfire coverage has not been a problem. Should it become increasingly difficult for homeowners to find insurance, creating a large burden on states, the federal government may be called on to intervene. For example, a federal flood insurance program offers policies directly to homeowners, and a federal terrorism program offers reinsurance to private companies. Many government programs, however, shift some of the costs of residing in high-risk areas from those at risk to others in the state or country. Empirical research on how insurance availability, pricing, and mitigation incentives alter homeowner behavior can inform how the government should (or should not) intervene in the insurance market.

The basic idea of any policy for public goods provision is to better align private incentives with the common good. To overcome the free-riding challenge, many local and state governments in fire-prone regions simply mandate certain risk-reduction efforts by homeowners, though such policies often focus on the construction of new subdivisions in the WUI rather than on the retrofitting of existing development. To further determine optimal levels of public and private risk reduction investments or the nature and extent of mandates for such actions, empirical evidence on when and where free riding is a problem in practice is needed.

Other approaches, which harness market forces more effectively than outright mandates, include reductions in insurance premiums to compensate homeowners for undertaking mitigating actions. For example, California's FAIR Plan provides lower rates for homeowners that clear brush or have an approved roofing material. Another market-based incentive is a requirement that homeowners share some liability for the costs of suppression with the public sector, if private mitigation activities are not sufficiently undertaken and fire ignition or spread can be reasonably attributed to a particular property. Oregon's Forestland-Urban Interface Fire Protection Act provides one example of this. Alternatively, the public sector can directly subsidize mitigation on private property. Empirical analysis suggests that both cost-sharing of mitigation activities and cost-sharing of suppression do provide incentives for fuel treatment by private non-industrial forest owners (Amacher et al. 2006). [13] Analysis regarding the effect of such policies, and the others we have discussed here, on private investment in fire mitigation by homeowners will inform policy formulation at the state and local levels in the future, when development in the WUI will be even more extensive.

Communicating the Contributions of Empirical Social Science Research on Fire Policy

In this chapter, we have advocated for the increased application of the tools of empirical microeconomics to the subject of wildfire policy. Researchers bringing a social science lens to these questions operate within the context of many decades of work on fire science and a public wildland fire policy apparatus that, to the extent that it draws upon peer-reviewed literatures at all in policy formulation, is grounded in the natural and physical sciences. If economists performing empirical analysis of policies regarding fire suppression, insurance, and the disclosure of risk information hope to influence the future direction of such policies, care must be taken to communicate results and underlying models in ways that are useful to policymakers who may be unfamiliar with our methods.

The central contribution that economists can make to policy analysis is a focus on causality above all else. Having operated since the beginning days of the discipline in a context in which observational data, rather than experimental data, is the subject of most analysis, the statistical techniques of modern microeconometricians have evolved to wring convincing causal effects out of noisy processes. In most cases, we have no choice—the randomized controlled experiments that are the gold standard of the scientific endeavor cannot be conducted in most economic contexts.[14] Thus, statistical techniques must employ identification strategies that simulate the workings of an actual experiment, using observational data.

These techniques, while valuable for policy analysis, can seem opaque to bench scientists, who tend to focus on causality when running experiments and description or prediction when using observational data. The analysis of observational data to estimate "associations," or correlational rather than causal relationships, between two variables is not at all uncommon in natural and physical science research. In contrast, natural experiments in economics typically "clean" away the effects of possible confounding variables through the use of sets of dummy variables (fixed effects), so that the coefficients of interest identify causal relationships. In doing so, economists can be confident in delivering unbiased estimates of policy impacts to the policy process—no small contribution.

However, these models may have little or no other descriptive power. For example, Kousky and Olmstead (2010) estimate the determinants of residential development in forested areas using a set of instruments for public fire suppression policies, as well as sets of fixed effects representing each parcel of land, state, and year (as well as interactions among these covariates). Their estimates suggest causal impacts of public suppression activities on development. But one cannot easily retrieve from such a model the effects of things like transportation networks or economic growth on development—things that most educated laypersons would expect to see included. These variables, and everything else that might vary over time and space and be correlated with development, are subsumed by the fixed effects, so we can be certain that they are not confounding our main result. But this fact may seem opaque to practitioners of statistics outside of economics.

There is much that economists can do to bridge this divide. We can discuss clearly the ways in which modern microeconometrics attempts to replicate, to the extent possible with observational data, the design of randomized experiments. We can introduce descriptive elements into models that treat all possible confounding variables with generic fixed effects, by estimating second-stage models that decompose these fixed effects so as to reveal the influence on the dependent variable of particular covariates. We can be explicit about the limits of the causal effects we estimate, which may be valid only within a narrow range or in particular cases. Using these approaches may make it more likely that economic analyses will have an impact on public policy toward wildland fire suppression, mitigation, and risk management. This is a critical endeavor. In the absence of convincing and well-communicated work by economists on the behavioral aspects of wildland fire policy, analyses by natural and physical scientists, which tend not to consider household and firm behavior or other economic phenomena, will remain the only contributions that are called upon in policy formulation.

Conclusions

Wildfire risk management has not received the attention from empirical economists that it has from researchers in other disciplines. This is unfortunate, as we argue here, since empirical economic research has much to contribute to the topic and much to offer policymakers. Fire suppression, information disclosure, insurance, and mitigation policies all create incentives that influence landowner behavior. The goal of these policies is usually to reduce the risk of damage from wildfire, but how well such policies do at achieving this goal, whether they have other unintended effects, and how they operate together are all questions that empirical economists can illuminate.

As discussed in this chapter, there are several challenges to addressing the many open research questions, perhaps explaining the relatively small literature to date. These include problems of endogeneity, limited data availability, and sample selection. These are not new problems to empirical economists, however. The focus of empirical economic research on establishing causality with observational data has led to the development of a host of tools that can be exploited to overcome these challenges. Coupled with new datasets, particularly GIS data on land use, much forward progress should be possible. With concerted effort on the part of economists at explaining their tools to policymakers and researchers in other disciplines, an improved understanding of the behavioral side of wildfire risk management can be developed and used to improve future policy at the federal, state, and local levels.

Notes

1. About 60 percent of the observed increase in large wildfires since 1970 has occurred in the Northern Rockies, and most of the remaining increase has been in the Sierra Nevada, Southern Cascades, and Coast Ranges of northern California and southern Oregon (Westerling et al. 2006). Whereas the increase in large western wildfire occurrence is well documented, there is less agreement over the causes of this increase (see Chapter 9).

2. An audit by the U.S. Department of Agriculture's Office of the Inspector General names WUI development, and the concomitant expectation of private property protection in suppression efforts, as the single biggest cause of increases in USFS large-fire suppression costs between 2000 and 2006 (USDA 2006).

3. Several analyses have recently drawn attention to the weak incentives for cost containment in reactive federal fire suppression (e.g., Donovan et al. 2008; NAPA 2002).

4. A growing literature models economically optimal public fire presuppression and suppression efforts (Mercer et al. 2007; Prestemon et al. 2001; Yoder 2004) but does not account for the interaction with development.

5. This Oregon policy is also related both to the location decision research described earlier and to fire insurance questions addressed later in the chapter. Once property owners have met the fuel-reduction standards required for their property under the Act, they obtain a certification form from the state Department of Forestry, which relieves the owner from liability for potential fire suppression cost recovery. If a landowner has property within the designated forestland-urban interface, but does not have a current certification for fuel reduction undertaken, the state can seek to recover some fire suppression costs (capped at $100,000) should a fire originate on the owner's property.

6. The premium for a property located outside designated areas of higher earthquake risk was about one-half the value of a swimming pool or one-third the value of a view (Brookshire et al. 1985).

7. Risk ratings can be readjusted by the department in response to homeowner investments in wildfire risk mitigation, such as the replacement of wood-shingle roofs with less flammable materials (Donovan et al. 2007).

8. The analysis used a contingent valuation survey of just over 1,000 households near Albuquerque, New Mexico, and laboratory experiments that recruited 72 subjects for 15 rounds, each representing a year of household decision-making (Talberth et al. 2006).

9. For a summary of the use of these methods in environmental economics and their advantages, see Greenstone and Gayer (2009).

10. One solution is to estimate a hedonic price function that controls for the underlying variables used to assign disclosed wildfire risk ratings, as well as the ratings themselves, as in Donovan et al. (2007).

11. The database is a set of randomly selected 10 × 10 kilometer sample blocks, with 30 to 40 sample blocks in each of the 84 Level III Ecoregions in the Lower 48 states. See Loveland et al. (1999) for a description of the Land Cover Trends project. Additional information is available from USGS (2010).

12. In at least one case, the selection problem has an upside—it may provide a source of variation that could be exploited by researchers. In California's VHFHSZ designation program, the fact that some jurisdictions altered these maps and some did not creates the opportunity to compare development on land that is technically high-hazard (as designated by CAL FIRE), and where the risk is accurately disclosed, with land on which the risk is the same, but risk information is not disclosed to buyers and sellers of property. Whether estimating such a model, while also accounting for the bias introduced by selection, would be empirically tractable is an open question.

13. Government cost-sharing of private fuel reduction does not always reduce social losses in the simulations in this study, but it can yield bigger reductions in social damages than requiring cost-sharing of suppression when fire risk is high (Amacher et al. 2006).

14. However, economists have also orchestrated an impressive and increasing number of actual social experiments, from early large-scale efforts such as the RAND Health Insurance Experiment of the mid-1970s (Newhouse 1993) and those involving the negative income tax, known today as the earned income tax credit (Ross 1970), to modern applications in labor (List and Rasul 2010), development (Banerjee and Duflo 2009), education (Angrist 2004), and other fields of economics (Levitt and List 2009).

References

Alig, R. J., and A. J. Plantinga. 2004. Future Forestland Area: Impacts from Population Growth and Other Factors That Affect Land Values. *Journal of Forestry* 102:19–24.

Allen, C. D., M. Savage, D. A. Falk, K. F. Suckling, T. W. Swetnam, T. Schulke, P. B. Stacey, P. Morgan, M. Hoffman, and J. T. Klingel. 2002. Ecological Restoration of Southwestern Ponderosa Pine Ecosystems: A Broad Perspective. *Ecological Applications* 12:1418–1433.

Amacher, G. S., A. S. Malik, and R. G. Haight. 2006. Reducing Social Losses from Forest Fires. *Land Economics* 82:367–383.

Angrist, J. D. 2004. American Education Research Changes Tack. *Oxford Review of Economic Policy* 20:198–212.

Banerjee, A. V., and E. Duflo. 2009. The Experimental Approach to Development Economics. *Annual Review of Economics* 1:151–178.

Beebe, G. S., and P. N. Omni. 1993. Wildland Burning: The Perception of Risk. *Journal of Forestry* 91 (9):19–24.

Bin, O., and S. Polasky. 2004. Effects of Flood Hazards on Property Values: Evidence before and after Hurricane Floyd. *Land Economics* 80:490–500.

Brookshire, D. S., M. A. Thayer, J. Tschirhart, and W. D. Schulze. 1985. A Test of the Expected Utility Model: Evidence from Earthquake Risks. *Journal of Political Economy* 93 (2):369–389.

Brown, D., and L. Schrader. 1990. Cholesterol Information and Shell Egg Consumption, *American Journal of Agricultural Economics* 72:548–555.

Burby, R. J. 2006. Hurricane Katrina and the Paradoxes of Government Disaster Policy: Bringing About Wise Governmental Decisions for Hazardous Areas. *ANNALS of the American Academy of Political and Social Science* 604 (1):171–191.

Busby, G., and H. Albers. 2010. Wildfire Risk Management on a Landscape with Public and Private Ownership: Who Pays for Protection? *Environmental Management* 45:296–310.

Calkin, D. E., K. M. Gebert, G. Jones, and R. P. Neilson. 2005. Forest Service Large Fire Area Burned and Suppression Expenditure Trends, 1970–2002. *Journal of Forestry* 103:179–183.

Carbone, J. C., D. G. Hallstrom, and V. K. Smith. 2006. Can Natural Experiments Measure Behavioral Responses to Environmental Risks? *Environmental and Resource Economics* 33:273–297.

Cardille, J. A., S. J. Ventura, and M. G. Turner. 2001. Environmental and Social Factors Influencing Wildfires in the Upper Midwest, United States. *Ecological Applications* 11:111–127.

Carle, D. 2002. *Burning Questions: America's Fight with Nature's Fire.* Westport, CT: Praeger.

Chivers, J., and N. E. Flores. 2002. Market Failure in Information: The National Flood Insurance Program. *Land Economics* 78 (4):515–521.

Cohn, P. J., D. R. Williams, and M. S. Carroll. 2008. Wildland-urban Interface Residents' Views on Risk and Attribution. In *Wildfire Risk: Human Perceptions and Management Implications*, edited by Wade E. Martin, Carol Raish, and Brian Kent. Washington, DC: Resources for the Future, 23–43.

Cordes, J. J., and A. M. J. Yezer. 1998. In Harm's Way: Does Federal Spending on Beach Enhancement and Protection Induce Excessive Development in Coastal Areas? *Land Economics* 74 (1):128–145.

Cross, J. A. 1989. Flood Insurance and Coastal Development. *Florida Geographer* 23:22–45.

Donovan, G. H., T. C. Brown, and L. Dale. 2008. Incentives and Wildfire Management in the United States. In *The Economics of Forest Disturbances: Wildfires, Storms, and Invasive Species*, edited by T. P. Holmes, J. P. Prestemon, and K. L. Abt. London: Springer, 323–340.

Donovan, G. H., P. A. Champ, and D. T. Butry. 2007. Wildfire Risk and Housing Prices: A Case Study from Colorado Springs. *Land Economics* 83:217–233.

Fenn, A., F. Antonovitz, and J. Schroeter. 2001. Cigarettes and Addiction Information: New Evidence in Support of the Rational Addiction Model. *Economics Letters* 72:39–45.

Foster, W., and R. Just. 1989. Measuring Welfare Effects of Product Contamination with Consumer Uncertainty. *Journal of Environmental Economics and Management* 17:266–283.

Galloway, G. E., G. B. Baecher, D. Plasencia, K. G. Coulton, J. Louthain, M. Bagha, and A. R. Levy. 2006. *Assessing the Adequacy of the National Flood Insurance Program's 1 Percent Flood Standard.* College Park, MD: Water Policy Collaborative, University of Maryland.

Gill, A. M., and S. L. Stephens. 2009. Scientific and Social Challenges for the Management of Fire-Prone Wildland-Urban Interfaces. *Environmental Research Letters* 4 (September), doi:10.1088/1748-9326/4/3/034014.

Goodwin, B. K., M. L. Vandeveer, and J. L. Deal. 2004. An Empirical Analysis of Acreage Effects of Participation in the Federal Crop Insurance Program. *American Journal of Agricultural Economics* 86:1058–1077.

Greenstone, M., and T. Gayer. 2009. Quasi-experimental and Experimental Approaches to Environmental Economics. *Journal of Environmental Economics and Management* 57: 21–44.

Gude, P., R. Rasker, and J. van den Noort. 2008. Potential for Future Development on Fire-Prone Lands. *Journal of Forestry* 106:198–205.

Hillyer, T. M., E. Z. Stakhiv, and R. A. Sudar. 1997. An Evaluation of the Economic Performance of the U.S. Army Corps of Engineers Shore Protection Program. *Journal of Coastal Research* 13 (1):8–22.

Holmes, T. P., J. Loomis, and A. González-Cabán. 2009. A Mixed Logit Model of Homeowner Preferences for Wildfire Hazard Reduction. In *Proceedings of the Third International Symposium on Fire Economics, Planning, and Policy; Common Problems and Approaches*, edited by A. González-Cabán. Washington, DC: USDA Forest Service, 124–136.

Klein, R. W., and S. Wang. 2007. Catastrophe Risk Financing in the US and EU: A Comparative Analysis of Alternative Regulatory Approaches. Paper presented at the SCOR-JRI Conference on Insurance, Reinsurance and Capital Market Transformations. September 2007, Paris, France.

Kotchen, M. J. 2005. Impure Public Goods and the Comparative Statics of Environmentally Friendly Consumption. *Journal of Environmental Economics and Management* 49:281–300.

Kousky, C. 2010. Learning from Extreme Events: Risk Perceptions after the Flood. *Land Economics* 86 (3):395–422.

Kousky, C., and S. M. Olmstead. 2010. Induced Development in Risky Locations: Fire Suppression and Land Use in the American West. Working paper. Washington, DC: Resources for the Future.

Krutilla, J. V. 1966. An Economic Approach to Coping with Flood Damage. *Water Resources Research* 2 (2):183–190.

Kumagi, Y., S. E. Daniels, M. S. Carroll, J. C. Bliss, and J. A. Edwards. 2004. Causal Reasoning Processes of People Affected by Wildfire: Implications for Agency-Community Interactions and Communications Strategies. *Western Journal of Applied Forestry* 19 (3): 184–194.

Kunreuther, H. 2006. Disaster Mitigation and Insurance: Learning from Katrina. *Annals of the American Academy of Political and Social Science* 604:208–227.

Lefcoe, G. 2004. Property Condition Disclosure Forms: How the Real Estate Industry Eased the Transition from Caveat Emptor to Seller Tell All. *Real Property, Probate and Trust Journal* 39:193–250.

Levitt, S. D., and J. A. List. 2009. Field Experiments in Economics: The Past, the Present, and the Future. *European Economic Review* 53 (1):1–18.

List, J. A., and I. Rasul. 2010. Field Experiments in Labor Economics. NBER Working Paper No. 16062. Cambridge, MA: National Bureau of Economic Research.

Loomis, J. 2004. Do Nearby Forest Fires Cause a Reduction in Residential Property Values? *Journal of Forest Economics* 10:149–157.

Loveland, T. R., T. L. Sohl, K. Sayler, A. Gallant, J. Dwyer, J. E. Vogelmann, and G. J. Zylstra. 1999. *Land Cover Trends: Rates, Causes, and Consequences of Late-Twentieth Century U.S. Land Cover Change*. EPA/600/R-99/105. Washington, DC: U.S. Environmental Protection Agency, Office of Research and Development.

McKee, M., R. P. Berrens, M. Jones, R. Helton, and J. Talberth. 2004. Using Experimental Economics to Examine Wildfire Insurance and Averting Decisions in the Wildland-Urban Interface. *Society & Natural Resources* 17:491–507.

Mercer, D. E., J. P. Prestemon, D. T. Butry, and J. M. Pye. 2007. Evaluating Alternative Prescribed Burning Policies to Reduce Net Economic Damages from Wildfire. *American Journal of Agricultural Economics* 89:63–77.

Miller, C. 2007. Wildfire Underwriting in California: An Industry Perspective. In *Living on the Edge: Economic, Institutional and Management Perspectives on Wildfire Hazard in the Urban Interface*, edited by A. Troy and R. G. Kennedy. Amsterdam: Elsevier, 121–125.

Monrovia Fire Safe Council. 2004. *Fire Safety and Fire Insurance Guide in the Fire Hazard Areas of Monrovia*. Monrovia, CA: Monrovia Fire Safe Council.

NAPA (National Academy of Public Administration). 2002. *Wildfire Suppression: Strategies for Containing Costs*. Washington, DC: NAPA.

Newhouse J. P. 1993. *Free for All? Lessons from the RAND Health Insurance Experiment.* Cambridge, MA: Harvard University Press.

ODF (Oregon Department of Forestry). 2010. Oregon Forestland-Urban Interface Fire Protection Act. www.oregon.gov/ODF/FIRE/SB360/sb360.shtml (accessed April 21, 2011).

Palm, R. I. 1981. Public Response to Earthquake Hazard Information. *Annals of the Association of American Geographers* 71 (3):389–399.

Prestemon, J. P., D. E. Mercer, J. M. Pye, D. T. Butry, T. P. Holmes, and K. L. Abt. 2001. Economically Optimal Wildfire Intervention Regimes. Paper presented at the *American Agricultural Economics Association Annual Meeting.* August 2001, Chicago.

Prestemon, J. P., J. M. Pye, D. T. Butry, T. P. Holmes, and D. E. Mercer. 2002. Understanding Broadscale Wildfire Risks in a Human-Dominated Landscape. *Forest Science* 48:685–693.

Radeloff, V. C., R. B. Hammer, S. I. Stewart, J. S. Fried, S. S. Holcomb, and J. F. McKeefry. 2005. The Wildland-Urban Interface in the United States. *Ecological Applications* 15:799–805.

Ross, H. L. 1970. An Experimental Study of the Negative Income Tax. *Child Welfare* 10:562–569.

Shafran, A. P. 2008. Risk Externalities and the Problem of Wildfire Risk. *Journal of Urban Economics* 64:488–495.

Shimshack, J. P., M. B. Ward, and T. K. M. Beatty. 2007. Mercury Advisories: Information, Education, and Fish Consumption. *Journal of Environmental Economics and Management* 53 (2):158–179.

Sloan, F., V. Smith, and D. Taylor. 2002. Information, Addiction, and "Bad Choices": Lessons from a Century of Cigarettes. *Economics Letters* 77:147–155.

Stavins, R. N., and A. B. Jaffe. 1990. Unintended Impacts of Public Investments on Private Decisions: The Depletion of Forested Wetlands. *American Economic Review* 80 (3): 337–352.

Talberth, J., R. P. Berrens, M. McKee, and M. Jones. 2006. Averting and Insurance Decisions in the Wildland-Urban Interface: Implications of Survey and Experimental Data for Wildfire Risk Reduction Policy. *Contemporary Economic Policy* 24 (2): 203–223.

Theobald, D. M., and W. H. Romme. 2007. Expansion of the US Wildland-Urban Interface. *Landscape and Urban Planning* 83:340–354.

Thomas, J. W. 2000. What Now? From a Former Chief of the Forest Service. In *A Vision for the U.S. Forest Service: Goals for Its Next Century,* edited by R. A. Sedjo. Washington, DC: Resources for the Future, 10–43.

Troy, A. 2007. A Tale of Two Policies: California Programs That Unintentionally Promote Development in Wildland Fire Hazard Zones. In *Living on the Edge: Economic, Institutional and Management Perspectives on Wildfire Hazard in the Urban Interface,* edited by A. Troy and R. G. Kennedy. Amsterdam: Elsevier, 127–140.

Troy, A., and J. Romm. 2006. *An Assessment of the 1998 Natural Hazard Disclosure Law (AB 1195)* . Berkeley: California Policy Research Center, University of California.

USDA (U.S. Department of Agriculture). 2006. *Audit Report: Forest Service Large Fire Suppression Costs.* Report No. 08601-44-SF. Washington, DC: USDA Office of the Inspector General, Western Region.

USGS (U.S. Geological Survey). 2010. Land Cover Trends Project. http://landcovertrends.usgs.gov (accessed April 21, 2011).

Westerling, A. L., H. G. Hidalgo, D. R. Cayan, and T. W. Swetnam. 2006. Warming and Earlier Spring Increase Western U.S. Forest Wildfire Activity. *Science* 313 (August), doi:10.1126/science.1128834.

Whitlock, C. 2004. Forests, Fires and Climate. *Nature* 432:28–29.

Winter, G., and J. Fried. 2000. Homeowner Perspectives on Fire Hazard, Responsibility, and Management Strategies at the Wildland Urban Interface. *Society and Natural Resources* 13:33–49.

Wu, J. 1999. Crop Insurance, Acreage Decisions, and Nonpoint Source Pollution. *American Journal of Agricultural Economics* 81:305–320.

WUIWT (Wildland/Urban Interface Fire Working Team). 2008. Wildland/Urban Interface Fire Hazards: A New Look at Understanding Hazard Assessment Methodologies. www.firewise.org/resources/files/wham.pdf (accessed April 21, 2011).

Xu, W., and J. Wu. 2009. Wildland Fire Hazard and Urban Development Pattern: Why California Civil Code 1103 Fails to Protect Households from Wildfires. Paper presented at the Agricultural and Applied Economics Association 2009 Annual Meeting. July 2009, Milwaukee.

Yoder, J. 2004. Playing with Fire: Endogenous Risk in Resource Management. *American Journal of Agricultural Economics* 86:993–948.

INDEX